On Property and Ownership Relations

Polish Contemporary Philosophy and Philosophical Humanities

Edited by Jan Hartman

Volume 12

PETER LANG

Wiesław Gumuła

On Property and Ownership Relations

A Return to the Social Theory of Karl Marx

PETER LANG

Bibliographic Information published by the Deutsche Nationalbibliothek
The Deutsche Nationalbibliothek lists this publication in the Deutsche Nationalbibliografie; detailed bibliographic data is available in the internet at http://dnb.d-nb.de.

Library of Congress Cataloging-in-Publication Data
A CIP catalog record for this book has been applied for at the Library of Congress.

ISSN 2191-1878 (Print)
ISBN 978-3-631-66736-1 (Print) · E-ISBN 978-3-653-06321-9 (E-PDF)
E-ISBN 978-3-631-71339-6 (EPUB) · E-ISBN 978-3-631-71340-2 (MOBI)
DOI 10.3726/978-3-653-06321-9

Peter Lang – Berlin · Bern · Bruxelles · New York · Oxford · Warszawa · Wien

This publication has been peer reviewed.

www.peterlang.com

Table of Contents

Introduction

The volume at hand comprises a systematic analysis of the reasoning of Karl Marx on the subject of ownership. In truth, ownership is one of the central categories found in his theories and doctrines, and, more pertinently here, it continues to arouse great interest and emotions among politicians and scholars alike. Scores of authors past and present make reference to Marx when writing about property, regardless of whether they accept or reject his views. Nonetheless, their selection of sources and interpretations thereof are often so biased that one could conclude that Marx – as the author of an original and novel theory of ownership – is yet to be discovered.

Such a state of affairs in discussions regarding Marx's concept of ownership stems from implications of an either social or theoretical nature. Among the former are mostly polemics of ideological and political consequence. Among the latter, theoretical resolutions have become ensnared in practical contexts and concrete effects which have hampered impartial academic analysis. After all, for the whole of the 20th century, the works of Marx were reshaped and twisted into a primitive political doctrine. Thus, a significant segment of his views has been moved into the shadows and suppressed. Even critics of Marxism were uninterested in stepping beyond a simplistic interpretation of the words of Karl Marx.

Among the dilemmas in this investigation, it is worth noting the great difficulties that result from an unequivocal reception of Marxist thought. Property and ownership comprise a running theme throughout the entirety of his substantial writings – from the earliest to the last – yet not one position incorporates a systematic discourse on this specific topic. Admittedly, only a certain fragment of his output is of a scholarly nature: dominating many texts is the ideological or programmatic aspect in connection with his political convictions or his involvement in the Communist movement. Furthermore, subtle, complex, or ambiguous analyses intertwine with clear and simple declarations. Crucial here is that Marx the creator of a theory which was to describe and elucidate social reality is a different animal from Marx the creator of a doctrine which was to alter the world.

Naturally, Marx himself would disagree with this last statement. After all, he assumed from the outset a unity of critical theory and practice. Still, between Marx's theory and the practice thereof, there is a dark realm of inattention and inconsistency; proof of which is, truth be told, the concept of the communist society. When designing a better world, Marx ignored the threats which social property ownership bears, despite having skillfully identified them in investigations of diverse pre-capitalistic forms of common ownership.

In this presentation of Marx's views on ownership, I will make full use of voluminous sources, recurrently citing Marx – as well as Engels and others – or referring the reader to original texts. After all these decades, far too frequently we find references to secondary materials in contemporary explorations of Marx, to oft-repeated interpretations, and to the same quotations. It is my deduction that these references usually include citations copied from secondary analyses and not from the primary texts penned by Karl Marx himself. Evidence to this effect can be the limited assortment, which now comprises a sort of banal canon of *WikiQuotes*. I, therefore, strive to delve into materials less cited; none too difficult, considering how neglected this topic and approach is. Reception of Marx's opinions on the subject of ownership is superficial and interpretations are fraught with many an error. Only a thorough and comprehensive presentation of the available body of material permits accurate analysis and safeguards against imputations of statements never uttered.

Analysis of Marx's conception here will be from that intellectual perspective, which emphasizes the elasticity and openness found in his own research approach. This is a reaction to scholastic and dogmatic readings of his works; a tendency initiated by Engels as he consolidated Marx's legacy and, subsequently, continued by Lenin and other Marxists of various ilk.

In first order, I will concentrate on analysis of the multiplicity of meanings assigned to the terms "private ownership" and "common ownership," or "social ownership." After all, private and common ownership have assumed many historical forms, which fundamentally differ from one another. Principally, I will try to break through the primitive interpretations, which discern in Marx a decisive critique of private property and an apologia for ownership in common. In fact, his approach to these matters was much more complicated. On several occasions, Marx spoke both encouragingly about specific forms of private ownership and disparagingly about specific forms of common ownership.

Secondly, I will treat with equal consideration both the processes of privatization and socialization of ownership as analyzed by Marx. Thusly, I aim to break through a sort of monoculture when it comes to interpretations of the works of Marx; a propensity to discuss and deliberate upon socialization to a rather limited degree.

Thirdly, I aim to shed light on Marx's conclusions and opinions regarding the diverse ways, in which a person may become an owner within different forms of private or common ownership. It is not true that individuals come in two categories; they are not simply owners and non-owners, as commentators on Marx would often have it; again, regardless of whether they advocate or oppose Marxism.

Fourthly, I focus strongly on that aspect of Marx's theory of ownership which pertains to interpersonal relations. For Marx, each form of ownership is a system of complicated relations between concrete individuals, and not some abstract institutional construct in which some are owners while others are not. Here, too, I break through a certain interpretative stereotype according to which Marx is simply the creator of an abstract theory, beyond which one may expect no individual actions or interpersonal relations. In fact, Marx's approach is closer to the sociology of social relations, which is evidenced by his theory of ownership.

The main objective of the inquiry and analysis conducted herein is ownership perceived as a socioeconomic category. Of course, one cannot ignore issues belonging more to the philosophical or legal categories. Although, these do not constitute – from my perspective – a distinctly separate matter, but rather complement deliberations of a more socioeconomic vein.

So much has been written on the subject of ownership that, no matter the guidelines, any bibliography will be less than complete. Already the classic thinkers of antiquity spoke of property and ownership; it was, and continues to be, the subject of reflection in Christian philosophy. The Renaissance, Reformation, and Enlightenment also witnessed a bounty of treatises on this topic; suffice it to mention Saint Thomas Aquinas, Thomas Hobbes, John Locke, David Hume, Jean-Jacques Rousseau, and Georg W.F. Hegel. At the turn of the 18th and 19th centuries, several new disciplines evolved out of the social sciences – including economics – and many of them also saw ownership as a topic of its interest (see Adam Smith, for instance).

This was also the moment, in which the most significant works appeared by representatives of utopian socialism; for instance, Robert Owen and Pierre-Joseph Proudhon. It was also in the 19th century, when Karl Marx penned the socioeconomic theory of ownership. Subsequently, at the turn of the 19th and 20th centuries, sociological theories of ownership appeared in the works of Ferdinand Tönnies, Georg Simmel, and Max Weber.

In the 20th century, ownership was the subject of research conducted as part of the most significant theoretical schools and trends; it was also an important playing field for their conflicts and resolutions. A few of these schools of thought deserve special mention here. One of these is the liberal-ethical school, which discerns the core problem in answering the question as to how it is possible to justly distribute private property and civil rights. The standard bearers for this group included Robert Nozick, though inspiration came from Thomas Hobbes and John Locke. A second school, which I will here call the liberal-pragmatic, posed the question as to which configurations of ownership rights and privileges would enable an efficient economy and utility maximization. This current of theoretical reflection on ownership was developed by, among others, representatives of the Property Rights School and the new institutionalized economics (e.g., Armen Alchian, Steven Cheung, Ronald Coase, and Harold Demsetz). The predecessors of this group may be found in classic economics or the psychological school in economics. Certain representatives have been inspired by the works of Max Weber and Karl Marx as well.

In Central and Eastern Europe, it was orthodox Marxism – concentrating on an apologetics for sundry forms of common and state ownership – which spread in the 20th century. This school of thought in various ways reproduced the concept of ownership found in works by Lenin or signed by Stalin. Against this regional backdrop, the Polish applicative-analytical trend was unique and assumed the traits of a theoretical school. Representatives of this line of thinking gathered around Stanisław Kozyr-Kowalski and his writings; they also attempted to use Karl Marx and other theorists dealing with ownership – such as Max Weber – to develop new research instruments. Such instruments were to facilitate critical diagnosis and elucidation of property relations in state socialism societies as well as in postmodern market economy societies.

Noticeable in the scholarly reflections of the first two decades of the 21st century are ever more studies inspired by the works of Karl Marx. This especially pertains to the creation of theoretical tools, which are to serve in the interpretation of processes currently underway in global finances and of the influence of finances on real economics. It is my feeling, however, that this renaissance of interest in Marx's output is a rerun in the history of oversimplifications and a deconstruction of his views and convictions. Interpreting Marx anew, sociologists and economists alike are replicating the same generalizations and falling into the same traps as their predecessors in the previous century. This is yet another reason why I decided to return to the issue of property and ownership, reexamine Marx in the original, and publish this volume.

Allowing oneself to be inspired by the writings of Marx is, from a theoretical point of view, a promising scholarly venture. Similarly, there is profound sense in delving into the views on ownership held by St. Thomas Aquinas, Max Weber, and Georg Simmel, representatives of the Property Rights School, and many another thinker. The ideas of our predecessors should serve to stimulate and incite. As Robert Merton said, a scholar is a dwarf standing on the shoulders of giants from whom he learns. In the case of Karl Marx, such a declaration is all the more warranted: even if he wrote in the 19th century, his thinking continues to be up-to-date. The processes that Marx identified and elucidated in his day manifest loud and clear in the 21st century and, so, it is worth verifying the applicability of his research perspective.

As for thinkers and politicians who would seek to find something in his program for changing the world, I admonish one and all to refer to his analyses of common and social ownership known from history. A thorough reading of Marx's views on the subject of the socialization of property also serves as a word of caution, albeit indirectly and implicitly, even if Karl Marx himself directly and explicitly recommends such a socialization. The volume at hand focuses not only on the opportunities but, foremost, on the dangers which Marx identified as borne by specific forms of common ownership. Already in his times, changes in property and ownership relations signaled both great hopes and expectations as well as great disquiet and unease.

Chapter I: What is Ownership?

On the Nature of General Concepts

In the 19th century, Pierre-Joseph Proudhon posed the question – "What is property?" – which was met by an audacious reply from Karl Marx: "The question is so badly formulated that it cannot be answered correctly."[1] Against this backdrop, the title of this chapter is perhaps incongruous and inapt particularly if this volume is to comprise a deliberation on Marxist theory of property and ownership.

Such a point of departure for these deliberations is justified, however, by the approach employed by the very author of the above-cited rebuke. Marx sketches out his methodology further into his just quoted *Letter to J. B. Schweizer* as well as in his *Letter to Pavel Vasilyevich Annenkov*, in *The Poverty of Philosophy*, and in *Contribution to the Critique of Political Economy.*[2] Quite interestingly, in all these works, Karl Marx presents his approach to general concepts against the backdrop of these considerations of Proudhon. Therein, Marx affirms that deliberations on such generally phrased problems are most often burdened by *a priori* formulas which have little in common with reality; and Proudhon's error was to be of this type. Instead of recognizing economic categories as a theoretical expression of historic social relations, Proudhon saw them as perpetual concepts independent of such concrete relationships; such an interpretation could only hinder a cognitive access to reality. Furthermore, Proudhon regarded the legal definition of capitalist private property as a general concept which might be applied to all historic forms of economic property relations:

> Ancient 'property relations' were superseded by feudal property relations and these by 'bourgeois' property relations. Thus, history itself had expressed its criticism upon past property relations. What Proudhon was actually dealing with was modern bourgeois property as it exists today. The question of what this is could have only been answered

---

1 Karl Marx [1865], *Letter to J B Schweizer: "On Proudhon"*, <http://marxists.catbull.com/archive/marx/works/1865/letters/65_01_24.htm> [accessed August 2017].

2 Karl Marx [1846], *Letter to Pavel Vasilyevich Annenkov*, <http://marxists.catbull.com/archive/marx/works/1846/letters/46_12_28.htm> [accessed August 2017]; Karl Marx [1847], *The Poverty of Philosophy: Answer to the "Philosophy of Poverty" by M. Proudhon*, <https://www.marxists.org/archive/marx/works/download/pdf/Poverty-Philosophy.pdf> [accessed August 2017]; Karl Marx [1859], *A Contribution to the Critique of Political Economy*, <https://www.marxists.org/archive/marx/works/download/Marx_Contribution_to_the_Critique_of_Political_Economy.pdf> [accessed August 2017].

> by a critical analysis of 'political economy', embracing the totality of these property relations, considering not their legal aspect as relations of volition but their real form, that is, as relations of production.[3]

In contrast, Marx's methodology is anchored in a belief that the genesis of general terms must be sought in reality itself. The definition of a general concept does not conclude the research process, but is rather a theoretical stage leading to answers about the concrete historical form of the phenomenon under study. It is therefore a mistake to attribute the content of a general concept, as Proudhon does, to real relations. In fact, quite the opposite is true: it is general concepts which are the theoretical expression of real phenomena. From the perspective of Marx,

> [Proudhon] fails to see that economic categories are but abstractions of those real relations, that they are truths only in so far as those relations continue to exist. Thus, he falls into the error of bourgeois economists who regard those economic categories as eternal laws and not as historical laws which are laws only for a given historical development, a specific development of the productive forces. Thus, instead of regarding politico-economic categories as abstractions of actual social relations that are transitory and historical, Mr. Proudhon, by a mystical inversion, sees in the real relations only the embodiment of those abstractions.[4]

On the basis of production, Marx provides a utilitarian validation for the use of general concepts:

> All periods of production, however, have certain features in common: they have certain common categories. Production in general is an abstraction, but a sensible abstraction in so far as it actually emphasises and defines the common aspects and thus avoids repetition. Yet this general concept, or the common aspect which has been brought to light by comparison, is itself a multifarious compound comprising divergent categories. Some elements are found in all epochs, others are common to a few epochs. The most modern period and the most ancient period will have (certain) categories in common.[5]

The function of general concepts is met by terms which: (a) permit delineation of the sphere of the identity of phenomena, regardless of the degree of variation between the forms which they can take; (b) facilitate demarcation of the sphere of reality, in which phenomena may be identified without fear of referring to things different than intended; i.e., demarcation of the boundaries within which a phenomenon occurs; and (c) afford a keystone for the study of differences and historical transformations, to which these phenomena succumb. The definition

3 Marx, *Letter to J B Schweizer: "On Proudhon"*.

4 Marx, *Letter to Pavel Vasilyevich Annenkov*.

5 Marx, *A Contribution to the Critique of Political Economy*, 113.

of a general concept cannot posit a specific historical shape for the phenomenon under investigation; again, it can only provide the basis for such research.

Does Marx employ a general concept of ownership? In truth, no such general definition of this concept can be found in his works, which could meet the abovementioned specifications. To be more precise, no straightforwardly articulated definition is to be found. It is, nevertheless, possible to distinguish descriptions of a lesser degree of generalization – adequate for some historical forms of ownership – or descriptions so very general that other social facts fit in the spectrum. Yet such overall concepts in his thinking are more discretely assumed, embedded in that layer of his theory which Piotr Sztompka calls the "theoretical-methodological orientation."[6]

It is worth delving into this further. According to Sztompka, each theory contains at least two layers of meaning: the superficial which comprises everything that is written *expressis verbis*, and the deep-seated which consists of everything that a conception implicitly assumes. It is the latter layer which bears the basic ontological and epistemological principles, key to the realm of the phenomenon that a theory describes and elucidates. The set of these principles constitutes the theoretical-methodological orientation, and anyone who proclaims a conception undertakes – consciously or subconsciously – such an orientation. To cite Sztompka, "I claim that the true uniqueness of each cognitive conception manifests itself only when we extricate the theoretical-methodological orientation at its base. This claim I use with reference to the analysis of Marxism."[7]

Indeed, Marx's general definition of property can be found in the ontological assumptions and presuppositions of his theory of ownership. A search for the underlying premises of statements and declarations requires, as Sztompka suggests, reverse extrapolation that refers to the tenet illustrated in the conventional saying: "Since you say B, then you had to have said A." And if reverse extrapolation is applied simultaneously to many different assertions and statements which constitute middle range theories, then that intersection of broad-spectrum statements – revealed through reverse extrapolations – constitutes the common premise for all middle range assertions and, hence, their generalized formulation. The same refers to the path for reconstruction of the general concept of ownership.

The core section of this chapter constitutes the search for Marx's general concept of property as a socioeconomic category. Yet, in fact, these deliberations will

6 Piotr Sztompka, "O marksistowskiej koncepcji rozwoju – nieco inaczej", *Studia Filozoficzne*, 145/12 (1977), 81.

7 Ibid.

be preceded by a sketch of legal understandings of ownership, necessary for the exposition of the unique socioeconomic content of this concept.

Property in a Legal and Socioeconomic Sense

Karl Marx used the concept of ownership in at least three senses: legal, socioeconomic, and philosophical. In doing so, Marx regularly accented the need to go beyond the legal understanding and reference economic analyses because capitalist law obscures economic relations instead of displaying their true content.

Marx states directly that, when capitalist relations of production have developed to such an extent that the legal institutions of feudalism have begun to stymie further development of capitalism, then Roman private law – which spotlights full and exclusive property rights – begins to be applied. This was a perfect instrument for the elimination of institutions of divided ownership which gave different persons different rights to the same things. Landlords used the formula of Roman private law to expropriate peasants from their property rights to the parcels of land they cultivated. Thus, Marx distinguishes various capitalist legal definitions for property as stemming from Roman law and taking on several traits thereof.

Above all, these definitions take on the abstract and generalized nature of the Roman law. The Roman formula for property rights endows the owner, according to Justinian code, with full reign over an object [*plena in res protestas*]. The proprietor accumulates, among other things, the following rights and privileges with regards to things: the right to possess, to use and abuse, to enjoy benefits, and to have command over things (*ius possidendi, ius utendi et abutendi, ius utendi fruendi*, and *ius disponendi*). Additionally, legislation in the capitalist countries of Marx's times aimed to bestow upon owners full and exclusive rights over objects, thus destroying feudal legal institutions:

> As soon as industry and trade developed private property further, first in Italy and later in other countries, the highly developed Roman civil law was immediately adopted again and raised, to authority. When later the bourgeoisie had acquired so much power that the princes took up its interests in order to overthrow the feudal nobility by means of the bourgeoisie, there began in all countries – in France in the sixteenth century – the real development of law, which in all countries except England proceeded on the basis of the Roman Codex. In England, too, Roman legal principles had to be introduced to further the development of civil law (especially in the case of movable property).[8]

---

8 Karl Marx, Friedrich Engels [1845–1846], *The German Ideology*, <https://www.marxists.org/archive/marx/works/download/Marx_The_German_Ideology.pdf> [accessed August 2017], 32.

Recognition of property relations as relations of free will is, according to Marx, the most obvious sign of a legal approach. This thesis runs so often throughout his works that it becomes something of a truism. On several occasions, Marx renders a more precise definition of property as will over people and things. Firstly, these relationships are realized via things which function as mediating elements in the transmission of the proprietor's free will onto other people. Secondly, a specific type of interest accompanies this volition, one which manifests itself in normatively regulated possibilities for the acquisition of goods through their various usages: "The mere legal property of land does not create any ground-rent for the owner. But it does, indeed, give him the power to withdraw his land from exploitation until economic conditions permit him to utilise it in such a manner as to yield him a surplus, be it used for actual agricultural or other production purposes, such as buildings, etc."[9] Thirdly, the will of the owner cannot be solely the result of some internal game, playing out his motives; the opportunity to control things is assigned by law and/or by customary or moral norms; e.g., for a while, in colonial America legal title was a rarity. Fourthly, realization of the owner's will depends upon the nature of economic relations. In order to sensibly apply the legal category of ownership, one needs to take into consideration the extralegal conditions of the economic relations. Marx solves this problem, for instance, when discussing the Hegelian concept of ownership: "This much at least is evident: the individual cannot maintain himself as a landowner by his mere 'will' against the will of another individual, who likewise wants to become a real individual by virtue of the same strip of land. It definitely requires something other than goodwill."[10]

A legal meaning for ownership can also be extracted from this analysis of the economic relationships of exchange:

> It is plain that commodities cannot go to market and make exchanges of their own account. We must, therefore, have recourse to their guardians, who are also their owners. Commodities are things, and therefore without power of resistance against man. If they are wanting in docility he can use force; in other words, he can take possession of them. In order that these objects may enter into relation with each other as commodities, their guardians must place themselves in relation to one another, as persons whose will resides in those objects, and must behave in such a way that each does not appropriate the commodity of the other, and part with his own, except by means of an act done by mutual consent. They must therefore, mutually recognise in each other the rights of private

9 Karl Marx, *Capital: A Critique of Political Economy*, Volume III, <https://www.marxists.org/archive/marx/works/download/pdf/Capital-Volume-III.pdf> [accessed August 2017], 555.

10 Ibid., 476.

proprietors. This juridical relation, which thus expresses itself in a contract, whether such contract be part of a developed legal system or not, is a relation between two wills, and is but the reflex of the real economic relation between the two. It is this economic relation that determines the subject-matter comprised in each such juridical act.[11]

This quote patently documents the fact that Marx utilized, among others, legal terminology referencing ownership. More significantly, these were not legal analyses of legal status, but legal analyses of the economic relationship of ownership. Marx did this relatively rarely because he placed the economic theoretical perspective above the legal one. After all, Marx was decisively critical of the hegemonic legal approach; an opinion he expressed, for instance, in his critique of Proudhon's and Hegel's views. Nevertheless, it would be inaccurate to interpret Marx's views and state that he entirely overlooks the advantages of legal analyses of ownership. It is worth underlining the stance of Marx because many Marxists, including Jarosław Ładosz, a well-known Polish materialist, stated that ownership is essentially a category that is exclusively economic.[12]

Taking the above into consideration, it is also true that Karl Marx criticizes, on many occasions, an approach relying solely on the legal sense of ownership. Marx argues that if one were to accept as true that free will is constitutive for ownership, then it could turn out that an owner would cease being one when confronted with the free will of another individual. Yet ownership is a rather permanent element in the social order.

In his day, German legal philosophy asserted that the law shapes and affixes economic order; it also influences and limits individual will. But, in Marx's eyes, such an argumentation does not signify a difference in the nature of volition. In this case, too, the content of free will remains the same because legal codes also are constituted by the will of the people – collectively. Nonetheless, ownership relations cannot be created in contradiction to economic processes solely by way of legislation, or individual will. We find this in Marx's writings, when he condemns Hermann Kriege who proposed that private ownership of parcels of land

11 Karl Marx [1867], *Capital: A Critique of Political Economy*, Volume I, <https://www.marxists.org/archive/marx/works/download/pdf/Capital-Volume-I.pdf> [accessed August 2017], 60.

12 Jarosław Ładosz, "Własność jako kategoria ekonomiczna a prawo własności", in *Własność, gospodarka a prawo: Studia o marksistowskiej teorii własności*, ed. by Stanisław Kozyr-Kowalski (Warsaw: Państwowe Wydawnictwo Naukowe, 1977), 170–171.

be made universal by the passage of comprehensive legislation.[13] Marx notes that this would result, paradoxically, in a re-concentration of landholdings. This is, in fact, what occurred in 19th-century France. This suggests that underpinning the power of both the owner as well as the legislature is the system of economic relations. Thus, the owner cannot bring his own will to fruition against the actual mode of production. If, however, the owner attempts to do so, then, most often, his rights and privileges are reduced to the immaterial letter of the law because his decision leads to the loss of the very thing which was his property. As Marx puts it, the proprietor possesses nothing more than his *uti et abuti*.

Such must be the conclusion as one is an owner not due to legalized opportunities to impose one's will, but due to participation in specified social and economic relations. Free will can be a means, by which these relations are realized, but not their cause. Marx and Engels elaborate:

> In civil law the existing property relationships are declared to be the result of the general will. The *jus utendi et abutendi* itself asserts on the one hand the fact that private property has become entirely independent of the community, and on the other the illusion that private property itself is based solely on the private will, the arbitrary disposal of the thing. In practice, the *abuti* has very definite economic limitations for the owner of private property, if he does not wish to see his property and hence his *jus abutendi* pass into other hands, since actually the thing, considered merely with reference to his will, is not a thing at all, but only becomes a thing, true property in intercourse, and independently of the law (a relationship, which the philosophers call an idea). This juridical illusion, which reduces law to the mere will, necessarily leads, in the further development of property relationships, to the position that a man may have a legal title to a thing without really having the thing. If, for instance, the income from a piece of land is lost owing to competition, then the proprietor has certainly his legal title to it along with the *jus utendi et abutendi*. But he can do nothing with it: he owns nothing as a landed proprietor if in addition he has not enough capital to cultivate his ground. This illusion of the jurists also explains the fact that for them, as for every code, it is altogether fortuitous that individuals enter into relationships among themselves (e.g. contracts); it explains why they consider that these relationships [can] be entered into or not at will, and that their content rests purely on the individual [free] will of the contracting parties.[14]

To describe property relations, Marx departs from considering them as legal relations of will ("volition") and approaches them as economic relations of production. Descriptions of property as an economic relationship surface very frequently in the works of Karl Marx. He speaks, too, of the "economic title to

13 Karl Marx, Friedrich Engels [1846], "Circular against Kriege", in *Marx and Engels, Collected Works* (Moscow: Progress Publishers, 1976), Volume VI, 35–51.

14 Karl Marx, Friedrich Engels [1845–1846], *The German Ideology*, 32.

property" as something different from the legal title. Sometimes he refers to ownership as a cornerstone of the social system. What all these descriptors share in common is that the property relations are established by people who are active and who are executing a broad spectrum of economic and non-economic activities. Looking at this in yet another way, whoever participates in relations of production, distribution, exchange, and consumption – and whoever undertakes political, cultural, religious, and friendship relations – concurrently and diversely, becomes party to ownership relations. At this point, the objects of ownership fulfill diverse economic and non-economic functions: they can, for instance, function as the property of the means of production, exchange, coercion, or play.

Property as an economic relationship is reflected in many legal institutions. Property law is but one of many normative regulators of activities associated with the economic appropriation of things. Suffice it to recall inheritance law or privileges as a consequence of a hiring, leasing, or credit contract. Marx expresses his position through an analysis of a diverse spectrum of legal acts. A person taking advantage of the above-referenced rights can have similar economic status as a proprietor although the legal status of their positions might differ. For instance, an economic owner of the means of production can be not only the legal owner of a business, but also a relative without title to these goods; or a lessee, stockholder, tenant, creditor, feudal serf, or somebody else. Marx lists numerous legal privileges permitting the appropriation of surplus product and, as a result, allowing achievement of the position of a proprietor of the means of production.

Production and Ownership

Ownership – A Social Relationship Shaped through Production

In *Grundrisse*, Marx speaks of two aspects of appropriation: (a) as a presupposition of labor and (b) as mediated by labor. This highlights the dual nature of the relationship between labor and ownership.

The first type of appropriation may be illustrated by looking at tribal societies in which natural working conditions dominate: the ownership of land and of nature's yield. The community treats the territory it seized as the object of its ownership. This comprises the prerequisite for unrestricted undertakings by members of the community within that territory; at the same time, it excludes such undertakings by persons not belonging to that community.

Looking at any society, it has its own social structure and, therefore, its unique system of ownership relations. The possibilities for action are, thus, already delineated by the *status quo* system of ownership relations. This pertains to the above-described community which, in order to begin living on some terrain, must be its owner. This also pertains to the owner of an individual farm who performs work on that farm only if he is its owner. And this pertains, too, to the wage laborer who makes use of a workshop by permission of its owner. In this sense, ownership precedes any kind of activity.

Even the appropriation of the fruits of nature requires at least some effort, such as harvesting. Without this, the owner will reap no benefits from ownership. The process of production – the process of any and all kinds of activities – is what makes someone the owner in a socioeconomic sense. The economic realization of the ownership relation, thus, transpires in action. Ownership is therefore more than just a psychological or legal fact. Marx writes of this when investigating tribal communities:

> Property, in so far as it is only the conscious relation – and posited in regard to the individual by the community, and proclaimed and guaranteed as law – to the conditions of production as *his own,* so that the producer's being appears also in the objective conditions *belonging to him* – is only realized by production itself. The real appropriation takes place not in the mental but in the real, active relation to these conditions – in their real positing as the conditions of his subjective activity.[15]

Marx emphasized this aspect of ownership very vividly through his description of the fate of a certain English capitalist who moved to the United States with the whole of his enterprise. This industrialist took with him all his machinery, money, and even three hundred wage laborers. Yet, upon arrival to the New World, his workers did not undertake jobs with him, but moved deep into continent in order to work for themselves on their own farms. All was lost, leading Marx to ironically comment: "Unhappy Mr. Peel who provided for everything except the export of English modes of production to Swan River!"[16]

It is likewise with each object of ownership. Only activity directed towards that object – meaning a situation in which that object becomes the factor of labor – permits its classification as an object of economic ownership. Objects of ownership in the socioeconomic sense are those material and non-material things which are applied in work and towards which human activity is directed, expressed in a wide variety of economic and non-economic actions. However, a thing or any other good which lays useless ceases to be an object of ownership;

---

15 Karl Marx [1857–1861], *Grundrisse: Foundations of the Critique of Political Economy* (Rough Draft), <https://www.marxists.org/archive/marx/works/download/pdf/grundrisse.pdf> [accessed August 2017], 417.

16 Marx, *Capital: A Critique of Political Economy,* Volume I, 543.

correspondingly, its legal and rightful owner loses his position as an owner, socioeconomically speaking. This owner can, however, be the possessor in a legal, psychological, moral, or any number of other understandings. For example, a buried, hidden treasure becomes the secret of a single individual. It is therefore a fact without any social value, and, as such, stops being a socioeconomic object of ownership; it can neither mediate in any relationship between people nor can it evoke any socially significant reaction.

Owners of Conditions of Labor and Owners of Labor Power

The considerations presented thus far permit a general, socioeconomic description of the owners of the means of production; something extricated from the foreshadowing of Marx's theory of ownership, sometimes manifestly articulated. The owner of the means of production is someone who employs himself or other people in the service of those means. This description can be extended to other spheres of activity. The owner of the conditions of labor is someone who employs himself and/or others within the scope of these conditions. Worth underlining here is that the term "conditions of labor," appears as often in Marx's writings as the terms "means of production," "conditions of production," and "means of labor." Marx treats them as synonyms.

Hence, only an owner of the means of production can employ himself or others. No non-owner can undertake work without the owner's permission, and no non-owner is capable of exchanging conditions of labor for a factor of production. Of course, this does not entail a normatively regulated possibility, but rather a structural situation which exists regardless of normative declarations.

Socioeconomically understood, objects of ownership are such things, which function as factors in all kinds of productive or nonproductive labor. Since the crucial factors of labor are not only the material elements of the working conditions, but also the talents and skills of human beings, then the labor power also becomes an object of ownership as long as the carrier of these skills is working. Marx explains that, "By labour-power or capacity for labour is to be understood the aggregate of those mental and physical capabilities existing in a human being, which he exercises whenever he produces a use-value of any description."[17] Noteworthy, the owner of labor power as a factor of production is always an owner of labor conditions. Such is the case with the individual owner of a small business who is self-employed in his own workplace. And such is the case with the capitalist who employs a worker by purchasing the latter's work capacity:

17 Ibid., 119.

"The capitalist buys labour-power in order to use it; and labour-power in use is labour itself."[18]

But the keystone in being an owner of conditions of labor differs between a tribal community and capitalism. In any case, regardless of the distinctions between specific historical forms of ownership, at the root of Marxist descriptions of these forms hides a general formula for being an owner which dictates that the owner is an employer. It is worth analyzing a few of Marx's statements in connection with various, completely contrasting forms of ownership.

When investigating ownership relations in primitive, tribal communities, Karl Marx asserts that property entails belonging to a community:

> *Property* therefore means *belonging to a clan* (community) (having subjective-objective existence in it); and, by means of the relation of this community to the land and soil, [relating] to the earth as the individual's inorganic body; his relation to land and soil, to the external primary condition of production – since the earth is raw material, instrument and fruit all in one – as to a presupposition belonging to his individuality, as modes of his presence. *We reduce this property to the relation to the conditions of production.*[19]

Thus, a person is an owner to the extent that he is a member of a community: "His *property*, i.e. the relation to the natural presuppositions of his production as belonging to him, as *his*, is mediated by his being himself the natural member of a community."[20] This thought is repeated and developed in numerous variations.[21] But what does it exactly mean to be an owner in this concrete situation?

No one from outside a community can undertake production; no one from outside can transform the land, its yield, or any capabilities to be economically effective. This is so even if the given territory flourished in the means of labor and natural products ready to eat, and even if an individual was an exceptional hunter, farmer, or shepherd. Such an opportunity can only be mediated by membership in the community. The ownership relation can only be established through the community: being a member of a community means to work, and through that work – to be an owner. Hence, a description of this relationship has been rendered as a general formula. Ownership described as belonging to a community means, more generally, ownership described as the chance to be self-employed on the lands controlled by the community, and, in consequence, the possibility to transform the land and one's own labors into factors of labor.

18 Ibid., 127.

19 Marx, *Grundrisse: Foundations of the Critique of Political Economy*, 416.

20 Ibid., 414.

21 Ibid., 397–438.

When dealing with 19th century petty bourgeoisie ownership, Marx writes as follows:

> The lower strata of the middle class – the small tradespeople, shopkeepers, and retired tradesmen generally, the handicraftsmen and peasants – all these sink gradually into the proletariat, partly because their diminutive capital does not suffice for the scale on which Modern Industry is carried on, and is swamped in the competition with the large capitalists, partly because their specialised skill is rendered worthless by new methods of production. Thus the proletariat is recruited from all classes of the population.[22]

The above-cited suffices for a portrayal of the position of the owner; both its positive and negative qualities:

1) If his tools, machinery, land, etc. function as a factor of production, then he is the owner of the means of production;
2) If he applies his skills inside his own workshop, he is the owner of his own labor power as a factor of labor;
3) If his means of production is not employed in production, then he stops being the owner in the socioeconomic meaning of this word; and
4) If he does not utilize his skills in his own workshop, then he is no longer an economic owner of his labor power as the factor of production.

A similar depiction of the owner emerges from Marx's note on the small peasant proprietorship of land parcels. Here, the owner appears as an employer and individual responsible for the transformation of the conditions of labor into factors:

> When an independent labourer – let us take a small farmer, since all three forms of revenue may here be applied – works for himself and sells his own product, he is first considered as his own employer (capitalist), who makes use of himself as a labourer, and second as his own landlord, who makes use of himself as his own tenant. To himself as wage-worker he pays wages, to himself as capitalist he gives the profit, and to himself as landlord he pays rent.[23]

It is precisely in the third volume of *Capital*, where Marx recurrently describes the nominal landowner as someone who permits others to farm on land in his possession; e.g., rural capitalists. Hence, even such minimal social activity on the part of the landowner – i.e., permitting a lessee to change the land into a factor of labor – makes him the owner in the economic sense. Land thus becomes

---

22 Karl Marx, Friedrich Engels [1847], *Manifesto of the Communist Party*, <https://www.marxists.org/archive/marx/works/download/pdf/Manifesto.pdf> [accessed August 2017], 18.

23 Marx, *Capital: A Critique of Political Economy*, Volume III, 626.

the object of economically understood ownership since the activity of various persons is managed and directed thereon.

The presented general formula for a proprietor also characterizes, however conversely, the wage laborer who cannot employ himself. This appears in a speech by Marx:

> Our efforts must be directed to the end that no instruments of production should be private property. The private property in these things was a fiction, since the proprietors could not use them themselves; they only gave them dominion over them, by which they compelled other people to work for them. In a semi-barbarous state, this might have been necessary, but it was no longer so. All the means of labor must be socialized, so that every man has a right and the means to exercise his labor power.[24]

On the one hand, among the owners of the conditions of labor and labor power are members of the tribal community, the craftsmen, the independent peasants who cultivate their own land, the capitalist-industrialists, the shopkeepers, etc. Each of them employs himself or other people within the framework of their conditions of labor; each of them transforms the conditions of labor and labor power into factors of work. Yet, some are owners of their own labor power, while others are owners of someone else's labor power. This last distinction is not a play on words. Marx frequently differentiates the owner of his own labor power from the owner of somebody else's labor power in order to describe diverse social relations. The owner of human capabilities is an owner of the conditions of labor: in his hands, these abilities are converted into labor power functioning as a factor of production. Nonetheless, the adjectives "own" or "somebody else's" indicate who is the actual bearer of the labor power. Underscored here is that labor power is seen in these deliberations as a factor of labor, and not as a commodity.

On the other hand, those who are not owners of labor power – neither theirs nor that of others – include the Roman slave, the Roman plebeian, or the 19th-century free wage laborer. With regards to the first of these, along with his talents, skills, and body, he has been sold to a patrician; the second does not work at all and, hence, does not transform his capacities into a factor of labor; and the third has sold his labors to a capitalist, albeit for a set period of time. It is true that the worker is an owner of labor power as a commodity; he owns the exchange value of his labor power. He is, however, never an economic owner of the use value of

24 Record of Marx's Speech on The right of inheritance, The International Workingmen's Association, From the General Council minutes of July 20, 1869, as taken by George Eccarius, <https://www.marxists.org/archive/marx/iwma/documents/1869/inheritance-speech.htm> [accessed August 2017].

his labor power. The use value of a laborer's capacities belongs to a capitalist who consumes this in the process of production.[25] It can happen that ownership of labor power is in the hands of the bearer of capacities plus another person. An example of this can be the peasant serf and the feudal lord: both are owners of the labor power of the peasant to the extent that the peasant is obliged to work on both the lord's land as well as on his own field. Such enumeration of the many types renders an image of the diversity and multitude of ways by which a human being can or cannot be an owner of the conditions of labor and of labor power.

The owner of the means of production is linked to the laborer by a relationship of power. Less important here is whether this is a slave, a serf, or a wage laborer; all of them are subordinated by the power of the owner of the conditions of labor. This is one of the general laws accentuated by Marx multiple times. The power of the owner over the worker stems from the fact that the owner of the conditions of labor is simultaneously the owner of the use value of the labor power of the producer. Thus, it is no surprise that the owner decides about the way in which the talents and skills of the worker will be utilized: "the man who possesses no other property than his labor power must, in all conditions of society and culture, be the slave of other men who have made themselves the owners of the material conditions of labor. He can only work with their permission, hence live only with their permission."[26]

Distribution and Ownership

Ownership – A Social Relationship Shaped through Participation in the Distribution of Product

Distribution – in the more common meaning of the word – seems to denote the division and distribution of product. Yet, in order for that to happen, distribution is firstly a condition of labor. For the purposes of this analysis, it is useful to take a closer look at the distribution of the conditions of labor as a prerequisite for production. The initial distribution does not make owners of human beings in the socioeconomic sense. Such a title of ownership would certainly be without economic meaning, although it could bear psychological meaning; here, this could also refer to a legal title or customary norm.

---

25 Marx, *Capital: A Critique of Political Economy*, Volume I, 119–147.

26 Karl Marx [1875], *Critique of the Gotha Programme*, <https://www.marxists.org/archive/marx/works/download/Marx_Critque_of_the_Gotha_Programme.pdf> [accessed August 2017], 7.

The first economic and social confirmation of the distribution of labor conditions among proprietors transpires in the activity of people who lay claim to such moral, political, psychological, or legal titles. Even minimal activity suffices, such as blocking or permitting other persons from taking advantage of these conditions. As mentioned earlier, it is at this (production) stage that the economic owners of the conditions of labor and owners of labor power itself emerge. But it would be a mistake to claim that this type of activity completely corroborates the position of the owner of the conditions of labor: appropriation of product is a prerequisite necessary for the realization of his position as such an owner.

In the socioeconomic sense, the owner of the conditions of labor – the owner of the means of production – is he who obtains products created via the use of those conditions and not always he to whom those conditions legally belong. Marx explains:

> For instance, land gives the living proprietor the power to transfer to himself, under the name of rent, without any equivalent, the produce of other people's labor. Capital gives him the power to do the same under the name of profit and interest. The property in public funds gives him the power to live without labor upon other people's labor, etc.[27]

Marx definitively solves this problem, among other things, by characterizing the position of the French peasant in the first half of the 19th century. During this period, that peasant was the legal owner of the parcel which he tended. These French peasants defended and independently cultivated their land, but were expropriated – by taxes, usury, unprofitable prices for agricultural goods, etc. – of so significant a portion of their products that their economic position became worse than that of the land lessee or the hired worker. Ultimately, this led to the loss of even their right of ownership:

> This process was accelerated in France by the ever growing *burden* of *taxes*, by *court costs* called forth in part directly by the formalities with which French legislation encumbers the ownership of land, in part by the innumerable conflicts over parcels everywhere bounding and crossing each other, and in part by the litigiousness of the peasants, whose enjoyment of property is limited to the fanatical assertion of their title to their fancied property, their *property rights*.[28]

---

27 Karl Marx [1869], *The Right of Inheritance: Report of the General Council*. Written by Marx on August 2–3, 1869, Endorsed by General Council of The International Workingmen's Association on August 3, 1869. <https://www.marxists.org/archive/marx/iwma/documents/1869/inheritance-report.htm> [accessed August 2017].

28 Karl Marx [1870–1871], The Civil War in France, <https://www.marxists.org/archive/marx/works/download/pdf/civil_war_france.pdf> [accessed August 2017], 61.

Does this mean that the peasant above was not the owner in the economic sense? No, he was the owner. After all, he employed himself to work on his land and appeared before other peasants as the owner. These are all forms by which the position of ownership is realized. But the peasant only partially asserted his position because a significant portion of the fruits of his labors was assigned to others. Thus, the latter became the economic owners of his land without being the legal owners. It was precisely about this group that Marx and Engels write in their *Circular against Kriege*: "And is it not then immaterial whether 'the land' or the *produce* of the land 'falls into the hands of rapacious speculators'?"[29]

In the social sciences, there is a tendency to contrast distribution relations with ownership relations. A representative of this school of thought is, for instance, Czesław Strzeszewski who asserts, in his extensive book on ownership, that economic reforms can be conducted either by regulating the means of distribution or of ownership. He adds, "The regulation of ownership is a revolutionary method, whereas the regulation of the distribution of the social profit is an evolutionary method."[30] This seems to mean that the ranges of these two types of relationships are inextricable, and, therefore, intervention in distribution relations will not alter anything in ownership relations. Marx often underscores that an individual's participation in the distribution of the social product testifies and proves his position as an owner of the conditions of labor. This act of division and distribution is one which shapes the relations of ownership.

The Marxist conception of ownership clearly declares that distribution is a key area of social life, in which the position of the owner of the conditions of work is affirmed. Moreover, this is not only key, but conclusive. Arrival at such a conclusion is substantiated by Marx's statements regarding those forms of ownership, within which people limit their activity only to the appropriation of the product: they are neither passively nor actively engaged in production; they employ neither themselves nor others; and, yet, they are described by Marx as the owners of the conditions of labor. Owners in this sense are owners of money, commodity, merchant, usury, and financial capital. This type of owner can also be a feudal lord who does not maintain any direct contact with his real estate and whose economic activity is reduced to ground rent collection. Naturally, in order for there to be something to appropriate, there must be production and, hence, owners who act in the field of that production; this does not, however, contradict

29 Marx, Engels, *"Circular against Kriege"*.

30 Czesław Strzeszewski, *Własność: zagadnienie społeczno-moralne* (Warsaw: Ośrodek Dokumentacji i Studiów Społecznych, 1981), 8.

the thesis about the existence of owners of the conditions of labor who are utterly alienated from the process of production.

Owners of the Conditions of Labor as Appropriators of Product

Two completely opposite situations are possible. People participate in distribution of the social product either as owners or as non-owners of the conditions of labor. Consequently, each and every person is in various ways the economic owner of product, depending upon the given form of ownership. Even a beggar or a slave is, in this sense, the owner. Of course, the product is then consumed personally, not productively, and disappears in the course of that consumption; meaning that the consumer is no longer an owner. Of course, such economic status as the owner should not be mistaken for the legal situation, which may be defined by other concepts such as property rights. Yet, the very act of appropriating even so minimal a part of the product renders each an individual economic owner. Whoever is incapable of participating, at least periodically and recurrently, in the distribution of the product, natural or manmade, perishes. It is possible to not be the owner of the conditions of labor, but to be an owner of product is a universal, economic condition of all living creatures. There must thus be crucial differences in the way the owner and the non-owner of the conditions of labor participate in the distribution relations.

A member of the ancient type of community is the proprietor of the conditions of labor. His economic status as the proprietor of the conditions of labor is mediated through his membership in this community. So, he is allowed to make use of that community's consumption funds – regardless of whether he works or not – and, by appropriation of products that come from common land and soil, he once again validates his position as economic proprietor of common property. For example, the Roman patrician leases state land (*ager publicus*) and, thus, from the legal point of view, he is a tenant. Yet from the economic point of view he is an economic proprietor of the means of labor; he is the person who appropriates the product that is produced by the use of land belonging to him. Therefore, he also authenticates his position as the economic proprietor of the means of production with respect to distribution of the resulting human labor. The free owner of a craftsman's workshop, the peasant serf, and the individual proprietor of a small parcel of land all fit into this category.

As Marx notes,

> The free ownership of the self-managing peasant is evidently the most normal form of landed property for small-scale operation, i.e., for a mode of production, in which possession of the land is a prerequisite for the labourer's ownership of the product of his

> own labour, and in which the cultivator, be he free owner or vassal, always must produce his own means of subsistence independently, as an isolated labourer with his family. Ownership of the land is as necessary for full development of this mode of production as ownership of tools is for free development of handicraft production. Here is the basis for the development of personal independence.[31]

The feudal lord who shares product with the peasant by appropriation of feudal rent is this type of a proprietor of the means of production. This also refers to the epoch of capitalism, in which the legal landowner permits the large-scale, agricultural capitalist farmer to utilize tenant land through employment of agricultural laborers. The legal landowner appropriates – in exchange – a lease or ground rent in some form, thus confirming his position as the economic proprietor of land. Furthermore, the agricultural capitalist magnate who leases land from the legal landowner corroborates his position as the economic proprietor of the same land because he appropriates a part of the surplus product of his agricultural laborers.

In the case of the owner of capital, the property of the conditions of labor and the property of someone else's labor power constitute the presupposition for the appropriation of product obtained by utilizing these two factors of production. As Marx notes in the third volume of *Capital*,

> By the purchase of labour-power, the capitalist incorporates labour, as a living ferment, with the lifeless constituents of the product. From his point of view, the labour-process is nothing more than the consumption of the commodity purchased, i.e., of labour-power; but this consumption cannot be effected except by supplying the labour-power with the means of production. The labour-process is a process between things that the capitalist has purchased, things that have become his property. The product of this process belongs, therefore, to him, just as much as does the wine which is the product of a process of fermentation completed in his cellar.[32]

In fact, the capitalist is such a proprietor regardless of the field of capital circulation in which he functions. Profit in various forms – interest, dividends, industrial profit, trade profit, etc. – confirms the capitalist's position as the owner of the conditions of labor. Access to the conditions of labor is direct in the case of the agricultural or industrial capitalist. Owners of trade capital and owners of financial capital – stockholders, creditors, traders, financial investors, etc. – do not maintain direct contact with the conditions of labor. Thanks to a unique social and financial mediator, they become proprietors of the material conditions of labor: it is money which fulfills this go-between function when assuming the

31 Marx, *Capital: A Critique of Political Economy*, Volume III, 485.
32 Marx, *Capital: A Critique of Political Economy*, Volume III, 131.

form of monetary capital. In the process of the circulation of capital, money capital is transformed into industrial capital by purchasing labor power and the means of production. These are then exchanged for factors of labor and, subsequently, into a product which, when sold as a commodity, returns to the owner of capital as profit in the form of currency capital.

Each of the abovementioned players ceases to be the owner of the conditions of labor, if he does not appropriate at least such a portion of the product as would suffice to assure his survival and also his reproduction of the conditions of labor. If the nominal landowner wishes to preserve his position as the owner, then he should receive a high enough ground rent to guarantee that he will not be forced to sell the land in order to assure his household of the means of existence. The capitalist should appropriate such an amount of product whose capitalization will allow him at least a simple reproduction of capital; that is, the reproduction of money functioning as capital. The peasant is an owner of a farm only as long as he appropriates the product, which permits him to cultivate the land again and physically survive until the next harvest.

Hence, being an owner of the conditions of labor requires more than just the employment of oneself and/or others, and running an economic activity. The owner needs to obtain the product produced via those conditions of labor, too. In the form of new potential conditions of labor and the means of subsistence, the product should be available before embarking on a new economic cycle and its temporal duration, meaning the time before the new product is created. The one, who appropriates less, cannot realize his position as the owner of the conditions of labor. As Karl Marx pens to Vera Zasulich,

> In order to expropriate the agricultural producers, it is not necessary to drive them from the land, as happened in England and elsewhere; nor to abolish communal property by some ukase. If you go and take from the peasants more than a certain proportion of the product of their agricultural labour, then not even your gendarmes and your army will enable you to tie them to their fields. In the last years of the Roman Empire some provincial decurions, not peasants but actual landowners, fled their homes, abandoned their land, and even sold themselves into bondage – all in order to be rid of a property that had become nothing more than an official pretext for exerting quite merciless pressure over them.[33]

In their *Manifesto*, Marx and Engels write:

> The average price of wage-labour is the minimum wage, i.e., that quantum of the means of subsistence which is absolutely requisite to keep the labourer in bare existence as a

33 Karl Marx [1881], *Letter to Vera Zasulich: The "First" Draft*, <https://www.marxists.org/archive/marx/works/1881/zasulich/draft-1.htm> [accessed August 2017].

> labourer. What, therefore, the wage-labourer appropriates by means of his labour, merely suffices to prolong and reproduce a bare existence. We by no means intend to abolish this personal appropriation of the products of labour, an appropriation that is made for the maintenance and reproduction of human life, and that leaves no surplus wherewith to command the labour of others. All that we want to do away with is the miserable character of this appropriation, under which the labourer lives merely to increase capital, and is allowed to live only in so far as the interest of the ruling class requires it.[34]

The worker is, thus, not the owner of the conditions of labor because the way he participates in the distribution of the product does not afford him the chance to accumulate potential means of production and means of subsistence that would suffice for the next period of production.

Moreover, the wage laborer does not appropriate the product, which is created by his own labor power; he appropriates the product created earlier, which is already in the hands of the capitalist in the form of so-called variable capital. In the case of the wage laborer, the ownership of the exchange value of his labor power mediates the possibility for expropriation of someone else's product. The worker sells his commodity – his labor power – and acquires products that take the form of wages.

It is similar with other non-owners of the conditions of labor. They obtain the means of subsistence by entering into many diverse kinds of relationships with proprietors of the conditions of labor, and, at the same time, with previous expropriators of products. The transfer of the product can take place on the basis of, for instance, a relationship of ruler-subject, superior-subordinate, slavery, kinship, inheritance, charity, donation, or even theft.[35]

Therefore, two traits distinguish the owner of the conditions of labor from the non-owner, when it comes to the way in which they usurp the product. Firstly, only the owner acquires enough product to be able to transform it into a means of employment – of himself and others – until such time as new product will be ready. In contrast, the product appropriated by the non-owner acts only as a means of subsistence. Secondly, only the owner of the conditions of labor appropriates the product created within the context of these conditions. In contrast, the non-owner gains such product only from someone who has previously appropriated it. Thus, the owner and the non-owner of the conditions of labor are linked by a relationship of power. This is the power of the appropriator of the product over the person who cannot appropriate that product in any other way than to become beholden to the owner of the conditions of labor.

---

34 Marx, Engels, *Manifesto of the Communist Party*, 23.

35 Marx, *Grundrisse: Foundations of the Critique of Political Economy*, 397–438.

Exchange and Ownership

Ownership – A Relationship Shaped through Exchange

Even the work of a single individual may be considered – as Marx does – as a process of exchange between that person and nature: the human being transfers his skills and capabilities for the sake of nature and, in exchange, gains certain goods from nature. This pertains as well to simple collective behavior and interpersonal relations inside the tribal community. The individual grants some of his labor power on behalf of the community and, as part of the barter, receives the means of subsistence. The communist society designed by Marx operates similarly:

> Here, obviously, the same principle prevails as that which regulates the exchange of commodities, as far as this is exchange of equal values. Content and form are changed, because under the altered circumstances no one can give anything except his labor, and because, on the other hand, nothing can pass to the ownership of individuals, except individual means of consumption. But as far as the distribution of the latter among the individual producers is concerned, the same principle prevails as in the exchange of commodity equivalents: a given amount of labor in one form is exchanged for an equal amount of labor in another form.[36]

Hence, exchange can take the form of an exchange of goods in happenstance proportions with respect to volume and number. And finally, exchange can assume the form of an exchange of commodities in fixed proportions (barter). Subsequently, this becomes an exchange of commodity equivalents with the use of currency as a mediator for transactions within the framework of the goods and money market. Marx explains in volume 1 of *Capital*:

> In order that this alienation may be reciprocal, it is only necessary for men, by a tacit understanding, to treat each other as private owners of those alienable objects, and by implication as independent individuals. But such a state of reciprocal independence has no existence in a primitive society based on property in common, whether such a society takes the form of a patriarchal family, an ancient Indian community, or a Peruvian Inca State. The exchange of commodities, therefore, first begins on the boundaries of such communities, at their points of contact with other similar communities, or with members of the latter. So soon, however, as products once become commodities in the external relations of a community, they also, by reaction, become so in its internal intercourse. The proportions in which they are exchangeable are at first quite a matter of chance. What makes them exchangeable is the mutual desire of their owners to alienate them. Meantime the need for foreign objects of utility gradually establishes itself. The constant repetition of exchange makes it a normal social act. In the course of time, therefore,

36 Marx, *Critique of the Gotha Programme*, 10.

> some portion at least of the products of labour must be produced with a special view to exchange. From that moment the distinction becomes firmly established between the utility of an object for the purposes of consumption, and its utility for the purposes of exchange. Its use-value becomes distinguished from its exchange-value.[37]

In tribal communities, all products of labor and gifts of nature are consumed collectively, sometimes consumed by individuals directly, or distributed among members of a community for individual consumption. Products have a use value for their possessors and are thus non-exchangeable; no one is interested in getting rid of them. The situation changes in those historic modes of production that are founded upon private property. Wherever private owners hold specialized positions in the social division of labor or produce in excess, a product loses use value for its creator. Instead, it becomes something desired by someone else; moreover, another product that is in the hands of the latter is simultaneously desired by the former.

Hence these products must be exchanged; only then do they become usable for their owners. Exchange then becomes more fixed and permanent, and is executed in strict numerical proportions. Additionally, the relationship in which one product is exchanged for another becomes more fixed and permanent in the form of trade value. Therefore, a split emerges between the usefulness of the object for consumption and its usefulness for exchange. To capture this dual nature of products, Marx uses the concepts of use value and exchange value. The means of exchange appear: commodities and money as a general social equivalent for goods. And so, too, private owners of the means of exchange appear. Marx elaborates that

> The appearance of products as commodities pre-supposes such a development of the social division of labour, that the separation of use-value from exchange-value, a separation which first begins with barter, must already have been completed. But such a degree of development is common to many forms of society, which in other respects present the most varying historical features. On the other hand, if we consider money, its existence implies a definite stage in the exchange of commodities. The particular functions of money which it performs, either as the mere equivalent of commodities, or as means of circulation, or means of payment, as hoard or as universal money, point, according to the extent and relative preponderance of the one function or the other, to very different stages in the process of social production.[38]

Marx writes that distribution demarcates the relationship, in which products are assigned to individuals; in turn, exchange demarcates the products, which individuals would want to receive in the distribution. During an exchange, an

---

37 Marx, *Capital: A Critique of Political Economy*, Volume I, 61–62.
38 Ibid., 120.

individual acquires the products that bear use value for him. If a product is capable of functioning as use value, then the usefulness of individual labor is socially confirmed. Otherwise such work is of no use; it exits the social division of labor, and the owner of the pertinent conditions of labor loses his status. To him, a product which he cannot divest is useless.[39]

The private owners of various commodities – that is, owners of the means of exchange – are those who engage in goods trading.[40] Naturally, each of them is the owner only inasmuch as he has something to sell and inasmuch as he actually unloads goods of no use to him and, simultaneously, procures the resources he needs. If the private owner does not sell his goods, then he does not authenticate his position as the owner of the means of exchange. In fact, it may happen that he is no longer the owner in other senses. Participation in the exchange contributes to the transformation of the owners of the means of exchange into owners of the factors of work as well as owners of the means of subsistence.

In certain forms of ownership – especially those in which commodities are produced for the market – realization of the position of the owner of the means of exchange is the prerequisite for the realization of the position of owner in other spheres. For example, a capitalist who does not sell his product ceases to be the owner of capital because he will not possess the resources to purchase the means of production and labor power. A laborer who does not sell his labors will not gain the resources needed for survival. The craftsman who does not sell his crafts will cease being the owner of his workshop.

Hence, being the owner of the means of exchange facilitates being the owner in other realms. Commodities mediate the entry into diverse ownership relations. The range of that mediation depends upon the boundaries in which the exchange value operates; that is, the range of the functioning of certain products in the form of commodities. For instance, since the Asian community did not sell its land, then the owners of the means of exchange could not acquire it and could not become landowners. The same may be said of the master craftsman's workshop in the guild mode of production. Yet, that same land and that same workshop could, under the conditions of a commodity-currency market, also become a means of exchange. And since the product, which is the object of exchange, is most often loaded with surplus value – emphasized on many an occasion by Marx – then, via the means of exchange, it can appropriate the effects of the labor power of someone else and participate in the relationship

39 Ibid., 26–125.

40 Ibid., 61–62.

of exploitation. No direct connections – to either the conditions of labor or the laborer – are thus necessary for assuming the position of the owner of the conditions of labor and of the labor power of others. Such a relation is mediated through ownership of the means of exchange.

Marx stresses many times that the ownership of exchange value not only facilitates the possibility of acquiring desired products and services but also creates the possibility for expropriating the fruits of the surplus labor of other people. The owner of exchange value – commodities or money – can acquire more than he sold. This is very visible in the case of the owner of currency. Money is a special kind of economic instrument that performs not only functions of measure, the mere equivalency of commodities, and means of payment. In the capitalist formation, money also performs the function of a means of expropriation of surplus value and the function of exploitation of partners in an exchange. Owners of money use it as a means for the circulation of capital. Acquiring the conditions of labor and labor power, such an owner facilitates production and creation of surplus value because he pays only for a part of the labor power. By selling products, he transforms the surplus value born in the products into profit in the form of a greater amount of money than he introduced into the process of circulation in the beginning of his activity as the owner of money.

Owners of the Means of Exchange

Marx's concept of ownership clearly assumes that the owner of the means of exchange is that very person who can sell something. The law will tend to underline the acquisition of things as crucial in the ownership title. Economically speaking, however, this aspect is less important: a thing can be stolen, occupied by force, or extorted. In each of these cases, the usurper can effectively play the role of the owner. Most important here is that aspect of exchange which lies in the selling.

Marx states that even the wage laborer is an owner of the means of exchange. He is the owner of a specific commodity: his labor power. As Marx notes, "The labourer is the owner of his labour-power until he has done bargaining for its sale with the capitalist; and he can sell no more than what he has i.e., his individual, isolated labour-power."[41] Elsewhere, Marx adds, "Consequently, labour-power is a commodity which its possessor, the wage worker, sells to the capitalist. Why does he sell it? It is in order to live."[42]

---

41 Ibid., 232.

42 Karl Marx [1847], Wage Labour and Capital, <https://www.marxists.org/archive/marx/works/download/pdf/wage-labour-capital.pdf> [accessed August 2017], 9.

It would be worth underscoring here the difference between labor as a factor of labor and as a commodity. The worker is the owner of his labor power as a commodity and thus sells it. The amount at which he sells it is the exchange value of his labor power. The person acquiring this labor power is its owner as a factor of labor, and, therefore, makes use of someone else's capabilities in production. What the capitalist purchases is the use value of someone else's labor power.

The position of the wage laborer is determined by the commodity he vends (his labor power), and not by the commodity acquired (the means of existence). Moreover, that same worker is not the owner of the fruits of his labors which means that – in accordance with the abovementioned – he cannot sell that product. If the worker was the owner of the conditions of labor, then he would appropriate the product and sell it rather than his own capabilities.

The term "owner" as the person qualified to sell Marx also applies – albeit negatively – when speaking about the position of the Roman slave. Marx's assessment is that the Roman law accurately describes the slave as a person who cannot acquire anything by way of exchange. "In Roman law, the *servus* is therefore correctly defined as one who may not enter into exchange for the purpose of acquiring anything for himself."[43] He has nothing to sell, and therefore cannot be the owner of any commodity. In *Wage Labour and Capital*, Marx recounts:

> Labour-power was not always a commodity (merchandise). Labour was not always wage-labour, i.e., free labour. The slave did not sell his labour-power to the slave-owner, any more than the ox sells his labour to the farmer. The slave, together with his labour-power, was sold to his owner once for all. He is a commodity that can pass from the hand of one owner to that of another. He himself is a commodity, but his labour-power is not his commodity.[44]

This description of the owner as someone who sells a commodity is expedient when investigating ownership relations typical of societies with a commodity or commodity-currency economy. Yet, it has limited use in the case of societies with a narrow exchange market. For instance, the feudal lord can sell land only to another feudal lord. The exchange market is also limited under the circumstances of a natural economy, in which individual homesteads produce things for direct consumption. Such is also the case with tribal communities. In all of these cases, the product does not assume the form of a commodity, or only rarely appears as a commodity.

---

43 Marx, *Grundrisse: Foundations of the Critique of Political Economy*, 174.

44 Marx, *Wage Labour and Capital*, 9.

We can then say that the formula that the owner is a potential seller assumes a more general definition of the owner of things befitting not only market societies, but also other historic forms of society and modes of production. Wherever there is the issue of taking products, there is also the issue of giving. From this point of view, the owner is the one who distributes, gives, and vends goods; in other words, the owner is someone who provides other people with the use value of a good. Such person is the owner of slaves and the feudal lord; each provides other people with access to a portion of his goods. The first of these feeds his slaves, the latter allows his retinue to consume the surplus product of the feudal village. An owner in this sense is also a member of the community – be it tribal or Communist – because as its member, he participates in the apportionment of the product in common. He will not protest to keep others from consuming product which also comprises a use value for him. All the abovementioned owners realize their title of ownership, providing some of their own goods to others. In exchange, these owners gain certain real or symbolic compensation.[45]

As a result, access to use value provided to others may assume various forms. This may rely on the sale of goods, entail a simple exchange of use values, and even assume the form of a gift. After all, even commodities exchange often has an unequal form. Some of the goods progress in one direction without the same amount returning in the opposite direction. Gifting constitutes precisely such a rudimentary exchange, albeit lacking even the pretense of equivalency. A gift heralds an obligation; it heralds a commodity by which one could get to the fruits of someone else's labors. As Jacek Kurczewski described this,

> Such is the resourceful man who successfully hunted much or who, along with his family, toiled in his garden. He held a feast from which he benefited perhaps less than his jealous fellow merrymakers who fare worse. Now they lie engorged under a tree. Let them lie there in peace before a permanent relationship of social dependency is shaped: we may discern its spark even among the pre-state societies.[46]

Thanks to the gifts of the donor, the resourceful man's status as the owner and superior is affirmed.

---

45 Marx, *Grundrisse: Foundations of the Critique of Political Economy*, 422–426.

46 Jacek Kurczewski, "Stosunki własności w społeczeństwach przedpaństwowych", in *Własność, gospodarka a prawo: Studia o marksistowskiej teorii własności*, ed. by Stanisław Kozyr-Kowalski (Warsaw: Państwowe Wydawnictwo Naukowe, 1977), 406.

Consumption and Ownership – Owners of the Means of Subsistence

In the process of reproduction, some relationships are converted into others. Ownership relations, which people create in production or distribution and exchange, are subject to conversion into ownership relations befitting the sphere of consumption. Consumption depends upon the nature of the mode of production, as well as the mode of distribution and exchange, and, simultaneously, initiates the process of production. Consequently, the way in which someone is the owner of the means of subsistence impacts the way in which he is the owner of the conditions of labor, labor power, and the means of exchange.

According to Marx, the economic owner of the means of subsistence is each and every living human being. He is the beggar, slave, capitalist, and any other person; regardless of the resources upon which he draws to survive. The very act of consumption attests to the holding of this position, although the economic appropriation of the means of subsistence can, in each case, essentially differ. It can, for example, be immediate consumption of a given item and thus lead to its obliteration; it can also be a recurrent act such as the wearing of garments or the inhabitance of a domicile. The consumption can involve regular acquisition or sporadic obtainment. Naturally, for a short while, a person can go without being the owner of the means of subsistence, but the very fact of existence means that, in one way or another, every individual alive is the owner in this manner.

We should consider here three theoretically possible situations. In the first, the owner of the means of consumption is not the owner in any other sense. In the second, he is the owner of a specific good, meaning labor power as commodity, but is not the owner of the conditions of labor. In the third case, he is the owner of the conditions of labor and labor power itself, his own or someone else's, which, in his hands, function as factors of labor. In fact, Karl Marx analyzed all three of these.

Marx labels the first of the situations above as the "third possible form;" distinct from the "historic states" number I and II.[47] Comparing this form to earlier, prehistoric forms of ownership, Marx explains:

> The third *possible form*, in which the worker relates as owner only to the necessaries of life, finding them on hand as the natural condition of the working subject, without relating to the land and soil, or to the instrument, or even (therefore) to labour itself as his own, is at bottom the formula of slavery and bondage, which is likewise negated, posited as a historically dissolved condition, in the relation of the worker to the conditions of production as capital.[48]

---

47 Marx, *Grundrisse: Foundations of the Critique of Political Economy*, 422–424.
48 Ibid., 424.

As this type of owners Marx saw, among others, slaves, manor servants, Roman plebeians sustained by alms, his contemporary lumpenproletariat, and beggars. Each of them is the owner of the means of survival, though not the owner in any other respect. In the case of these persons, a significant difference unveils: the legal and the socioeconomic title of ownership. Each of them takes advantage of shelter and food offered by the whim and will of someone else and, mainly, in the interest of someone else. Not being owners from the normative perspective, they are nonetheless owners from the socioeconomic one.

The social doctrine of the Roman Catholic Church applies the legal denotation of ownership. Not everyone is an owner and, yet, those who are not deserve at least the right of usage: "It is therefore understood that the right of usage is an element of the primary law of nature. In other words, each human being – simply because one is human – has the right to avail oneself of material resources to the extent necessary to preserve human existence."[49] Hence, what in Catholic social doctrine constitutes usage, in Marx's perspective constitutes economic ownership of the means of subsistence.

In the second type of ownership of the means of consumption, on quite a different basis, the wage laborer is an owner of the "necessaries of life." He is the owner of labor power functioning as a commodity; he hence acquires the means of consumption in the process of an exchange in which he sells his labor power. As Marx writes, the laborer transforms labor power belonging to him into the means of subsistence: "The value of labour-power resolves itself into the value of a definite quantity of the means of subsistence."[50] However, because of the transaction, the laborer acquires the means of consumption of lower use value than the use value of the labor power that he sold.

The third situation is different; that is, the situation of the owner of the conditions of labor. The owner of the conditions of labor is assured of the means of subsistence at each stage of his activity. Marx describes this in discussing various forms of common and individual ownership of land and instruments which precede capitalist production: "Included in both is the fact that he has the means of consumption in his possession before production, which are necessary for him to live as producer – i.e. during production, *before* its completion."[51] Next, Marx describes how it is that various owners of the conditions of labor are assured of the means of survival. On the one hand, members of a primitive society, as owners of the community property, are directly supplied with the means of survival

49 Józef Majka, *Etyka życia gospodarczego* (Wrocław: Wydawnictwo Wrocławskiej Księgarni Archidiecezjalnej, 1982), 97.

50 Marx, *Capital: A Critique of Political Economy*, Volume I, 121.

51 Marx, *Grundrisse: Foundations of the Critique of Political Economy*, 421–422.

since their land is not only a natural means of production but also a natural reservoir of food. On the other hand, the master craftsman appropriates the earlier created product and therefore possesses the means of survival for the new production cycle.

Elsewhere Karl Marx asserts that what is decisive in the position of the capitalist is not only the conditions of labor which belong to him but also the means of consumption. The latter, in the form of variable capital like a wage fund should be in the hands of the capitalist before undertaking production; if he wants his conditions of labor to become a means for the employment of a hired worker: "The employer, by commanding the means of employment, commands the means of subsistence of the worker, i.e., the latter's life depends on him; just as the worker himself degrades his life activity to a mere means of existence."[52]

This is the variable capital that is precisely the means of subsistence of the worker, which the capitalist owner of the conditions of labor holds prior to the initiation and for the whole duration of the production; or any other capitalist activity. This is a requirement because the employee does not possess such resources and cannot grant his employer a long-term credit in the form of unpaid wage. Consequently, each owner of the conditions of labor is the owner of the means of subsistence before and during production, before its completion. Here, it is less significant whether this activity is undertaken by himself personally or with the services of others: the owner's means of subsistence permits him to economize his conditions of labor.

We should now consider the viewpoint popular among the Marxists: when defining the position of the owner, the category of the means of consumption is less important than that of the conditions of labor. This is not confirmed by the concepts of Karl Marx; in his eyes, these two categories are mutually complementary. A correct depiction of ownership relations comes to light only when they are scrutinized through both these lenses.

Conclusions: General Concepts of Ownership

From the deliberations above, it appears that the question of "what is ownership" can be understood twofold. On the one hand, this can be taken as a question as to who exactly is the owner. On the other hand, it can be taken as a query as to the form of ownership or system of ownership relations.

52 Karl Marx [1846], "Wages", in *Własność, gospodarka a prawo: Studia o marksistowskiej teorii własności*, ed. by Stanisław Kozyr-Kowalski (Warsaw: Państwowe Wydawnictwo Naukowe, 1977).

Evidently underpinning a Marxist analysis of the historical forms of ownership is a stable set of elementary categories which include:

1) the owner of the means of production (also known as the owner of the conditions of labor);
2) the owner of labor power functioning as a factor of labor;
3) the owner of labor power functioning as a commodity;
4) the owner of the means of exchange; and
5) the owner of the means of consumption (also known as the owner of the means of subsistence, of the means of survival, or of the necessaries of life).

Whenever Marx writes about a form, type, or system of ownership, it is possible to identify these fundamental components in the structure; all forms of ownership are composed of these categories. Although people are distinctly different owners in each of the historical forms, all the components appear within those forms of ownership; the only exception is the owner of the means of exchange, who appears in a few of the systems of ownership. A form of ownership comprises a system of relations found among people occupying owner positions in the meanings above.

We can now identify the relationships, in which owners participate in correspondence with different forms of ownership. Albeit a very generalized construct, anchored in the investigation presented in this chapter heretofore, it can be summarized as follows:

1) The owner of the means of production (i.e., the conditions of labor): (a) employs himself and/or others facilitating the utilization of such means as factors of labor (in other words, transforming the means of production and his own or someone else's labor power into factors of labor); (b) appropriates the product created under those conditions of labor; (c) sells that product or otherwise provides others with access to the use value of the conditions of labor and of that product; and, finally, (d) is the owner of the means of consumption before and during the period of labor, until the new product is ready. Thus, the owner of the means of production converts objects of his property into the means of employment and the means for appropriation of the fruits of his own or others' labor.
2) The owner of labor power functioning as a factor of labor is the one who simultaneously applies talents and skills – his own or those belonging to others – in the process of working, and appropriates the product created thereby.

3) The owner of labor power functioning as a commodity realizes his position, as does the owner of any other means of exchange, by selling his labor capabilities in exchange for the means of subsistence.
4) The owner of the means of exchange is someone who sells such means; more generally, someone who provides others with access to the use value of those means in exchange for other goods which are of need to him.
5) The owner of the means of subsistence is someone who consumes or who provides other people with access to consumption of those means.

The owner of the conditions of labor is also the owner in other meanings. Firstly, and above all, he is the owner of his own labor power – functioning as a factor of labor – and/or that of others depending upon whether he himself is working, and/or if he is employing others. Secondly, he is the owner of product which, in his hands, functions as a factor of labor, as a means of consumption, as a commodity – in an exchange economy – or as something else. Thirdly, he is the owner of the means of subsistence in a fashion unique only to him because he owns them before, during, and after the completion of the process. This description also refers to the owner of capital who can play all those roles as one person. Depending on what he acquires, his money allows him to play the role of the owner of the means of production (constant capital), the owner of the means of consumption, and the owner of the use value of someone else's labor power (variable capital), and/or the owner of commodities (trade capital). When he uses his money as financial capital, he is the owner in all those meanings simultaneously, without maintaining direct contact with real economy.

There are such forms of ownership within which it is common that each member of the community plays all these ownership roles together. Such is the case with individual private ownership as well as with certain forms of common ownership.

Still, there are such forms of ownership, in which a part of the population plays only certain ownership roles. This would be, for example, the wage worker who is neither the owner of the conditions of labor nor the owner of labor power as a factor of production, nor the owner of the fruits of his own labors. In his hands, labor power is merely a good of which he is the owner. His ownership position is realized in the selling of his labor power as a commodity and in his consuming of the means of survival gained in the form of wages. Rather than employ someone, he is employed; rather than appropriate the product of his labor, he is divested of it. Moreover, he is not the owner of the means of existence before or after his engagement in an employment relationship; he is only such an owner over the course of his employment; a situation which forces him to renew this type of relationship.

The configuration of mutual relationships, in which the owners above enter, distinguishes explicit systems of ownership. Marx describes this, among other places, in *Capital*:

> Whatever the social form of production, labourers and means of production always remain factors of it. But in a state of separation from each other either of these factors can be such only potentially. For production to go on at all they must unite. The specific manner in which this union is accomplished distinguishes the different economic epochs of the structure of society from one another.[53]

Regardless of whether these factors converge in one person, or whether their linkage is the outcome of interdependencies amongst many people, the form of ownership is fulfilled only in the sum of all the interconnected ownership roles above. This aspect of ownership is rarely undertaken when interpreting the theories of Karl Marx.

Most often, investigations probe into ownership of the petty bourgeoisie, capitalist, feudal, cooperative, common, or peasant farming types. Or, even more generally, there is talk of private or social ownership. However, none of this delves deeper into the internal structure of these synthesized concepts. Yet forms of ownership also differ from one another, since individuals can be owners in diverse ways within them; individuals can enter and remain in various ownership relationships. For Karl Marx, the form of ownership was more than a system of relationships between owners and non-owners of the means of production. Marx analyzed the complex configurations of relationships amongst varying kinds of owners: owners of the conditions of labor, owners of labor power, owners of the means of exchange (including money), owners of the means of subsistence, etc. Applying much more precise theoretical instruments in the analysis of ownership relations, Marx went further than has been presented by his successors with roots in sundry strands of Marxism.

53 Karl Marx [1863–1878], *Capital: A Critique of Political Economy*, Volume II, <https://www.marxists.org/archive/marx/works/download/pdf/Capital-Volume-II.pdf> [accessed August 2017], 22.

Chapter II: A History of Privatization: Pre-Capitalistic Forms of Ownership

Historical Systems of Ownership

Marx applies a few typologies for historical systems of ownership. Consequently, specialized literature provides many different interpretations of his position in this regard. The most frequently presented – especially in political economy textbooks – is the one which identifies the five basic "modes of production": (a) primitive, tribal, pre-class community; (b) slavery; (c) feudalism; (d) capitalism; and (e) socialism. However, this set is only partly in accord with the positions of Karl Marx. For instance, in *A Contribution to the Critique of Political Economy*, Marx states: "In broad outline, the Asiatic, ancient, feudal, and modern bourgeois modes of production may be designated as epochs marking progress in the economic development of society."[54] Yet his manuscripts from 1857 to 1859, the so-called *Grundrisse*, reveal an even greater number of modes of production and corresponding types of ownership. These include, among other things, the ownership of the tribal community, the Asiatic, the classical ancient, and the Germanic types; in addition to the slavery, feudal, and capitalistic.[55] Furthermore, certain works reveal his thoughts about more than one communist type of ownership.[56] In fact, *Capital* is rank with explications regarding several historical types of property relations.[57]

---

54 Karl Marx [1859], *A Contribution to the Critique of Political Economy*, <https://www.marxists.org/archive/marx/works/download/Marx_Contribution_to_the_Critique_of_Political_Economy.pdf> [accessed August 2017], 4.

55 Karl Marx [1857–1861], *Grundrisse: Foundations of the Critique of Political Economy* (Rough Draft), <https://www.marxists.org/archive/marx/works/download/pdf/grundrisse.pdf> [accessed August 2017], 397–440.

56 Karl Marx [1844], *Economic & Philosophic Manuscripts of 1844*, <https://www.marxists.org/archive/marx/works/download/pdf/Economic-Philosophic-Manuscripts-1844.pdf> [accessed August 2017]; Karl Marx [1875], *Critique of the Gotha Programme*, <https://www.marxists.org/archive/marx/works/download/Marx_Critque_of_the_Gotha_Programme.pdf> [accessed August 2017]; Karl Marx, Friedrich Engels [1847], *Manifesto of the Communist Party*, <https://www.marxists.org/archive/marx/works/download/pdf/Manifesto.pdf> [accessed August 2017].

57 Karl Marx [1867], *Capital: A Critique of Political Economy*, Volume I, <https://www.marxists.org/archive/marx/works/download/pdf/Capital-Volume-I.pdf> [accessed August 2017].

That noted, the historical types of ownership distinguished by Karl Marx may be characterized by tracing his subsequent reflections. In more detailed analyses, it is clear that Marx refers to an irresolute number of types; including those just cited: "Property, then, originally means – in its Asiatic, Slavonic, ancient classical, Germanic form – the relation of the working (producing or self-reproducing) subject to the conditions of his production or reproduction as his own. It will therefore have different forms depending on the conditions of this production."[58] *Grundrisse* even mention a whole series of pre-capitalistic formations. For instance,

> Communal property has recently been rediscovered as a special Slavonic curiosity. But, in fact, India offers us a sample chart of the most diverse forms of such economic communities, more or less dissolved, but still completely recognizable; and a more thorough research into history uncovers it as the point of departure of all cultured peoples. The system of production founded on private exchange is, to begin with, the historic dissolution of this naturally arisen communism. However, a whole series of economic systems lies in turn between the modern world, where exchange value dominates production to its whole depth and extent, and the social formations whose foundation is already formed by the dissolution of communal property, without [Here the manuscript breaks off].[59]

In addition, on more than one occasion, Marx speaks of the so-called mixed or transitional forms of ownership. Marx further notes a peculiar formation of society which existed in most of the Western European countries, a form whose key trait was a predominance of individual private property. Ownership relations manifest in this form cannot be reduced to either the feudal or the capitalistic type.[60]

Nevertheless, in the course of more general analyses, the number of types diminishes to a handful of the most basic ones. These generalizations are of various sorts. One of these is rooted in encompassment, under one label, of the primitive, Asian, ancient, German, and Slavic forms of ownership. Marx will sometimes categorize these as the "archaic type of communal property." Furthermore, scholars discover a simplification of the traits of Asian, ancient, and Germanic ownership, described as "dualistic" and clearly differentiated from the primitive, common ownership.[61] Karl Marx also lists three types of historical formations: primary, secondary, and tertiary:

---

58 Marx, *Grundrisse: Foundations of the Critique of Political Economy*, 419.

59 Ibid., 800.

60 Marx, *Capital: A Critique of Political Economy*, Volume I, 541–547.

61 Karl Marx [1881], *Letter to Vera Zasulich: The "First" Draft*, <https://www.marxists.org/archive/marx/works/1881/zasulich/draft-1.htm> [accessed August 2017]; Karl Marx [1881], *Letter to Vera Zasulich: The "Second" Draft*, <https://www.marxists.org/archive/marx/works/1881/zasulich/draft-2.htm> [accessed August 2017]; Karl Marx [1881],

> Accordingly, the 'agricultural commune' every here presents itself as the most recent type of the archaic formation of societies; and the period of the agricultural commune appears in the historical course of Western Europe, both ancient and modern, as a period of transition from communal to private property, from the primary to the secondary formation.[62]

The first of these includes those communities in which common ownership dominates; the last two include those in which slavery, servitude (serfdom), and private ownership prevail:

> As [the most recent and] the latest phase in the [archaic] primitive formation of society, the agrarian commune [naturally represents the transition] is at the same time a phase in the transition to the secondary formation, and therefore in the transition from a society based on communal property to one based on private property. The secondary formation does, of course, include the series of societies which rest upon slavery and serfdom.[63]

It is evident that Marx does not propose some stiff and formal classification system. Hence, in analyzing his elucidations on the history of ownership relations, we emphasize more this more flexible and open quality of Marx's method. It encompasses the most cognitive content and, yet, is the most rarely extricated from his writings.

Indeed, precisely the diversity he ascertained in real-world ownership systems led Marx to avoid the establishment of stiff classifications, which could hinder the study of phenomena in their actual contours and, befitting a specific society, in a specific time and place. In turn, the models which Marx applies were continuously subject to various reconfigurations. With respect to this, Karl Marx was at profound variance with his continuators – including Engels and Lenin – who aimed to hem historical processes, to enclose them in an unambiguous and streamlined theoretical framework.

Each particular system of ownership has its own distinct structure. This structure can facilitate the formation of rather homogenous and uniform ownership relations; however, most often, a multitude of forms of ownership functions within the same system, with one dominating over the remainder. For instance, there is the ascendancy of communal property in Asian societies; of individual land ownership in Ancient societies; and of private ownership accompanied by a free labor market in capitalistic societies. The remaining, minor forms of

---

Letter to Vera Zasulich: The "Third" Draft, <https://www.marxists.org/archive/marx/works/1881/zasulich/draft-3.htm> [accessed August 2017].

62 Marx, *Letter to Vera Zasulich: The "First" Draft.*

63 Marx, *Letter to Vera Zasulich: The "Third" Draft.*

ownership endure despite the influence of the major one. This can manifest itself in the expropriation of individuals who work within a marginal form of ownership, accompanied by the rising liquidation of that form together with its corresponding mode of production. A somewhat less forceful means of interference is the subordination – but not elimination – of other forms by the dominant mode of production. Yet, another one can be the consciousness among owners who conduct business in a subsidiary form and begin to rationalize their activities in such a way as if they were working within the basic, dominant one. Marx provides an example:

> In a social order dominated by capitalist production even the non-capitalist producer is gripped by capitalist conceptions. Balzac, who is generally remarkable for his profound grasp of reality, aptly describes in his last novel, *Les Paysans*, how a petty peasant performs many small tasks gratuitously for his usurer, whose goodwill he is eager to retain, and how he fancies that he does not give the latter something for nothing because his own labour does not cost him any cash outlay. As for the usurer, he thus fells two dogs with one stone. He saves the cash outlay for wages and enmeshes the peasant, who is gradually ruined by depriving his own field of labour, deeper and deeper in the spider-web of usury.[64]

The dominant mode of production and its analogous type of ownership do have an impact on other contemporaneous ones. Government ownership of a capitalist type is different from that of the feudal type – and even more different from that of the Asian type. The same could be stated about other forms of ownership appearing at various stages of social development. For instance, land ownership based on slave labor survived until the modern times of Karl Marx and, yet, he calls the American plantation owners capitalists because the form of their ownership assumed a spectrum of traits associated with the form then dominant: "The fact that we now not only call the plantation owners in America capitalists, but that they *are* capitalists, is based on their existence as anomalies within a world market based on free labour."[65]

Even more rare are those peripheral forms which create an economic framework for the exploitation of the fundamental system. Marx identifies these ownership structures in most historical forms:

---

64 Karl Marx [1863–1883], *Capital: A Critique of Political Economy*, Volume III, <https://www.marxists.org/archive/marx/works/download/pdf/Capital-Volume-III.pdf> [accessed August 2017], 26.

65 Marx, *Grundrisse: Foundations of the Critique of Political Economy*, 437.

> To the extent that slavery prevails, or in so far as the surplus product is consumed by the feudal lord and his retinue, while either the slave-owner or the feudal lord fall into the clutches of the usurer, the mode of production still remains the same; it only becomes harder on the labourer. The indebted slave holder or feudal lord becomes more oppressive because he is himself more oppressed. Or he finally makes way for the usurer, who becomes a landed proprietor or a slave-holder himself, like the knights in ancient Rome. The place of the old exploiter, whose exploitation was more or less patriarchal because it was largely a means of political power, is taken by a hard, money mad parvenu. But the mode of production itself is not altered thereby. / Usury has a revolutionary effect in all pre-capitalist modes of production only in so far as it destroys and dissolves those forms of property on whose solid foundation and continual reproduction in the same form the political organization is based. Under Asian forms, usury can continue a long time, without producing anything more than economic decay and political corruption.[66]

In this chapter, I will discuss several Marx's viewpoints on pre-capitalistic systems of ownership, even though this will not comprise a comparison of his analyses with those of the latest commentators today. Deliberations of this sort are interesting, but would completely veer off the path of this volume. The point here is not to shed light on historical events and evolutions but to illuminate the uniqueness in Marxist thinking about these societies, demonstrate his methodology, and describe the research tools which served his studies of societies so completely different from the capitalist one.

Property Relations in the Primordial Community

General Characteristics

The starting point for an investigation into ownership is, for Karl Marx, any form of collective life, the simplest social group; meaning a family, clan, tribe, horde, etc. This is rooted in an assumption that ownership relations are, after all, relations between human beings. An individual can be a proprietor of a piece of land, if and only if he participates in the life of some collective. As Marx wrote,

> An isolated individual could no more have property in land and soil than he could speak. He could, of course, live off it as substance, as do the animals. The relation to the earth as property is always mediated through the occupation of the land and soil, peacefully or violently, by the tribe, the commune, in some more or less naturally arisen or already historically developed form.[67]

66 Marx, *Capital: A Critique of Political Economy*, Volume III, 445.
67 Marx, *Grundrisse: Foundations of the Critique of Political Economy*, 409.

The same refers to each human activity directed toward nature as the subject of property:

> In the process of production, human beings work not only upon nature, but also upon one another. They produce only by working together in a specified manner and reciprocally exchanging their activities. In order to produce, they enter into definite connections and relations to one another, and only within these social connections and relations does their influence upon nature operate – i.e., does production take place.[68]

Karl Marx often categorically asserted that the very first form of ownership in the history of societies – "historic state No. I" – was common property of land and soil.[69] The descriptors he applies vary: common property, communal ownership, primitive ownership, tribal ownership, or primitive forms of ownership. Moreover, Marx declares that the existence of this type is obvious and requires no elucidation. What does require, in his eyes, explication is the breakdown of primitive ownership.

The material conditions of life of primordial groups were overwhelmingly a consequence of nature; even rudimentary tools were delivered thereby. This low development of creativity paralleled the simplicity of relationships between human beings. Each individual lived as a member of a rather small community which, consequently, delineated the boundaries of his social life. As Engels recounted Marx,

> Man was bounded by his tribe, both in relation to strangers from outside the tribe and to himself; the tribe, the gens, and their institutions were sacred and inviolable, a higher power established by nature, to which the individual subjected himself unconditionally in feeling, thought, and action. However impressive the people of this epoch appear to us, they are completely undifferentiated from one another; as Marx says, they are still attached to the navel string of the primitive community.[70]

Constitutive for such an intimate group was kinship. The community was always a family, clan, or assembly of clans. Upon finishing Lewis Henry Morgan's *Ancient Society*, Marx was enthusiastic about the theories he found therein.[71] Quite

---

68 Karl Marx [1847], *Wage Labour and Capital*, <https://www.marxists.org/archive/marx/works/download/pdf/wage-labour-capital.pdf> [accessed August 2017], 13.

69 Marx, *Grundrisse: Foundations of the Critique of Political Economy*, 422–424.

70 Friedrich Engels [1884], *Origin of the Family, Private Property, and the State*, <https://www.marxists.org/archive/marx/works/download/pdf/origin_family.pdf> [accessed August 2017], 52.

71 Karl Marx [1880–1881], *Conspectus of Lewis Morgan's Ancient Society*, <https://www.marxists.org/archive/marx/works/1884/origin-family/marx-conspectus.htm> [acces

frequently and at various points in his life, Karl Marx emphasizes the foremost meaning of the familial-clan structure in the life of communities.

Common Ownership

Belonging to a community constitutes a prerequisite for the appropriation of land and its products by the members thereof. It is not the individual, but the community which first takes ownership of the land; only a community can remove another community from a territory occupied by the latter and only a community can be deprived of its own property. The community appears as the collective owner vis-à-vis other groups and vis-à-vis its own members. Each person becomes the owner solely as a member of a collective. As Marx put it, "His *property*, i.e. the relation to the natural presuppositions of his production as belonging to him, as *his*, is mediated by his being himself the natural member of a community."[72] An individual can be evicted from his living conditions only when the property of the entire community is seized or when he or the community severs the ties that bind them together.

The land is the primary object of ownership. Yet it can only become such an object inasmuch as it is utilized and inasmuch as the community directs its activity towards it: "Only when tribes hunt upon it does a region of the earth become a hunting domain; only cultivation of the soil posits the land as the individual's extended body."[73] Communal ownership of the physical environment also encompasses ownership of tools, materials, water, uncultivated fruits, and nuts, etc. These are products of nature and even the first cultural products created by man are perceived as part and parcel of land ownership:

> Ownership of land and soil potentially also includes ownership of the raw material, as well as of the primordial instrument, the earth itself, and of its spontaneous fruits. Posited in the most original form, it means relating to the earth as proprietor, and finding raw material and instrument on hand, as well as the necessaries of life created not by labour but by the earth itself. Once this relation is reproduced, secondary instruments and fruits of the earth created through labour itself appear as included with landed property in its primitive forms.[74]

sed August 2017]; Marx, *Grundrisse: Foundations of the Critique of Political Economy*, 397–440.

72 Marx, *Grundrisse: Foundations of the Critique of Political Economy*, 414.

73 Ibid., 417.

74 Ibid., 422–423.

Every member of a community has the status of an owner of the communal land and soil. Marx clearly speaks about this when discussing the similarities between collective and individual private ownership: "In both forms, the worker relates to the objective conditions of his labour as to his property; this is the natural unity of labour with its material [*sachlich*] presuppositions. The worker thus has an objective existence independent of labour. The individual relates to himself as proprietor as master of the conditions of his reality."[75]

Each of the members is a proprietor of the conditions of labor because each member can render the territory inhabited by his community the object of his actions and activities. With the explicit or implicit permission of other co-owners, he employs himself within the realm of the available working conditions, and can, furthermore, agree or not to a partaking by others of the goods found on the terrain settled by the group to which he belongs.

Marx describes common ownership as a form "in which the worker is a proprietor, or in which the proprietor works" and as "natural unity of labour with its material presuppositions."[76] This form, therefore, assumes indistinguishability between the owner of the labor force and the owner of the means of production; this applies to both individual members as well as to the community as a whole.

The community organizes all the work to be done, decides how to make use of the skills and talents of each member, controls the products of collective labor, and, finally, distributes these products among its members. That which the individual loses, he gains as a member of the community. Hence one can speak of a dualistic relationship: on the one hand, each member is an owner via the collective intermediary; on the other hand, the group becomes such an owner via the day-to-day undertakings of its members.

Members of the commune enjoy their share of the production due to their belonging to the community. This even pertains to those who do not work; e.g., the elderly, children, those ill or with disabilities. Although such persons do not confirm their ownership position by their physical or mental efforts, they are owners by way of the group; something expressed in their participation in the distribution of the fruits of the earth gathered by the general population of tribesmen.

The oldest communities do not allot parcels of land amongst their membership. Exploitation of the land and its yield is of a collective nature. And even if a portion of the crops is reaped through the efforts of but a few individuals, still others bear access to all the territory and its resources. In sum, one cannot speak

75 Ibid., 398.

76 Ibid., 398, 421.

here of individual ownership of tools which are used by all the members of the community. At this stage, too, the distribution of produced goods is not yet connected to the distribution of working conditions (distribution of land and tools). As Engels observes,

> At all earlier stages of society production was essentially collective, just as consumption proceeded by direct distribution of the products within larger or smaller communistic communities. This collective production was very limited; but inherent in it was the producers' control over their process of production and their product. They knew what became of their product: they consumed it; it did not leave their hands. And so long as production remains on this basis, it cannot grow above the heads of the producers nor raise up incorporeal alien powers against them, as in civilization is always and inevitably the case.[77]

Initially, there is a lack of permanent, socially constructed principles regarding unequal apportionment. These are only being shaped and, hence, nature dominates (strength, health, etc.) or social norms step in (tradition, customs, habits, etc.). To a certain degree, the products are not even divided and distributed but directly internalized by consumption.

Nevertheless, that part of the production, which is absorbed by the community, is distributed at least partly along the lines of an inscribed and generally known set of principles. This looks differently in every society, as the rules of distribution are influenced by the personal traits of individual members, how a product was obtained, coincidence, circumstance, etc. Kinship relations, family-clan structures, and social hierarchies affect this as well. It can be assumed that, as of a certain stage of development, this becomes the core factor in tribal communities.

A product of common labor is intended to be consumed and so it is. Therefore, it should not remain in circulation. Even if there were to be an overproduction – "the first spontaneously evolved form of wealth"[78] – then it was most often one coming from nature and not from man. As such, this surplus does not lend itself to a transformation into accumulated wealth, into a commodity; it does not function as a means of exchange, but is rather wasted. For a product to become a means of exchange, it should be of a useful, practical value for someone who does not possess it. In this case, however, no one is interested in taking control of it because the feasible excess product affects one and all. This form of wealth, although not comprising a practical value for any party, is sometimes an object of exchange; above all, between communities, and often fulfilling some symbolic function. It is only at

77 Engels, *Origin of the Family, Private Property, and the State*, 94.
78 Marx, *A Contribution to the Critique of Political Economy*.

a later stage of development that an exchange of useful valuables appears. Yet this takes place at the borderlines between communities, each of which perceives the other as the sole proprietor of its product. Initially, such products are exchanged in completely happenstance proportions:

> So long as, instead of two distinct use-values being exchanged, a chaotic mass of articles are offered as the equivalent of a single article, which is often the case with savages, even the direct barter of products is in its first infancy.[79]

Moreover, there are limits: land does not become an object of exchange, neither do the most indispensable tools nor other key elements of the working conditions:

> But such a state of reciprocal independence has no existence in a primitive society based on property in common, whether such a society takes the form of a patriarchal family, an ancient Indian community, or a Peruvian Inca State. The exchange of commodities, therefore, first begins on the boundaries of such communities, at their points of contact with other similar communities, or with members of the latter. So soon, however, as products once become commodities in the external relations of a community, they also, by reaction, become so in its internal intercourse. The proportions in which they are exchangeable are at first quite a matter of chance. What makes them exchangeable is the mutual desire of their owners to alienate them. Meantime the need for foreign objects of utility gradually establishes itself. The constant repetition of exchange makes it a normal social act.[80]

A characteristic trait of a primordial community is a correspondence between the means of work with the means of subsistence. As Marx puts it, "the consumption fund appears as a component part of the original production fund."[81] Therefore, a member of a community is an owner of the means of survival prior to undertaking a job and during the course of his work, up until the new product is created. In this case, of secondary meaning is the fact that these means might be available in quantities barely sufficient for existence. Despite this, it is also via consumption that a member affirms his position as the owner of the working conditions.

Movable Property

The primitive, tribal community is one of the most permanent social forms. But, along with the development of creative energy and productive forces, the group succumbs to various transformations and, ultimately, disintegration. In specific societies, these transformations run in different directions, but certain similarities can be identified.

---

79 Marx, *Capital: A Critique of Political Economy*, Volume I, 64.

80 Ibid., 61.

81 Marx, *Grundrisse: Foundations of the Critique of Political Economy*, 416–417.

The first of these is the appearance of new, manmade elements of the forces of production. In the economy, alongside the natural working conditions and objects created by the community, especially movable goods come to play a growing role. The second is the emergence of new methods for the execution of collective work and the shaping of new relationships in the division of labor; a "natural" one (according to age, gender, health, abilities, etc.), which yields way to other principles of division. Especially important here is the separation of those performing productive and nonproductive tasks. Third is the rise in work productivity which enables some persons to make supplementary products and others to engage in matters disassociated from the creation of the means of consumption. The fourth tendency is an increase in the resident population; fifth and final are changes in the shape of the family and, therefore, changes in kinship relations.

The beginnings of the disintegration of a community and its common property will be a new object of ownership emerging from within: mobile ownership of the means of production. Development of the tribal community will lead to a dualization of proprietary relations. As members of a community, people are still co-owners of the working conditions. Nonetheless, at least some of them start to concurrently be individual owners of instruments and tools – as well as other factors of labor – independent of the community.

The type of this mobile wealth depends upon the means of production. On the one hand, among nomadic peoples such property will be cattle, transportation modes (horses, camels, etc.), or weapons. Wandering groups will always perceive the land as shared by all and so its ownership will never congeal. Although control of the land comprises the foundation of their existence, the reproducing object which constitutes the crucial core of their activities is their herd (e.g., cattle, sheep, goats, reindeer, etc.). On the other hand, among farming peoples, their accumulated wealth includes their tools and their grain. All portable elements of their labor and their means of survival are initially used in common. But, with time, these objects more often fall into individual hands; first governed by specific clans or families within the community, later by the leaders of these groups.[82]

The distribution of tools leads to a differentiation in the capabilities of specific families, clans, and individuals to undertake specific tasks, activities, and endeavors. In turn, this will intrude upon the distribution of production, but this interference will not be of an obvious nature since the land will not yet have been parceled out. Hence, the partitioning of the product still depends above all on a

82 Ibid., 397–440; Engels, *Origin of the Family, Private Property, and the State*; Marx, *Letter to Vera Zasulich: The "First" Draft.*

person's place in the family and kinship structures. For instance, the position of the patriarch or matriarch is an element not only of kinship, but also of a special place in the relationships pertaining to the division of labor, the division of production, and the exchange and consumption of goods.

This state of affairs is reflected in new production goals. Whereas the primary and fundamental aim of production will always be the satisfaction of needs and the reproduction of the community; now, the production of goods for exchange emerges. The augmentation of moveable property means that exchanges along the boundaries between communities become more intense. Simultaneously, exchanges begin to take place within the home community itself – at first between clans and their representatives, later between individuals. Still, at the outset, these will be phenomena of marginal significance. In conjunction with the still dominant collective consumption, familial or individual consumption begins to play an increasingly larger role. The first signs surface from the individual ownership of permanent means of consumption (e.g., home ownership).[83]

Property Relations in the Asiatic Society

General Characteristics

The Asiatic mode of production and its corresponding type of ownership relations has appeared not only in Asia, but in other parts of the world as well. Marx applies this label to certain Slavic, Celtic, or even American communities such as the Inca and Aztec. This type of relations has generally developed on the Asian continent and, hence, the genealogy of the name by which Marx pools together communities separated from each other in space and time. Nonetheless, he does use other terminology on occasion, and here it would be worth mentioning: the oriental form, Hindu ownership, or the Eastern form of ownership. However, this broad-strokes employment of a single appellation for detached groups does not mean that Marx was implying the existence of some historical contact between them; even if in some concrete cases such contact could have occurred. These are basically social forms which are, to some extent, similar to one another; they are variations of a single type.[84]

---

83 Marx, *Capital: A Critique of Political Economy*, Volume I, 41, 46; Marx, *Grundrisse: Foundations of the Critique of Political Economy*, 419–423.

84 Marx, *Grundrisse: Foundations of the Critique of Political Economy*, 400, 418, 419; Marx, *Letter to Vera Zasulich: The "First" Draft*; Marx, *Letter to Vera Zasulich: The "Second" Draft*; Marx, *Letter to Vera Zasulich: The "Third" Draft*.

These subtypes vary in the levels of development of productive forces. They represent many different configurations of interpersonal relations between their members. They differ in the magnitude of their economic and political organisms, their scale of production, and many other traits. Some of them live at a level of development which – in the eyes of Morgan and Engels – could be called the barbarian epoch, while others represent a high level of civilizational development. Some still constitute pre-state, isolated social organisms; they are, at best, organized as associations of communities. In contrast, some function in the framework of archaic, despotic states.

Yet, there is such a dimension in which Marx perceives all manner of similarities among these communities: all these societies anchor their existence in the community. It is of less importance if the society is organized as a state, or not. Despite the development variation in the Asian type society, the commune functions as the keystone of economic and social life.

On more than one occasion, Marx underscored the strategic meaning of the commune for the functioning of the Asian type of society. If a commune exists within a despotic state, then it is an entity isolated from other communities and contacts between them are maintained by way of the state; that is, mediated by the functionaries of the state. Such a system is especially permanent because it is economically self-sufficient. Whereas other forms of social life succumb to change or even vanish, this form continues unaltered as the fundamental building block in this type of society. Marx spotlights this in the first volume of *Capital*:

> The simplicity of the organisation for production in these self-sufficing communities that constantly reproduce themselves in the same form, and when accidentally destroyed, spring up again on the spot and with the same name – this simplicity supplies the key to the secret of the unchangeableness of Asiatic societies, an unchangeableness in such striking contrast with the constant dissolution and refounding of Asiatic States, and the never-ceasing changes of dynasty. The structure of the economic elements of society remains untouched by the storm-clouds of the political sky.[85]

It is within the communal space that the most meaningful social ties are established, constitutive for this type of social relations. The individual lives as a member of the collective: the clan, tribe, village, etc. Membership in the community mediates his relationships with other people, the conditions of work, his means of survival, and the state as the superordinate political institution.

It is in this aspect that the Asiatic type of commune is like the primitive community. In both cases there is a dominance of the collective element over the

85 Marx, *Capital: A Critique of Political Economy*, Volume I, 247–248.

individual, the commune over the person. One can only survive as a member of the community; or as a functionary of the state, which is a novelty compared to primitive communities. Still dominating here are blood ties which connect each member of the commune. Wherever the state is already formed, the meaning of territorial divides and ties increase inside as well as outside the community.

These new bonds of a territorial nature, nevertheless, remain inextricably connected to kinship relations. Even a territorial group like a village is governed by the principles of life in a clan. One of the petrified forms which the kinship tie can take in a community or state is the caste. In each commune, the family and kinship structure takes on a different form, but it continues to impact the life of the group. This is evident in the division of labor, in ownership relations, and in the domination-subordination relationship. A privileged position in the kinship structure simultaneously means a privileged position in other systems. A presupposition for the first forms of enslavement are a concrete model of family and a concrete type of kinship. For instance, the institution of matriarchy (subsequently patriarchy) is precisely such a cultural form of slavery within a community.

The Asiatic type of community also distinguishes itself from the tribal one by new and fixed principles in the division of labor. There is no room within the commune for a division into the working and non-working. Such a split appears only later, within the entire country. Here it is worth recollecting Marx's description of just such a village, in which precisely the issue of the division of labor is in the foreground – the Hindu community:

> The constitution of these communities varies in different parts of India. In those of the simplest form, the land is tilled in common, and the produce divided among the members. At the same time, spinning and weaving are carried on in each family as subsidiary industries. Side by side with the masses thus occupied with one and the same work, we find the 'chief inhabitant,' who is judge, police, and tax-gatherer in one; the book-keeper, who keeps the accounts of the tillage and registers everything relating thereto; another official, who prosecutes criminals, protects strangers travelling through and escorts them to the next village; the boundary man, who guards the boundaries against neighbouring communities; the water-overseer, who distributes the water from the common tanks for irrigation; the Brahmin, who conducts the religious services; the schoolmaster, who on the sand teaches the children reading and writing; the calendar-Brahmin, or astrologer, who makes known the lucky or unlucky days for seed-time and harvest, and for every other kind of agricultural work; a smith and a carpenter, who make and repair all the agricultural implements; the potter, who makes all the pottery of the village; the barber, the washerman, who washes clothes, the silversmith, here and there the poet, who in some communities replaces the silversmith, in others the schoolmaster. This dozen of individuals is maintained at the expense of the whole community.[86]

86 Ibid., 247.

Communal Ownership of the Asiatic Formation

In the Asian state, the legal status of the community can vary. The community can be, for instance, the rightful owner of the territory which it occupies. This case, however, is rather rare; more frequently the owner in a legal sense is the state or the landlord as a personification of the state. Here, the commune possesses the status permitting legal inheritance and taking ownership of property. Yet such a depiction of a community is an obvious legal fiction which Marx surely applies to present descriptively the normative structure which regulates socioeconomic life. It may be a fiction, but Marx rectifies this situation as follows:

> Amidst oriental despotism and the propertylessness which seems legally to exist there, this clan or communal property exists in fact as the foundation, created mostly by a combination of manufactures and agriculture within the small commune, which thus becomes altogether self-sustaining, and contains all the conditions of reproduction and surplus production within itself.[87]

A community of the Asian type, as with the primitive, tribal one, constitutes the presupposition for the appropriation of land. The tribal community took control of the land, on which it dwelled. Land appropriation in the Asian community assumes a similar form, although the community, as a group of people or by way of its leader or chief, received an allotment from the rulers. The despotic state grants land to a community, not to individual members thereof. Again, consequently, no one can be an owner independent of the group, and no one who is not a member of the group can become an owner within its jurisdiction. Simultaneously, nobody who is a member of the group can be divested of property. Expropriation of a person's land can occur only when that individual is expelled from the local community or when the community itself is stripped of its property.

The economic realization of the position of owner by members of a community is mediated by their community. This can take on many a form. In the oldest form, work is of a collective nature and hence the fruits of labor are distributed according to various principles. In the youngest form, there is an allotment of the working conditions and each family individually works its own apportioned plot of land. The family keeps part of the crops and yield for the satisfaction of its own needs and transfers the rest to the community or its representatives. Additionally, between the extremes, numerous transitional variations appear:

> Now, in so far as it actually realizes itself in labour, this kind of communal property can appear either in the form where the little communes vegetate independently alongside one

87 Marx, *Grundrisse: Foundations of the Critique of Political Economy*, 399–400.

another, and where, inside them, the individual with his family work independently on the lot assigned to them (a certain amount of labour for the *communal reserves, insurance* so to speak, and to *meet the expenses of the community as such,* i.e. for war, religion etc.; this is the first occurrence of the lordly *dominium* in the most original sense, e.g. in the Slavonic communes, in the Rumanian etc. Therein lies the transition to villeinage [*Frondienst*] etc.); or the unity may extend to the communality of labour itself, which may be a formal system, as in Mexico, Peru especially, among the early Celts, a few clans of India.[88]

Regardless of that, in every one of these cases, there is a distinguishable set of shared characteristics typical of Asian style ownership. The community:

1) reigns over the conditions of labor as a group of people or by way of its agents; it is the community and not an independent person who is the key to appropriation;
2) makes the conditions of labor available to its members by either dividing the land amongst its members or organizing their employment;
3) requisitions the fruits of labor of its members in whole or in part;
4) distributes the product;
5) reproduces the conditions of labor in whole or in part;
6) represents itself as the owner and seller vis-à-vis other groups, protecting the goods used by its members and transferring to the state any surplus product (e.g., taxes); and
7) administrates the reserve supplies, including the means of maintenance.

Ownership Relations in the Asiatic Society

In *Grundrisse*, Karl Marx wrote that, in the "specifically oriental form," man is a private possessor of communal property:

> wherever property exists *only* as communal property, there the individual member is as such only *possessor* of a particular part, hereditary or not, since any fraction of the property belongs to no member for himself, but to him only as immediate member of the commune, i.e. as in direct unity with it, not in distinction to it. This individual is thus only a possessor. What exists is only *communal* property, and only *private possession*. The mode of this possession in relation to the communal property may be historically, locally etc. modified in quite different ways, depending on whether labour itself is performed by the private possessor in isolation, or is in turn determined by the commune or by the unity hovering above the particular commune.[89]

88 Ibid., 400.
89 Ibid., 403.

A double meaning can be found in the portrayal of the member as the owner. First, this is a normative trait of his position: he is a possessor because he utilizes land on the basis of someone else's will, that of the community who is the owner. Secondly, this is also an economic definition of the proprietor: he is a working owner who directly appropriates at least some of the fruits of his labors.

This does not, however, refute the fact that they are enslaved – something which Marx addressed up front. Still, subjugation does not signify a loss of property. When Marx writes that the relationship of each person vis-à-vis the community of which he is a member is never one of freedom, such assertions are always accompanied by a clarification regarding the impossibility of the member's expropriation: "In the oriental form this *loss* is hardly possible, except by means of altogether external influences, since the individual member of the commune never enters into the relation of freedom towards it in which he could lose his (objective, economic) bond with it. He is rooted to the spot, ingrown."[90] In fact, this kind of subjugation contributes to the solidification or even petrification of the communal ownership. It is only later, when and if the individual frees him- or herself from the commune, that expropriation becomes possible.

Depending upon the form of development of the group, people fulfill their ownership position in a diverse manner. As noted earlier, work is performed together in older forms, whereas there is allotment of land in the younger ones. In the former, members are co-owners while, in the latter, they are individual landholders. In more democratic forms, all members of the community participate in the collective appropriation of the means of production and its distribution. In more despotic forms, they have a passive right to own their plot; i.e. limited access to the means of production. In both cases, they can, however, undertake work on the territory belonging to the community. Within the community, no one is in such a situation as to be unable to find employment.

In each developmental variation, members are owners of results of production in a different sense. Wherever work is performed jointly, the product is wholly appropriated by the community and only subsequently divided. Wherever land has been parceled out, the product is appropriated individually:

> Finally, although the arable land remained communal property, it was periodically divided among the members of the agricultural commune, so that each farmer tilled on his own behalf the various fields allocated to him and individually appropriated their fruits. In the more archaic communities, by contrast, production was a common activity, and only the final produce was distributed among individual members. Of course, this

90 Ibid., 418.

primitive type of collective or co-operative production stemmed from the weakness of the isolated individual, not from socialisation of the means of production.[91]

The community of Asiatic type appropriates a portion of the fruits of an individual household's labors, in the form of taxes, so as to ensure resources to provide for the community, support its functionaries, and pay taxes to the state. This is a form of community in which the domination of the collective element over the individual appears in the subjugation of the residents. Hence, in the dispersal of the product, non-economic factors play a big role. Any and all connections blur between the division of working conditions, work contribution, and product distribution. It would be a mistake, however, to claim that coincidence and haphazardness decide about this division because it does bear the traits of a permanent relationship: the regularity and repetitiveness, without which no society is capable of existing over the longer duration. Yet, this does not preclude the appearance of more permanent forms of exploitation within the community although this will not take on some more drastic form since anticipated consumption limits production.

The goal of the activity undertaken by members of the community is not to expropriate other peers and get rich – though this could be a secondary goal – but rather to reproduce the community in unchanged form. Hence, no distribution of the product can lead to the loss by some residents of their position as owners of the working conditions. Even if the distribution is disadvantageous, still all members reaffirm their position as owners capable of assuring themselves of resources: "The aim of this work is not the *creation of value* – although they may do surplus labour in order to obtain *alien*, i.e. surplus products in exchange – rather, its aim is sustenance of the individual proprietor and of his family, as well as of the total community."[92]

In the Asian type of community, a phenomenon appears, rarely met in communities of the older type; initially the community, but then its members, begin to present themselves as owners of goods. At first, this will involve intercommunity exchanges in which a person can only represent his own community, not participating as a private individual. At the outset, individuals participate in exchanges of movable assets within their own group and only later make contacts outside it with, for instance, merchants from other communities. The land and other crucial factors in work remain common property, and the community does not divest itself of such holdings. Any exchange between individuals would be an

91 Marx, *Letter to Vera Zasulich: The "First" Draft.*

92 Marx, *Grundrisse: Foundations of the Critique of Political Economy*, 398.

expression of the advent of individual (family) ownership of movable assets. The rise of such a phenomenon would lead to the disintegration of the community.[93]

People who perform various specialized tasks – as well as the local functionaries, administrators, heads of family, etc. – all occupy ownership positions distinct from those of the "masses" and are owners of a somewhat different sort. On the one hand, their position does resemble that of all the rest. Regardless of whether it is the mayor, cobbler, or priest, the ownership locus continues to be mediated by membership in the community because of the particular function he fulfills within it. For instance, the craftsman is co-owner of the land which belongs to the community, but is also an individual owner of his workshop. On the other hand, however, at least some of these individuals hold a more privileged position than the average inhabitant. Due to his unique place in the division of labor, important function, or fortunate position in the kinship structure, such a person appropriates more than the rest, decides about the ways in which conditions of labor are utilized and the ways in which the labor force is employed, accumulates movable assets, and participates in the (over)consumption of surplus goods created by the community. Such persons constitute the exploiting party. Sometimes their privileged social position is commonly sanctioned by tradition. Sometimes they must resort to non-economic coercion. This explains the great significance of blood ties and personal dependencies as well as traditions which normalize relations between the exploiters and the exploited; it also explains the great significance of the leading role of the state. Marx explains:

> It is furthermore evident that in all forms in which the direct labourer remains the 'possessor' of the means of production and labour conditions necessary for the production of his own means of subsistence, the property relationship must simultaneously appear as a direct relation of lordship and servitude, so that the direct producer is not free; a lack of freedom which may be reduced from serfdom with enforced labour to a mere tributary relationship. The direct producer, according to our assumption, is to be found here in possession of his own means of production, the necessary material labour conditions required for the realisation of his labour and the production of his means of subsistence. He conducts his agricultural activity and the rural home industries connected with it independently. This independence is not undermined by the circumstance that the small peasants may form among themselves a more or less natural production community, as they do in India, since it is here merely a question of independence from the nominal lord of the manor. Under such conditions the surplus-labour for the nominal owner of the land can only be extorted from them by other than economic pressure, whatever the form assumed may be. This differs from slave or plantation economy in that the slave works under alien conditions of production and not independently. Thus, conditions

93 Marx, *Capital A Critique of Political Economy*, Volume III, 445, 451.

> of personal dependence are requisite, a lack of personal freedom, no matter to what extent, and being tied to the soil as its accessory, bondage in the true sense of the word. Should the direct producers not be confronted by a private landowner, but rather, as in Asia, under direct subordination to a state which stands over them as their landlord and simultaneously as sovereign, then rent and taxes coincide, or rather, there exists no tax which differs from this form of ground-rent.[94]

Also noteworthy is that, in the statement above, Marx differentiates the Asiatic form of society from that of slavery.

The ownership relations which are typical of the Asiatic style community are described by Marx as dualistic since they simultaneously bear the traits of both common and private ownership:

> It is easy to see that the dualism inherent in the 'agricultural commune' may give it a sturdy life: for communal property and all the resulting social relations provide it with a solid foundation, while the privately owned houses, fragmented tillage of the arable land and private appropriation of its fruits all permit a development of individuality incompatible with conditions in the more primitive communities. It is just as evident, however, that the very same dualism may eventually become a source of disintegration.[95]

In one sphere of their everyday activity community members appear as co-owners, in another as individual proprietors, and in yet another – as private owners exploiting their fellow tribesmen.

Other Forms of Ownership in the Asiatic Society

When a community exists independently, ownership relations manifest themselves solely in the dualistic form. However, if a state rises above the communities, then complications set in. Here, several new forms of ownership appear, in which people are different kind of owners than they are within the community.

Above all, this means state ownership. The legal status of the Asian state has already been described: it appears before other communities as the sovereign and titleholder. This is also the case, when the personification of the state is its ruler. But state holdings are not limited to a legal phenomenon, but also are an economic fact. The economic entity of the state as owner is expressed above all in the appropriation by the functionaries of the state of the surplus produced by individual communities: "E.g. it is not in the least a contradiction to it that, as in most of the *Asiatic* landforms, the *comprehensive unity* standing above all these

94 Ibid., 575–576.

95 Marx, *Letter to Vera Zasulich: The "First" Draft*;

little communities appears as the higher *proprietor* or as the *sole proprietor;* the real communities hence only as *hereditary* possessors."[96]

The status of the state as owner manifests itself in relationships wherein the state:

1) amasses a part of the means of production by way of its functionaries, and then employs some of the residents to operate it;
2) takes over the surplus product created by the communities (in the form of taxes) as well as the product created by use of state means of production;
3) distributes appropriated product;
4) carries out the reproduction of intercommunity infrastructure (e.g., irrigation equipment, roads, etc.);
5) fulfills, by way of its functionaries, the role of merchandise vendor; and
6) accumulates most of the means of maintenance.

The outline of state ownership just presented would, however, be deficient. The state is, after all, an abstract, heuristic category, and must be translated into the language of concrete institutions and social relations between groups and individuals. The state does not refer to some superhuman being but encompasses relationships regulated by a set of social institutions. From the economic point of view, state property is, therefore, not the property of some abstract individual, but a configuration of the property relationships between physical persons.

The worst position in the system of state property is taken up by the "slaves" – those working in publicly owned mines or construction projects and performing various services for the state and its functionaries. They are neither landowners nor tool owners, nor owners of their own labor power. They are but owners of the means of survival which they receive from the state. Underscored here is that their position is completely different from the position of members of the community who are also enslaved. Members of the community are still owners of their labor conditions while slaves are not. This state of affairs will become universal only in societies of the slave formation (for example, in Rome).[97] In Asiatic communities, however, this can only happen within a state ownership arrangement.

A different category of people which manifests itself in this form of ownership is emancipated wage laborers who own their manpower which they sell to the state in exchange for their means of consumption. Here reference should also be made to mercenary soldiers, representatives of certain professions, and those freemen (often foreigners) who have some more unique services to offer:

---

96 Marx, *Grundrisse: Foundations of the Critique of Political Economy*, 399.
97 Ibid., 399–405, 417, 419–420.

> The entire class of so called *services* from the bootblack up to the king falls into this category. Likewise the free day-labourer, whom we encounter sporadically in all places where either the oriental community [*Gemeinwesen*] or the western commune [*Gemeinde*] consisting of free landowners dissolves into individual elements – as a consequence of increase of population, release of prisoners of war, accidents by which the individual is impoverished and loses the objective conditions of his self-sustaining labour, owing to division of labour etc.[98]

State ownership of the Asiatic type also serves as a framework for private owners who exploit hired laborers, slaves, or specific other communities. Whatever specific categories of inhabitants do on behalf of the Asian state, they also do on behalf of those social groups privileged by the state. The legal form of this relationship is, in this case, less important, especially since the boundary between the state and its representatives controlling the most important state functions is rather tenuous. Actions taken by the state are, in fact, their actions, payments made to the state are payments delivered into their hands, and the consumption of the state is what they and their entourage consume. Appropriation of the country's product is what gives them real power over the populace; this power becomes complementary to the power they hold by virtue of their state function.

Marx speaks of yet another form of ownership which appears in Asian type societies: usury and trade capital which expand at the expense of community and state ownership. This is the only form of ownership in which people channel their energies towards the accumulation of wealth. Still, usury and trade capital is incapable of destroying the system of common ownership since money alone will not attract a sufficient number of emancipated wage laborers on the market, nor an accessible means of production. Most of the population is enslaved by the community and land, too, is unavailable for exchange – neither the community nor the state will allow this. Furthermore, the conversion of usury capital into productive capital is impossible. As a result, a community can thank this impotence of usury and trade capital for the long duration of its unchangeableness: "Under Asian forms, usury can continue a long time, without producing anything more than economic decay and political corruption."[99]

98 Ibid., 391–392.

99 Marx, *Capital: A Critique of Political Economy*, Volume III, 445.

Property Relations in the Ancient Society

General Characteristics

There is a tendency to associate the classical, ancient form of society with that of slavery. Such an interpretation of the views of Marx could arise from the fact that the embryonic stage of slavery existed in the ancient formation and Marx discusses this phenomenon as part of his analysis thereof. Still, this side effect of the ancient form of production cannot be seen as the dominant form.

The ancient formation, in the eyes of Marx, belongs to the primary while the slavery formation belongs to the secondary one. The first type is rooted in a specific kind of community in which people are working owners of land, whereas the latter assumes the disintegration of the community and expropriation of the producers since slavery is built upon the private ownership of slaves and their consequent exploitation. On more than one occasion, Marx pointed to a fundamental distinction between these two types of societies, such as in *Capital* wherein he straightforwardly writes:

> Peasant agriculture on a small scale, and the carrying on of independent handicrafts, which together form the basis of the feudal mode of production, and after the dissolution of that system, continue side by side with the capitalist mode, also form the economic foundation of the classical communities at their best, after the primitive form of ownership of land in common had disappeared, and before slavery had seized on production in earnest.[100]

Nonetheless, he devotes a long fragment of analysis in *Grundrisse* precisely to the relationships typical of ancient societies. A significant portion of Engels' work on classical societies is dedicated to similar matters.[101] Ownership, in the "ancient classical forms," "Roman, Greek form," or "the form of classical antiquity" emerged in the times of Homer and the "Greek period of heroes" (per Engels) as well as in ancient Rome at the beginnings of the Roman state. Indeed, Marxist analyses of the ancient type of ownership refer precisely to those societies and that time. Still, the period in which the slavery formation reached the epitome of its development is the times of the Roman Republic and the beginnings of the Roman Empire. Although these are completely different societies, the second was born of the first.

---

100 Marx, *Capital: A Critique of Political Economy*, Volume I, 263.

101 Marx, *Grundrisse: Foundations of the Critique of Political Economy*, 403–436; Engels, *Origin of the Family, Private Property, and the State*, 54–71.

Each of these modes of production arose much earlier and, in skeletal forms, did survive until the times of Marx. In fact, the ancient mode of production (and type of ownership) has lasted to modernity. "In so far as classical landed property reappears in modern small-parcel landownership, it itself belongs to political economy and we shall come to it in the section on landed property."[102]

Communities in the form of "classical antiquity" stand at a higher level of development than communities of the Asian form. This means that traces of the Asiatic form can be found in the ancient, and the process of privatization of ownership evolved further in the latter form. As Marx writes: "The original form of this property is therefore itself *direct common property (oriental form,* modified in the Slavonic; developed to the point of antithesis, but still as the secret, if antithetical, foundation in classical and Germanic property)."[103]

The foundation of existence for this social form, as with its predecessors, is the community which appears here in somewhat different character. Since the Asiatic community was primary, whereas the individual was of a secondary nature, then in the ancient type the community and its members are equal entities. The earlier, Asiatic form of community was an expression of extreme collectivism and even despotism; here in the classical, it is a more or less democratic unit which protects its freemen.

In the Asian formation, the center of assembly for the inhabitants was the village; the city was something beyond the community (as a center for the country's rulers). However, in the classical formation, the center of assembly for the inhabitants, the place where farmers go and where the most important matters for the society take place, is the city. Agricultural soil becomes urban territory; the city becomes the center of defense. The city is where the individual owners of land parcels live, and it is from here that crusades against other urban centers embark. By way of military campaigns, the city appropriates foreign territories and incorporates them within its boundaries. The urban community is shaped "in a warlike way;" it forms a community because war and military campaigns are waged together by all the citizens of the city:

> War is therefore the great comprehensive task, the great communal labour which is required either to occupy the objective conditions of being there alive, or to protect and perpetuate the occupation. Hence the commune consisting of families initially organized in a warlike way – as a system of war and army, and this is one of the conditions of its being there as proprietor.[104]

---

102 *Marx, Grundrisse: Foundations of the Critique of Political Economy*, 421.
103 Ibid., 421.
104 Ibid., 401

The ancient community takes on the form of a state (*polis*). In its earliest developmental variations, the political entity exists as a union of tribes which elects a group of persons who execute power. The tribal structure of such a state exemplifies a division into higher and lower tribes, which distinctions deepen as a consequence of interactions between the victorious and conquered tribes. The tribal-clan structure, anchored in blood ties, is increasingly supported by the territorial structure; ultimately, the tribes and clans succumb to disintegration. Marx claims that the transformation of communities in ancient Greece and Rome from bloodline to territorial communities occurred in such as a way that the new territorial partition of communities "took on an ancestral appearance" of a clan or kinship partition.[105]

The breakdown of tribal and clan communities results in the strengthening of the state. The dissolution of tribes leads to a new form of family: the monogamous couple unit which becomes the keystone of the social structure. Social differentiation – which used to constitute distinctions within a clan or between clans as bearers of state mandate – begins to take on the form of differentiation between monogamous couple families. Naturally, various groups of citizens do represent the state to some degree and have varied rights, but the basic principle holds true. As a result, the state evolves into a community of citizens rather than tribes. The citizens decide about public affairs and hold power over non-citizens (because such are found in every state). This is the classic mode of development for the ancient type of community. Marx dedicates most of his time to this; Engels, in turn, primarily investigated the earlier phases of development in ancient communities.[106]

The ancient state differs from that of the Asian. Firstly, on the one hand, the classical state of antiquity appears as a community of citizens, even if a leader reigns over them. On the other hand, the Asian state manifests itself as an external factor concerning communities and takes on a hierarchical, despotic shape, rising above them. Secondly, a member of a community in the state of antiquity is a free citizen; the member of the Asian community is enslaved. Thirdly, the ancient state, by transformation into a territorial unit, puts an end to the clan and tribe as socioeconomic units. The Asian state fixes the commune's status as the fundamental and (sometimes the only) economic organism, underpinned by blood ties.

105 Ibid., 405.

106 Engels, *Origin of the Family, Private Property, and the State*, 54–71.

The classical commune thus exists doubly in its two, equivalent economic units – the family and the state. The life of an individual is also concentrated upon the fulfillment of two social roles – as a member of a family and as a citizen of the state. Alongside the privileged category of citizens of the commune (the *polis*) are also persons lacking the status of citizen: plebeians, *Metoikoi*, slaves, etc. When the fall of an ancient society begins, these groups will become the winds of change.[107]

The Dualism of Property Relations in the Ancient Society

At the foundation of socioeconomic life in the ancient community is a split in the sphere of property relations. Both the family and the state have their own autonomous existence on the ground of a separate form of ownership – individual private ownership by citizens and public ownership by the state. These two forms constitute the framework for social life. In the Asian community, the border between shared property and property that is private has been difficult to delineate, whereas in the ancient community it is very clear and evident. This fact Marx emphasizes multiple times, including this fragment from the *Grundrisse*:

> in the Roman, Greek form (in short, the form of classical antiquity) – in this case, the land is occupied by the commune, Roman land; a part remains to the commune as such as distinct from the commune members, *ager publicus* in its various forms; the other part is divided up and each parcel of land is Roman by virtue of being the private property, the domain of a Roman, the part of the *laboratorium* belonging to him; but, also, he is a Roman only in so far as he possesses this sovereign right over a part of the Roman earth.[108]

Each citizen of an ancient state is the owner of a land parcel, but in a different sense than a member of an Asian community. The latter was at most an individual possessor whereas the citizen of the *polis* is legally a private proprietor. As a citizen (a member of a state community), he is entitled to a specific parcel. The state bestows such upon the citizen, but does not interfere with the means by which that property is utilized; at the same time, it is only as a landowner that the individual can be a citizen of the state.

Nevertheless, the citizen is not an owner with respect to state property: "But this *ager publicus* does not appear, as with the Romans e.g., as the particular economic presence of the state as against the private proprietors, so that these latter are actually *private* proprietors as such, in so far as they are *excluded*, deprived,

107 Marx, *Grundrisse: Foundations of the Critique of Political Economy*, 425.
108 Ibid., 403.

like the plebeians, from using the *ager publicus*."[109] The classical community does not constitute the simple sum of its citizens. It is an independent organism, a union of citizens, which is its own distinct entity in the existence of the city (the *polis*) and its administrators. The large possessor of state land (in other words, a tenant of a large landholding of the *ager publicus*) can only be such a person who is something more than simply an individual, private owner: namely, he must be a functionary of the state, a patrician.

An antagonism between the private and public property of land is expressed in the fact that the augmentation of one form entails the diminishment of the other. On the one hand, citizens are interested in obtaining the largest plots of state land and, thus, to thin out the range of public holdings; on the other hand, the state and patricians who act on behalf of the state are interested in distributing the least part of its lands among the citizens. Comprising the social power which counteracts any distribution of state land amongst the citizens are also the functionaries of the Greek *polis*. They utilize state land due to the public functions they fulfill; part of the profits they appropriate, and part is assigned to state aims and purposes. Exclusion of citizens from public land usage toughens antagonism and ratifies the boundary between the public and private sectors.

Marx writes, "In antiquity (Romans as the most classic example, the thing in its purest, most fully developed form), the form of state property in land and that of private property in land [are] antithetical, so that the latter is mediated by the former, or the former itself exists in this double form."[110] In the heyday of the ancient form of community, both types were balanced – at least neither of them gained decisive superiority over the other. It was only a rocking of this balance which contributed to the emergence of the slave formation of society.

Individual Private Property of the Ancient Type

In ancient societies, a tight dependency appears between the economic entity of the state or community and that of the individual. The land ownership relation is mediated by belonging to a community, or, to be more precise, by possession of the status of a citizen of the *polis*. At one point, Marx even describes the position of the individual as "the double relation which makes him both an equal citizen, a member of the community, and a *proprietor*."[111] He also notes,

---

109 Ibid., 407.
110 Ibid., 408.
111 Ibid., 418.

> The commune – as state – is, on one side, the relation of these free and equal private proprietors to one another, their bond against the outside, and is at the same time their safeguard. The commune here rests as much on the fact that its members consist of working landed proprietors, small-owning peasants, as the peasants' independence rests on their mutual relations as commune members, on protection of the *ager publicus* for communal needs and communal glory etc. Membership in the commune remains the presupposition for the appropriation of land and soil, but, as a member of the commune, the individual is a private proprietor. He relates to his private property as land and soil, but at the same time as to his being as commune member; and his own sustenance as such is likewise the sustenance of the commune, and conversely etc.[112]

Therefore, even if the individual becomes an owner of the conditions of labor via the community to which he belongs, this is not a matter of co-owning, but rather private ownership. Communality expresses itself here as, above all, the universal access of each citizen to a piece of land on the territory of the state and in the collective defense of those lands. Yet, this is private ownership of a parcel of land since no one outside the family can render a piece of land the object of his activity without permission of that family.

A citizen of the state is a private owner in a dual sense. The citizen is an owner from a legal point of view since he holds most property rights to the land (including exclusivity). Nonetheless, as an owner in a socioeconomic sense, the citizen participates in all collective relations which signify ownership. In the hands of the citizen, a plot of land is transformed into a factor of labor: the citizen employs himself and his family on the farmstead which belongs to him. Together with his family he tends the lands and only inasmuch as he is an effective owner will he be able to cultivate it, reproducing thusly the conditions of his work, his family life, and his position as one of many private landholders and citizens on par with each other. If and when this is the status quo, then no one dominates or controls his labors; he is then a working owner of a parcel of land, an individual owner in the socioeconomic sense of that word:

> The presupposition of the survival of the community is the preservation of equality among its free self-sustaining peasants, and their own labour as the condition of the survival of their property. They relate as proprietors to the natural conditions of labour; but these conditions must also constantly be posited as real conditions and objective elements of the personality of the individual, by means of personal labour.[113]

Each citizen directly appropriates the product of his smallholding and not indirectly through the community as was the case in certain variants of the Asian type

112 Ibid., 401–402.
113 Ibid., 402.

community. The magnitude of the arrogated product depends upon the magnitude of the landholding, the quality of the soil, the equipment and livestock, and the workforce (the number of family members). This form of ownership bears yet another key trait which manifests itself in apportionment. As a matter of course, the farmer does not hand his produce over to the state (at most delivering a minimal share). The state, in turn, controls its own sector – the *ager publicus*. In this indirect fashion the citizen takes advantage of public property, but, as a citizen, delivers to the state some of his surplus labor in the form of services in defense of the country (e.g., military service).

This constitutes an appropriation of labor and product when the farm is self-sufficient and does not produce a surplus for trade. But wherever there is private property and division of labor, there also is a form of exchange, more or less developed. This form of ownership assumes as its primary goal (such is the internal logic of this form) production for household purposes and reproduction of the dual position of dwellers as citizens and owners. But it also entails production of commodities – for buying and selling – if for no other reason than to acquire necessary equipment for the citizen-soldier. Hence, the private landholding is at least partly inscribed in the general market of goods or even goods and currency. The citizen appears, therefore, in certain situations as the owner of commodities. The exchange of such commodities leads to a second division of the yield produced on a concrete farm. Regrettably, advantage may be taken of the owner; in fact, this is more frequently the case. Representatives of this social category are played on by merchants, usurers, craftsmen, and others with whom the citizen owner does business.

The owner in antiquity differed from his predecessors in that he treated land not only as a focus of production but also as a good in and of itself. Thus, he could increase his holdings, but could also lose them. He could, for example, be deprived of them by way of exchange. In preceding forms of ownership, such a loss was impossible. Here, however, a situation arose which facilitated the concentration of labor conditions on the one hand, and their loss on the other.[114]

The basic source of the means of subsistence in this form is the land and the owner's labor. Individual ownership of land is a precursor for personal (familial) ownership of the means of consumption. A typical characteristic of the position of the citizen is that he stands as the owner of the means of consumption at every moment of the process of production. In this case, the means of consumption, just as with the means of production, are an indispensable condition for production. To produce something on an individual farmstead, the owner and his family must be

114 Ibid., 397–437.

able to provide for themselves until the current crops are harvested – and such was the case at the height of antiquity's form of private ownership.

Yet, the forerunner for the expropriation of the citizen is already in place here. Be it due to natural disaster or illness or a disadvantageous market, the individual can find himself deprived of the conditions of labor and necessities of life. In communities of an earlier type, the means of subsistence were in the hands of the community; here, however, this is the task of each separate household. The ancient community does not protect the individual proprietor of the land parcel from dispossession. Hence, a citizen may be deprived of ownership of his conditions of labor. Either he will sell his parcel of land in order to be able to assure himself and his family of a minimum of foodstuffs or he will be dispossessed for payment of debts and/or even enslaved. This can, in fact, contribute to the downfall of the ancient community of citizens and the arising of a society of a new type – the slavery formation. Eventually, the dispossession of individual owners of small parcels of land in Greece and Rome became a reality. This process was not even hindered by the legislation of the Greek politician, Solon who wanted to halt the expropriation of private proprietors of land parcels.[115]

State Ownership of Land

Marx hails ownership of ancient communities as either communal or state ownership (i.e., *ager publicus*). This nomenclature is justified by the nature of this form of property: it is land belonging to a union or association of citizens (one which exists as a separate entity) and not a common property shared by individual owners. Therefore, it is impossible for each citizen to participate independently in the utilization of this land. Naturally, certain citizens can take advantage of it, but only as representatives of the state who have been selected from among the general population. The average citizen is, although a legal owner in a sense, excluded from access to the property; he can only take advantage of it indirectly as a citizen of the state. The state provides several services on behalf of the citizen: protecting his private property, his status as a citizen, etc. However, the citizen's most important indirect benefit is associated with the fact that he is not obliged to serve up the fruits of his labor on behalf of the state. Even if this were to happen, then only to a minimal degree because the state works its holdings in order to maintain its public institutions and the persons working in that sphere.

Due to the indirect nature of the property relation, the commonality of the landholding is very problematic. From a legal standpoint, no one is personally

115 Ibid., 397–437; Engels, *Origin of the Family, Private Property, and the State*, 63–64.

(as a physical person) its proprietor. According to legal criteria, state land is such a form of property regarding which concrete people take up various, more or less privileged social positions and become the economic owners of this land in highly diversified ways. Marx points to the special privileging of the state functionaries who act economically within the framework of this form. He comments: "The right of *using* the communal land through *possession* originally appertained to the patricians, who then granted it to their clients; the *transfer of property* out of the *ager publicus* appertained exclusively to the plebeians; all assignments in favour of the plebeians and compensation for a share of the communal property."[116] This is an idea to which he returns many a time: "Since the patrician represents the community in a higher degree, he is the *possessor* of the *ager publicus* and uses it through his clients etc. (and also appropriates it little by little)."[117] Thus what is communal ownership succumbs over time to economic privatization.

The social status of the patrician is much stronger than that of ordinary folk – even if it would seem otherwise from a legal point of view. The citizen is a legal private owner of a separate parcel of land; the patrician (or some other state representative) is only the legal possessor as a tenant of the *ager publicus*. Still, from a socioeconomic point of view, the patrician is also the proprietor with no need to come into physical contact with the land. Those actually at work are leaseholders, hired laborers, the semi-enslaved, conquered populations, and also a small number (in this formation) of slaves.

In fact, from an economic point of view, the patrician is an economic owner of state property since it is he who employs people to work the land assigned to him; it is by his decisions that the land and the labor power are transformed into factors of labor. As a representative of the state and a public functionary, he bears part of the power over the country's inhabitants. As the economic owner of state property, he bears an owner's power over an external workforce, over persons he has hired. By this token, his political power is confirmed by the economic power of an owner of the labor conditions and the labors of others. The patrician – as the functionary of state and the tenant of *ager publicus* – appropriates surplus product.

Noteworthy here is that, of this product which he agrees to take from its producers, a portion will be transferred to satisfy state needs – either in the form of taxes or in the form of his own expenses incurred as a consequence of fulfilling his official duties and representing the state. But it would be difficult to demarcate the boundary between that part which he has assigned himself and that part

116 Marx, *Grundrisse: Foundations of the Critique of Political Economy*, 404.
117 Ibid., 405.

which he assigns to the state aims. This stems from the fact that his personal consumption is partially public, and that the boundary between his private and public life is unstable. In fact, that boundary does not exist: state property is partially his own property. In the hands of the patrician, the appropriated product is relayed into goods for sale. This does not pertain to the land which he utilizes as a state functionary, although he can buy (and sell) private land, too.

This form of ownership encompasses yet other ways of being an economic owner. The overwhelming majority of the patrician's clients takes up positions as possessors in a socioeconomic sense, even if their legal position can be highly varied. This can be tenant farming led by free dwellers and other clients. This can also take on the form of a native enslaved population which the state has passed on, together with the land, to its functionaries. But the situation of these clients is similar in each of these two cases: together with their families, they tend their assigned parcels and appropriate the yield gained from these farms. Their economic position is, however, much worse than that of the free citizens of a state who are tending their own individually and privately-owned land. Both types of clients are dependent upon the patrician; moreover, they are forced to grant a significant portion of the fruits of their labors on behalf of the state – or, more precisely, of the patrician. So they are, therefore, exploited in part. But everything which they produce above and beyond these allotments does belong to them. They are also reproducing the conditions of labor which have been assigned to them. Their legal position has nothing in common with ownership title, but, in an economic sense of the term, they are recognized by Marx as individual possessors of land.

Another group of owners is the free wage laborers who possess their labor power which they exchange for means of survival. Finally, the last group which will constitute the most numerous one in the next formation are slaves who manifest themselves as owners solely of the means of consumption which they receive from their lords. They work on behalf of the patricians, but do not appropriate the product of their work; they themselves, as well as their labor, are the property of the patricians.

Property Relations in the German Commune

General Characteristics

Both Marx and Engels devoted much time to deliberations on the Germanic type of ownership, first mentioned in *German Ideology*. Marx himself refers to this type in *Capital*, in drafts of his letter to Vera Zasulich, and in *A Contribution to the Critique of Political Economics*. In *Grundrisse*, Marx performs a holistic analysis of this form, claiming that it comprises the foundation for a separate, historical type of social production. He also describes the then-contemporary German mark – a mode of production which had survived until his day and had preserved characteristics of its "prototype" with, e.g., traits of the archaic German type of ownership: "Communal property – always distinct from the State property just dealt with – was an old Teutonic institution which lived on under cover of feudalism."[118] Engels, too, writes of the German type of ownership in *Origin of the Family, Private Property, and the State.*

The Germanic type of ownership and its corresponding means of production are one of the many paths of development for societies anchored in communal life. This is a developmental variation completely at odds with the Asiatic or classical types. The height of development in this social form is found in early medieval times. Naturally, it arose much earlier and survived to our contemporary days, albeit subordinated to other historical systems of production, taking on many regional forms:

> Primitive communities are not all cut according to the same pattern. On the contrary, they form a series of social groups which, differing in both type and age, mark successive phases of evolution. One of these types, conventionally known as the *agrarian commune* (*la commune agricole*), also embraces the Russian commune. Its equivalent in the West is the very recent *Germanic commune*. This did not yet exist in the time of Julius Caesar, and no longer existed when the Germanic tribes came to conquer Italy, Gaul, Spain, etc.[119]

Marx writes that the history of antiquity is a history of cities rooted in individual land ownership and horticulture. Asian history is exceptionally undifferentiated between town and village while the city appears as an economic expansion superior to the commune. However, the starting point for the history of the medieval German period is the village which will only later be urbanized.

Within the society of antiquity, there were two distinct economic organisms: the community (the state) and the family. Here, in the Germanic mode of production, the economic whole is the family (and the household), whereas the community itself does not have a separate economic existence from that of the families of which it is composed. In the classical society, the community was a union of citizens which took on the form of a state; the community had its own independent entity through the existence of the city and its administrators. The German community, however, is not a union, but rather an association of free and independent families. The ancient community exists regardless of its citizens,

118 Marx, *Capital: A Critique of Political Economy*, Volume I, 512.
119 Marx, *Letter to Vera Zasulich: The "Third" Draft.*

and the position of a citizen is mediated by the prior existence of the community as a state organization. The German community, however, exists because its residents (family representatives) gather together to make decisions about common problems; the existence of this community is mediated by the prior existence of sovereign families. Commonality does not express itself in the creation of a state organization but in the assemblies devoted to discussions regarding war, rituals, religious cults, justice and the courts, and the assurance of mutual safety. It manifests itself further in culture and language as well as in descent from the same, primordial clan or tribal community. In *Grundrisse*, Marx compares further:

> Dissimilar, too, is the position of the individual vis-à-vis the community. The individual is neither an addition to the community as was the case in the Asian community, nor a citizen dependent upon the state as was the case in the ancient community. The life of the individual and his family constitute the starting point for the emergence of interpersonal and interfamilial relationships. Among the Germanic tribes, where the individual family chiefs settled in the forests, long distances apart, the commune exists, already from *outward* observation, only in the periodic gathering-together [*Vereinigung*] of the commune members, although their unity-*in-itself* is posited in their ancestry, language, common past and history, etc.[120]

Individual Private Property and Communal Ownership of Land

The cornerstone of the existence of the German type of community is individual ownership of parcels of land and soil. A member of a community is an individual owner, and a principal portion of the economic activity takes place on individual, familial farms. Alongside this dominant form of ownership, there is also communal property which differs profoundly from the Asian or ancient types. The communal property does not dominate here as was the situation in the Asiatic society (which led to the exploitation of the individual by representatives of the commune and the state), nor is this an antagonistic form of state property to which the citizen has no access as was the situation in the classical type of community. The communal property appears among the Germans as an appendix to the individual: it comprises that part of the group territory which was never divided among individual owners, but which is defended by the community and of which one and all can take advantage (the same as with his own plot of land). As objects of communal ownership, Marx mentions meadows, forests, fishing and hunting grounds, and fallow land. Therefore, community ownership is derived from a relationship with the families which comprise the community:

---

120 Marx, *Grundrisse: Foundations of the Critique of Political Economy*, 407.

> Among the Germanic tribes, the *ager publicus* appears rather merely as a complement to individual property, and figures as property only to the extent that it is defended militarily as the common property of one tribe against a hostile tribe. Individual property does not appear mediated by the commune; rather, the existence of the commune and of communal property appear as mediated by, i.e. as a relation of, the independent subjects to one another.[121]

Each of the members of a community is an individual owner of that part of the land which he cultivates together with his family. He is an owner in a normative sense since he holds the most (more than anyone else) rights and privileges with regards to this land, and is an owner in an economic sense. In his hands, the parcel of land becomes a factor of work for him and his family, and then a means of appropriation of product. Each member of a community is also an owner of shared territory. He is such an owner since he has the chance to utilize it independently. This does not mean a political or normative possibility since he already enjoys this as a member of the community. This entails an economic chance which is conditioned, for example, by workforce resources at the disposal of the family or its livestock which grazes on communal lands. The commonality of these territories bears, therefore, a somewhat different character than what was found amidst the primitive community wherein work is of a collective nature and is performed by the whole group. Here, solidarity is expressed in the shared defense of territory and access by each tribal member to the natural resources – yet the process of labor itself is of an individual nature. In the words of Marx,

> For the commune to come into real existence, the free landed proprietors have to hold a *meeting*, whereas e.g. in Rome it *exists* even apart from these assemblies in the existence of the *city itself* and of the officials presiding over it etc. True, the *ager publicus*, the communal or people's land, as distinct from individual property, also occurs among the Germanic tribes. It takes the form of hunting land, grazing land, timber land etc., the part of the land which cannot be divided if it is to serve as means of production in this specific form. But this *ager publicus* does not appear, as with the Romans e.g., as the particular economic presence of the state as against the private proprietors, so that these latter are actually *private* proprietors as such, in so far as they are *excluded*, deprived, like the plebeians, from using the *ager publicus*. Among the Germanic tribes, the *ager publicus* appears rather merely as a complement to individual property, and figures as property only to the extent that it is defended militarily as the common property of one tribe against a hostile tribe.[122]

121 Ibid.
122 Ibid.

The family is an independent and self-sufficient economic unit within which its members perform their various functions. The division and assignment of labor conditions is the basic element in the distribution of the product. The product of labor is appropriated by explicit families and not by the community. Movable property is, therefore, the property of specific families and individuals belonging to it. Moreover, each of the families individually appropriates product obtained on community territory. Ultimately, however, this leads to a situation about which Engels spoke: a barrier in the exploitation of a workforce is the magnitude of the household because of an increase in the population size. Nonetheless, as long as this form of ownership is in full bloom stage, the longer it will create conditions conducive to the requisitioning of the fruits of its own labors.

In this form, just as in most of other forms of ownership rooted in communal life, land cannot be merchandised. No family will rid itself of the keystone of its very existence – something which will only happen at a time of community disintegration and dissolution. That said, goods for sale can be a mobile property such as livestock and other products of the land or cottage industry. Merchandising of these products leads to significant differences in wealth between particular members of the community.

Property Relations in the Slavery Formation of Society

The Dual Nature of Enslavement

A common opinion in sociology and economics is that societies in which producers are enslaved should be counted as falling under the category of the slavery formation. If so, then this leads to an association of both the ancient and the Asiatic formations with the slavery formation, or to an acknowledgment of the first two as variations of the last formation. It appears that Marx's understanding of this matter is quite different. Two different types of ownership relations can lie at the foundation of enslavement. Earlier, in the Asiatic formations, even the captive human is the owner of his labor condition. "This differs from slave or plantation economy in that the slave works under alien conditions of production and not independently."[123] Hence, in the later formation, the slave is expropriated from the conditions of labor; dealt with here are completely different types of economic formations.

In drafts of his letter to Vera Zasulich, Karl Marx wrote that, just as in geological formations, there are historical types of ownership which are primary, secondary,

123 Marx, *Capital: A Critique of Political Economy*, Volume III, 576.

and tertiary. And it is precisely ownership of the slavery type which comprises an outcome of the fall of the first order formations which are based upon different forms of common property: "The secondary formation does, of course, include the series of societies which rest upon slavery and serfdom."[124]

Marx develops this line of thinking further on more than one occasion. For instance, he writes,

> Slavery, bondage etc., where the worker himself appears among the natural conditions of production for a third individual or community (this is *not* the case e.g. with the general slavery of the Orient, *only* from the European point of view) – i.e. property no longer the relation of the working individual to the objective conditions of labour – is always secondary, derived, never original, although [it is] a necessary and logical result of property founded on the community and labour in the community.[125]

As is made clear, none of these societies "founded on the community and labour in the community" qualifies for assignment to the slavery formation since the producers (even those who are enslaved) are owners of the labor conditions. This is what, in *Grundrisse*, Marx describes as the historic state number I. In turn, those societies in which the free worker is the private proprietor of instruments or devices (and is, at the same time, the individual proprietor of the means of consumption) are identified as historic state or situation number II. Finally, he describes the state of slavery (accompanying expropriation from the means of production, including land and tools) and the situation of Roman *plebs* as "the third possible form."[126]

For the fall of an archaic form to occur, it would be necessary to create a situation in which a person is an owner distinct and independent of the community. The extreme collectivism in the communal life of an Asiatic society inhibits such processes. The enslavement of the individual within the community hampers expropriation. Only the classical ancient form of collective life – in which a member of the community and citizen of the state became a free individual landowner and acted independently of the community – opened such a possibility. The slavery formation, therefore, emerges from the ancient formation. The very community which protected the free citizen and the individual owner of a plot of land from external threats stopped protecting him from internal threats of divestment (expropriation) by other members of the community.

124 Marx, *Letter to Vera Zasulich: The "Third" Draft.*

125 Marx, *Grundrisse: Foundations of the Critique of Political Economy*, 419–420.

126 Ibid., 423–424.

The period of the greatest flourishing of the slavery formation was in the times of the Roman Republic and Empire. It was then that, on the one hand, there was a stripping of property and enslavement of the majority of the population, and, on the other hand, a transformation of a significant segment of state-owned land into a privately owned, grand plantations the functioning of which depended upon slaves.

Large Landownership Based upon the Work of Slaves

In this type of ownership, the lord as the owner of the means of production enslaves the non-owner and exploits him. The patrician expropriates the surplus labor of working slaves. He possesses a dualistic type of power over slaves: (a) normative power anchored in legal regulations and (b) economic power stemming from the fact that the lord directs the production process, appropriates the entire product, and provides the means of consumption.

The owner of slaves appropriates products differently than did the Roman patrician or the Greek dignitary in the period of ancient classical society who only garnered the surplus product of the captured possessors and whose position was realized in a land rent. The owner of slaves, however, takes the whole of the product of the slave and only afterward provides the means of consumption. Finally, the enslaver holds power as an owner of someone else's labor power. This is different power than in the case of a capitalist who purchases labor power instead of purchasing a slave who can later be sold like any other merchandise:

> Labour-power was not always a commodity (merchandise). Labour was not always wage-labour, i.e., free labour. The slave did not sell his labour-power to the slave-owner, any more than the ox sells his labour to the farmer. The slave, together with his labour-power, was sold to his owner once for all. He is a commodity that can pass from the hand of one owner to that of another. He himself is a commodity, but his labour-power is not his commodity. The serf sells only a portion of his labour-power. It is not he who receives wages from the owner of the land; it is rather the owner of the land who receives a tribute from him. The serf belongs to the soil, and to the lord of the soil he brings its fruit. The free labourer, on the other hand, sells his very self, and that by fractions.[127]

The slave, however, is neither the owner of the means of production nor of his labor power, nor of the fruits of his labors, nor of the means of exchange. The slave appears in this relationship solely as the owner of the means of consumption. The slave receives the necessaries of life from his lord. He can neither commandeer them directly as does any owner of working conditions nor gain them by way of barter as the owner of the means of exchange. His existence is

127 Marx, *Wage Labour and Capital*, 9.

guaranteed by the very fact of captivity and forced labor on behalf of the owner of the working conditions. Comparing the position of the slave to that of the hired worker, he writes,

> The third *possible form,* in which the worker relates as owner only to the necessaries of life, finding them on hand as the natural condition of the working subject, without relating to the land and soil, or to the instrument, or even (therefore) to labour itself as his own, is at bottom the formula of slavery and bondage, which is likewise negated, posited as a historically dissolved condition, in the relation of the worker to the conditions of production as capital.[128]

Description of the slave as an owner of the means of subsistence is not some singular or coincidental aspect of his position. Marx repeats this formula a few times in different variations. For example, in *Value, Price and Profit*, he notes,

> The slave receives a permanent and fixed amount of maintenance; the wage-labourer does not. He must try to get a rise of wages in the one instance, if only to compensate for a fall of wages in the other. If he resigned himself to accept the will, the dictates of the capitalist as a permanent economical law, he would share in all the miseries of the slave, without the security of the slave.[129]

Other Forms of Ownership

Private ownership of land based upon the work of slaves naturally constitutes the dominant form in slavery formation societies. Still, alongside this form of ownership, there are many others: some are vestiges of earlier formations while others are harbingers of ones to come. Taken all together, these elements shape a heterogeneous and complicated system of ownership.

For instance, there is a very numerous class of the Roman plebs (proletariat). Their economic position in the structure of ownership relations is characterized by, according to Marx, the same formula which describes the position of slaves: they are only owners of the means of maintenance:

> The third form, ownership of the necessaries of life – if it does not reduce itself to slavery and serfdom – cannot contain a relation by the *working* individual to the conditions of production and hence of existence; it can therefore only be the relation of a member of the original community based on land ownership who has lost his landed property

128 Marx, *Grundrisse: Foundations of the Critique of Political Economy*, 424.

129 Karl Marx [1865], *Value, Price and Profit*, <https://www.marxists.org/archive/marx/works/download/pdf/value-price-profit.pdf> [accessed August 2017], 26.

and not yet proceeded to variety No. II of property, such as the Roman *plebs* at the time of the bread and circuses.[130]

The Roman proletariat were once individual owners of land who constituted the dominant class in the classical formation of society but was subsequently divested of their property. They lost what they had owned, but they did not lose their political rights and privileges. They continued to be freemen (citizens of the state), did not undertake any work, and lived off the foodstuffs distributed by the state and its functionaries.

Within the slavery formation – alongside the dominant form of enslavement wherein the slave is not the owner of the conditions of labor – other forms are also to be found, which does not, in principle, assume expropriation of workers of the means of production. The captive population has, in such cases, the status of possessors and tenants (e.g., certain clientele, colonies, etc.). These possessors directly appropriate the fruits of their own labors and only later will be forced to transfer some part to the nominal owners as a result of surplus labor. Some slaves will even attain high economic positions and, with time, will become the exploiting side. These are, nevertheless, ancillary forms of ownership here. There is, too, individual private ownership – for example, the property of freed peasants, of *decurions*, and individual ownership of the craftsmen's workshop.

Developing, too, will be capital in various nonproductive forms:

> The development of usurer's capital is bound up with the development of merchant's capital and especially that of money-dealing capital. In ancient Rome, beginning with the last years of the Republic, when manufacturing stood far below its average level of development in the ancient world, merchant's capital, money-dealing capital, and usurer's capital developed to their highest point within the ancient form.[131]

The intrusion of all these forms into the basic means of production is significant, but, up to a certain moment, they do not alter its fundamental content. Although usury capital does contribute to a rise in exploitation within a system of private ownership underpinned by the work of slaves, and although this can even lead to the divestment of the property of some slave owners, this does not alter the relationship itself because, ultimately, the usurer himself becomes the slave owner. Otherwise, usury contributes to the creation of a limited class of slaves, and to the strengthening of the system of slavery:

> Moreover, the usury which sucks dry the small producer goes hand in hand with the usury which sucks dry the rich owner of a large estate. As soon as the usury of the

130 Marx, *Grundrisse: Foundations of the Critique of Political Economy*, 424.
131 Marx, *Capital: A Critique of Political Economy*, Volume III, 443.

Roman patricians had completely ruined the Roman plebeians, the small peasants, this form of exploitation came to an end and a pure slave economy replaced the small-peasant economy.[132]

Property Relations in Feudal Societies

General Characteristics

The society of the feudal formation underpins its economy by an arrangement of two modes of production: feudal farming with its specific form of private land ownership, and the guild system for which individual ownership of the craftsmen's workshop is emblematic. These two types will constitute the basis for a conflict between the town and village which takes place on both the economic and political levels of social life. On the one hand, the village will politically dominate over the town; on the other hand, the town will economically exploit the village. This exploitation of the latter by the former intensifies – particularly, in the later stages of feudal development when benefits of landlords take on the form of a feudal rent in money. These two components are, obviously, not the sole means of production and the sole forms of ownership, but they do, nonetheless, shape the character of social life in the town and village.

In the countryside, the land is the fundamental object of ownership, and this imparts a natural character to the rural economy. Natural here means that the newly created product form meddles only to the slightest degree in the essence of the previous conditions of production. In other words, land ownership potentially encompasses ownership of raw resources and materials, tools and instruments, as well as the crops and yields whose attainment depends, to a great degree, on nature. Therefore, even exploitation takes on a primordial form because the producer provides the landlord with, above all, feudal rent in the form of rent in labor or rent in kind. As a consequence, the end product is still something of use value. Production of commodities is a side effect of the rural economy, but, over the course of time, it begins to increase, accompanied by the development of the goods and money market and propagation of rent in money.[133]

Surplus labor here comprises the work of concrete persons for concrete persons among whom dependencies are of a personal nature. Such dependencies are regulated either by written law or by tradition. In certain cases, this can lead to arbitrariness on the part of the feudal lord, yet the limits of this phenomenon

132 Ibid., 444.

133 Marx, *Grundrisse: Foundations of the Critique of Political Economy*, 431–436.

are delineated by the economic demands made upon the mode of production (as well as the economic culture).

Urban production is organized on completely different principles. Marx underscores especially the difference in the object of ownership. Here the conditions of labor are an invention of a historical process. Dominant is ownership of tools, instruments, and machines; moreover, this means of production already assumes the production of goods which are not intended for direct consumption, but for the market. Nevertheless, the upper limits of this exchange are not yet the conditions of demand, but the rules and regulations of guild institutions. These, in turn, are subject to the reproduction of the down-to-earth craftsman's workshop and anticipated consumption by the master, his family, and his journeymen and apprentices:

> With the urban crafts, although they rest essentially on exchange and on the creation of exchange values, the direct and chief aim of this production is *subsistence as craftsmen*, as *master-journeymen*, hence use value; not *wealth*, not *exchange value as exchange value*. Production is therefore always subordinated to a given consumption, supply to demand, and expands only slowly.[134]

Borough societies are organized in the form of guild corporations conjoining individual owners of their own workshops. But because urban communities are more susceptible to change than rural ones, guilds begin to take on the form of stiff, restrictive institutions opposing the introduction of any changes. Guild corporations regulate the majority of issues connected with the operation of each workshop: "The guilds of the middle ages therefore tried to prevent by force the transformation of the master of a trade into a capitalist, by limiting the number of labourers that could be employed by one master within a very small maximum."[135] They demarcate the upper limits of production, the number of persons employed in one workshop, and even the methods by which goods are produced. Relations in the workshop are characterized by patriarchy.

The guild and feudal modes of production constitute the framework for the feudal formation society. Marx points to the existence of many forms of feudal land ownership as well as many forms of individual crafts workshop ownership. The number types of feudal ground rent are, for instance, an expression of the fundamental differences between diverse forms of land ownership. Additionally, there was individual property of small parcels of land which was completely independent of feudal landlords. Persons working in this form were freemen and

---

134 Ibid., 436.

135 Marx, *Capital: A Critique of Political Economy*, Volume I, 216.

did not submit any servitude on behalf of the liege lords. The numbers of free wage laborers were on the rise.

Different ownership of capital (e.g., trade, usury, monetary, etc.) developed as well:

> Commercial wealth as an independent economic form and as the foundation of commercial cities and commercial peoples exists and has existed between peoples on the most diverse stages of economic development, and within the commercial city itself (e.g. the old Asian, the Greek, and the Italian etc. of the Middle Ages) production can continue on in the form of guilds etc.[136]

The slavery type of ownership continued, too. Hence property relations in feudal societies present a complicated mosaic of many forms. Some of them stem from earlier stages of development (and have been described in the course of those portrayals), while others would appear in a full and final shape only after the decline of feudalism (and will, therefore, be described in the following chapter). Nonetheless, this dichotomous, conflict-generating, rural-urban arrangement appears always.

According to Marx, feudal relationships achieved their "classic" form only in England to which these arrived from the continent; interestingly enough, that is where feudalism was earliest abolished. In fact, it was precisely the English case which provoked Marx to construct a theoretical model serving investigations into diverse variants of feudal development.

Feudal Land Ownership

Marx speaks of two variations in the birth of feudalism. In Western Europe, it appeared as a result of the decline of the slavery formation. The genesis of subjugation in Eastern Europe differed somewhat: in this region, it evolved from the deterioration of communities of individual owners which functioned in configurations seen as Germanic, Slavic, or Romanian.

In Western Europe, during the fall of the Roman slavery formation – as a consequence of internal transformations as well as the dissemination of the German mode of production – more effective, individual ownership of small land parcels began to universalize. This situation appeared in the form of free individual ownership of *colons*, individual ownership of the German type, individual possession of the provincial decurions, and many others. The interim period between slavery and feudalism was characterized by – worth noting and emphasizing – the domination of small-scale ownership by working producers.

---

136 Marx, *Grundrisse: Foundations of the Critique of Political Economy*, 778.

Many a cause impacted the decline of this form. Among these were the state's excessive exploitation of free ownership as well as the exploitation of small proprietors and tenants by large landholders; an unstable political situation and numerous wars which contributed to the ruin of individual farms; the collapse of the goods-currency market on the territories of the former Roman Empire; and other factors. For example, "During the reign of Charlemagne, the Frankish peasants were likewise ruined by wars, so that they faced no choice but to become serfs instead of debtors."[137] This led to a secondary enslavement of producers in a new feudal form, i.e., serfdom. Some of the ruined owners were forced into slavery; others surrendered to slavery on their own to protect themselves from even more drastic forms of exploitation. Also taking place was the transformation of earlier forms of slavery into serfdom:

> In order to expropriate the agricultural producers, it is not necessary to drive them from the land, as happened in England and elsewhere; nor to abolish communal property by some ukase. If you go and take from the peasants more than a certain proportion of the product of their agricultural labour, then not even your gendarmes and your army will enable you to tie them to their fields. In the last years of the Roman Empire some provincial decurions, not peasants but actual landowners, fled their homes, abandoned their land, and even sold themselves into bondage – all in order to be rid of a property that had become nothing more than an official pretext for exerting quite merciless pressure over them.[138]

In Eastern Europe, feudalism came as result of the dissolution of German, Slavic, and Romanian communes as well as the dissolution of archaic common property. Initially, members of these archaic communes (as individual possessors of households and parcels of land) submitted a portion of the yield from their farms on behalf of a communal fund of production and consumption. They offered products of their labor to accomplish common goals. In time, the communal dignitaries usurped for themselves the community property and the accompanying compensations. This economic fact found its authorization and justification in the normatively sanctioned relationship of serfdom dependencies.

Serfdom is not the only legal form which the feudal ownership relation can take. This can also be found among producers who, from a legal point of view, are freemen. Key to the feudal ownership relations is feudal annuities: in the form of direct work, product, or currency. Hence, feudal services can take on the form of labor rent, kind rent, and money rent. Wherever servitude takes on the form of labor rent, there will also be serfdom. This will be anchored in a direct enforcement of extra work and in being bound to the land. Wherever

137 Marx, *Capital: A Critique of Political Economy*, Volume III, 447.

138 Marx, *Letter to Vera Zasulich: The "First" Draft.*

feudal benefits are realized in the form of in-kind rent or money rent, serfdom fades away.

In Western Europe (for instance, in England), serfdom had already disappeared in the 14th century, replaced by various kinds of ground rent tenancy and then sharecropping. The peasant became a free owner of his land. However, in Central and Eastern Europe – where peasants were formally emancipated at the beginning of the 15th century and mainly delivered feudal rent in kind or money – serfdom was reintroduced after the aristocracy's victories during the peasant wars in Germany. Hence, whereas serfdom had already vanished in Western Europe, it appeared all over again in Central and Eastern Europe.

The legal situation of the parties in feudal ownership relations is highly complex. In various countries, various legal institutions regulated this relationship. In law, it is customary to label feudal landownership as "divided ownership"; the decadent, pre-capitalist variants are dubbed "incomplete." This notion indicates the fact that each of the parties of feudal relations is a user of different rights and privileges in reference to the same land. Thus, from a legal perspective, both the peasant and the feudal lord are, in a sense, partial owners of the conditions of labor. The feudal lord is owed, among other things, the right to make use of and manage the land, while the peasant has the right to possess the same parcel of land, cultivate it, and make use of the land since this does not collide with the rights of the lord. The feudal lord takes advantage of ground rent in several forms and can sell his land. This means that he can transfer his rights to another noble who, therefore, obtains rights and privileges, but to an extent no greater than the previous landlord. In the meantime, the peasant does not lose any of his rights and privileges during such a transfer; he continues to be a possessor of the land parcel as well as an owner of the movable property. The relationship just described is not to be mistaken for that of co-ownership in which all parties have similar or identical rights to land or goods. As has already been stated, in different countries, different legal institutions control feudal ownership relations, and hence the description above renders but a rough outline of this relationship. Additionally, all the rights and privileges in the legislation of those times were variously labeled, and various were their content and range.[139]

A philosophical-legal sketch of this relationship was conducted by St. Thomas Aquinas. Feudal ownership is reflected in his writings as the partitioning of the category of property into such elements as *dominium*, *possessio*, and *proprietas*. Generally speaking, *dominium* signifies the right of a feudal landlord to dispose

139 Anatoly W. Wieniediktow [Vieniediktov], *Państwowa własność socjalistyczna* (Warsaw: Wydawnictwo Prawnicze, 1952), 92–245.

of his land, manage it, make partition of it, distribute it amongst the peasants, and make use of its profits. *Possessio*, however, is more like today's tenant farming that is run by a working peasant. The *dominium* is rooted in divine and natural law (as states St. Thomas); the *possessio*, however, is rooted in positive (constitutive) law. In turn, the contemporary correlate for *proprietas* is the concept of free individual private property. Some peasants who delivered ground rent in kind or money might be defined as free individual owners of the parcels cultivated by them. Of course, a literal representation of the meaning of these categories in today's language is impossible; these are merely approximate facsimiles.[140]

However, focusing on the socioeconomic substance of feudal relationships, Karl Marx writes that the formula of slavery and that of serfdom are similar. This could suggest that the peasant serf holds only the position of an owner of the means of consumption; he is neither the owner of land or any other objects of ownership. Such a situation emulates the model version of the position of the slave, but, in all certainty, does not emulate the position of the peasant. Both the facts and Marx himself contradict this.

This formula does, however, match the position of the feudal manor servants. As Marx writes, manor servants were co-consumers of the surplus product paid by the village in the form of feudal rent and appropriated by the feudal lord. In exchange for real or symbolic services rendered, servants received the "necessaries of life" from their superior. Members of the manor house staff were, therefore, economic owners of the means of consumption, whereas, concerning other elements of their living conditions (including the means of production), they were non-owners.

The peasant was, nonetheless, the owner of his working conditions, even if his living conditions were far below the standards of the manor servants who were sole owners of their means of consumption. Feudal peasants were self-sustaining, individual proprietors of land parcels despite their serfdom: "This differs from slave or plantation economy in that the slave works under alien conditions of production and not independently. Thus, conditions of personal dependence are requisite, a lack of personal freedom, no matter to what extent, and being tied to the soil as its accessory, bondage in the true sense of the word."[141]

Regardless of the legal and political interpretation of their position, perhaps a better description of their socioeconomic position would be to say that they

140 Czesław Strzeszewski, *Własność: zagadnienie społeczno-moralne* (Warsaw: Ośrodek Dokumentacji i Studiów Społecznych, 1981), Volume XII, 141–163.

141 Marx, *Capital A Critique of Political Economy*, Volume III, 576.

were working possessors of plots of land. On more than one occasion, Marx calls the serf peasants as owners or possessors.[142] Nevertheless, when serfdom has disappeared, the position of the producers as proprietors of the means of production becomes all the more visible:

> In England, serfdom had practically disappeared in the last part of the 14th century. The immense majority of the population consisted then, and to a still larger extent, in the 15th century, of free peasant proprietors, whatever was the feudal title under which their right of property was hidden. In the larger seigniorial domains, the old bailiff, himself a serf, was displaced by the free farmer.[143]

Depending upon the form in which the producer submits the ground rent to the feudal lord, differently does the producer realize his position as an owner. What all these forms share is that the land parcel comprises – for the producer and his family – a workshop for their labor and independent farming. As every owner of the conditions of labor, the producer employs himself and others to work the land belonging to him. Thus he also holds the position of a proprietor of his own (and/or sometimes someone else's) labor power. Marx asserts straightforwardly that the peasant can be the owner of someone else's labor power – either that of free wage workers or that of his serfs. As Marx explains,

> The transformation of rent in kind into money-rent is furthermore not only inevitably accompanied, but even anticipated, by the formation of a class of property-less day-labourers, who hire themselves out for money. During their genesis, when this new class appears but sporadically, the custom necessarily develops among the more prosperous peasants subject to rent payments of exploiting agricultural wage-labourers for their own account, much as in feudal times, when the more well-to-do peasant serfs themselves also held serfs. In this way, they gradually acquire the possibility of accumulating a certain amount of wealth and themselves becoming transformed into future capitalists.[144]

The economic position of the peasant as the owner of the conditions of labor is also subject to confirmation at the stage of product distribution. Wherever feudal serfdom and labor rents exist, the peasant appropriates only those fruits of his labors which have been produced on his allocated parcel of land. The free peasant appropriates the entire product; this is not in contradiction with the fact that he is forced by the feudal lord to pass on a surplus product to the lord in the form of rent in kind or currency. The sole difference between him and the independent proprietor is that the latter is not obliged to share what he produces

142 Ibid., 575–576.

143 Marx, *Capital: A Critique of Political Economy*, Volume I, 510.

144 Marx, *Capital: A Critique of Political Economy*, Volume III, 580.

with anyone. Feudal rent in money contributes to the development of a market: the peasant is compelled to produce market goods and sell them. This leads to a second division of agricultural products among the participants in the exchange. Regrettably, this exchange usually acts to the detriment of peasants and to the advantage of the merchant capitalists who begin proliferating in the feudal society:

> Land is not a commodity for sale in the hands of a peasant. What does become such a market good is, however, the product of his labors, his mobile property. Market is still of limited range here. But, along with the introduction of a money rent, the role of market increases rapidly. The direct producer as before is still possessor of the land either through inheritance or some other traditional right, and must perform for his lord, as owner of his most essential condition of production, excess corvée-labour, that is, unpaid labour for which no equivalent is returned, in the form of a surplus-product transformed into money. Ownership of the conditions of labour as distinct from land, such as agricultural implements and other goods and chattels, is transformed into the property of the direct producer even under the earlier forms of rent, first in fact, and then also legally, and even more so is this the precondition for the form of money-rent. The transformation of rent in kind into money-rent, taking place first sporadically and then on a more or less national scale, presupposes a considerable development of commerce, of urban industry, of commodity-production in general, and thereby of money circulation. It furthermore assumes a market-price for products, and that they be sold at prices roughly approximating their values, which need not at all be the case under earlier forms.[145]

Ultimately, the peasant does manifest himself as the economic owner of the means of maintenance in a manner characteristic only of owners of the conditions of labor. Firstly, the peasant himself creates the means of consumptions and, as Marx puts it, submits a "wage" for these means to himself. In comparison, the slave receives such means from his master, the wage laborer receives them by way of his selling of his labor power, but the peasant is supplied with the necessaries of life as the owner of the product produced on his plot of land. Further, the peasant is supplied with a fund of consumption before undertaking production, a fund which will last for the whole vegetation cycle until the new product is actually ready. Such is the case even if the amount of those means constitutes the bare minimum, starvation rations. Moreover, the peasant manifests himself as the subject of product consumption. It is, after all, the peasant (and not the feudal lord) who invests and reproduces the conditions of labor (except sharecropping whereby both contribute to the renewal of the landholding). Reproduction usually takes on a simple form since the bulk of the product goes

145 Ibid., 579.

out as feudal rent; it is even often the case that remittance is at the cost of the family's living standards.[146]

In a totally different fashion, does the feudal superior (occasionally seen by Marx as the nominal owner) realize his position as the landholder. He is also an owner in the economic sense. On the one hand, wherever feudal compensation takes the form of labor rent, his position is confirmed in both production and distribution. On the other hand, wherever the compensation takes the form of in kind or money rent – and arable land is divided among producers – the feudal lord realizes his position only in the economic domain of distribution since he appropriates the surplus value produced by the peasants. In other words, "Whatever the specific form of rent may be, all types have this in common: the appropriation of rent is that economic form in which landed property is realized, and ground rent, in turn, presupposes the existence of landed property, the ownership of certain portions of our planet by certain individuals."[147]

As an owner of the working conditions, the feudal lord is also the owner of the labor power of others – the direct producers – to the degree to which they submit the surplus product to him. As a result of this, his position is measured not only by the amount of land belonging to him but also the number of producers (the number of souls) who deliver ground rent to him.

Guild Ownership of the Craftsman's Workshop

The fundamental form of property within whose scope the inhabitants of medieval cities conducted their production activities is the individually owned, private workshop of the craftsman. The guild master has the privileged position in this form of small-scale, private property. The master – through his constituency in a specific type of association, the guild corporation – is an individual owner of his workshop. He, too, is a working owner. Even if he employs the labors of others, this comprises a subordinate factor since the number of persons whom he can employ is limited by guild rules and regulations. He will hire at most a few apprentices and pupils. Relations among them will bear a strictly and normatively (by legal and traditional rules) delineated structure.

Karl Marx accents the meaning of the physical characteristics of the object of ownership in the relations formed within the framework of the craftsman's workshop. This is no longer land property (which consistently involved ownership of instruments). This type of ownership assumes that the producer has been

146 Ibid., 577–582.
147 Ibid., 473.

dispossessed of his land and is, therefore, the owner of tools and instruments as well as the owner of his labor power. As Marx says, this constitutes a new historical stage in the transformation of property relations: "As regards No. II, [there is] the particular kind of work – mastery of it, and, consequent upon that, an identity between property in the instrument and property in the conditions of production…."[148] The very nature of the object of ownership contributes to the fact that this is individual work which does not require a collective handling of conditions of labor:

> In short, the essential character of the guild-corporation system, of craft work as its subject, constituted by owners – can be resolved into the relation to the instrument of production – the instrument of labour as property – as distinct from the relation to the earth, to land and soil (to the raw material as such) as one's own. That the relation to this one moment of the conditions of production constitutes the working subject as owner, makes him into a working owner, this [is] historic situation No. II, which by its nature can exist only as antithesis to or, if one will, at the same time as complement of a modified form of the first – likewise negated in the first formula of capital.[149]

Marx also points to yet another crucial factor which distinguishes this relationship from other forms of individual private property. In other forms, ownership of the conditions of labor mediates the ownership of one's labor power: to be able to work, one must first possess a place to work. However, in the case of the craftsman's workshop, it is just the opposite. Here ownership of one's labor power mediates every other type of participation in the ownership relation. In the case of the guild craftsman, what counts the most is, above all, skilled labor (*die Kunst*) which has been tested in practice and accepted by the corporation. To start producing, the simple purchase of tools and devices is insufficient. A requirement is peer acceptance of the craftsman as a skilled owner of his labor power. At this point the privilege of being a master is certified by the guild, and, as of this moment, the master's position as the owner of his own personal workforce begins to mediate other ways of being an owner, including his ownership of a craftsman's workshop. Thus, the craftsman's workshop manifests itself only as a necessary confirmation of this privilege.

The position of the master as the proprietor of his workshop was like the position of the feudal landlord. To become a master, someone must be certified by a guild; to become a feudal landlord, someone must be knighted by the monarch or bear a hereditary title of belonging to the aristocracy or gentry. Belonging to

148 Marx, *Grundrisse: Foundations of the Critique of Political Economy*, 424.
149 Ibid., 423–424.

concrete, privileged estate mediates the possibility of being a proprietor of the means of production. Thus, feudal property relations are at the same time relations between social estates.

The economic situation of the master as an owner of a product was essentially the same as his legal situation. The entire production manufactured in his workshop was appropriated by him. Still – although production undertaken in this form of ownership was destined for the market – it did not, however, lead to the transformation of a workshop owner into a capitalist. This was so because his participation in exchange relations was limited by the rather small amount of goods created in his workshop. Furthermore, the guild system limited the possibilities for expanded reproduction of working conditions: "The guilds of the middle ages therefore tried to prevent by force the transformation of the master of a trade into a capitalist, by limiting the number of labourers that could be employed by one master within a very small maximum."[150] As a consequence of this situation, a significant portion of the workshop's product was consumed by the master and his family. The journeymen and apprentices were also co-consumers of the product found in the hands of the master. Overall,

> The guilds protect a workshop owner from exploitation by merchants, yet because they enforce monopolist prices for the products of their members, the situation becomes a basis for exploitation of, e.g., peasants and liege lords. The means of exploitation is a non-equivalent exchange. In such manner, the craftsman's workshop becomes for the master not only a means of employment, but also a means of intermediate exploitation of those who enter into exchange relations with him. But the circumstances can be reversed: the workshop, too, can succumb to intermediate exploitation. If the countryside exploits the town politically in the Middle Ages, wherever feudalism has not been broken down by exceptional urban development – as in Italy, the town, on the other hand, exploits the land economically everywhere and without exception, through its monopoly prices, its system of taxation, its guild organisation, its direct commercial fraudulence and its usury.[151]

150 Marx, *Capital: A Critique of Political Economy*, Volume I, 216.
151 Marx, *Capital: A Critique of Political Economy*, Volume III, 581.

Chapter III: Capitalistic Forms of Private Ownership and Other

Introductory Remarks

Naturally, the majority of the works of Karl Marx pertains to capitalism. This area of his interest has been thoroughly investigated by historians of economic and social thought. The literature discussing the views of Marx on capitalism is characterized by a single trait: they primarily investigate capital seen as a historical mode of production. Significantly fewer analyses address capital understood as a system of property relations.

Additionally, the vast majority of the interpretations of his viewpoints is limited to generalizations that take into consideration merely the basic mode of capitalist production. Nonetheless, there were many forms of ownership functioning simultaneously in 19th-century capitalist societies and, in fact, Marx observes and describes various of their modes of production. Serving as examples here are the mode of industrial capitalist production, the agricultural mode of capitalist production, the metayer (or sharecropping) system of production, and the cottage industry mode of capitalist production – all of which differ from one another with regards to several key characteristics. Karl Marx also devotes much attention to nonproductive forms of capital, subjecting each concrete form of productive and nonproductive capital (and forms of property) to deep analysis, and identifying distinctive traits.

Marx's outlook on this subject of capitalist property relations will be systematically discussed in this chapter, albeit also surfacing in partial analyses throughout the volume at hand. This will enable a spotlighting of the differences between the particular forms of private ownership.

Ownership Relations during the Transition between Feudalism and Capitalism in Western Europe

Individual Private Ownership

Nineteenth-century capitalism arose as a result of the disintegration of feudal socioeconomic structures. The majority of scholars agrees with such a reading of Marx's theory of social development, adopting this general thesis formally and then applying it systematically and consistently.

However, Karl Marx was far from a schematic application of theory to diverse European and non-European societies. After all, the birth of capitalism looked differently in each country or region. For instance, in Central and Eastern Europe where feudal relations lasted the longest, the fall of feudalism led to a direct switch from feudal dependencies to capitalist ones.[152] In contrast, the onset of capitalism in Western Europe was preceded by a rather long, provisional period during which such economic modes of production appeared as cannot be assigned either to agricultural feudalism or the urban guild, or handicraftsmen mode of production, or capitalism. As Marx states,

> It will suffice merely to refer to certain intermediate forms, in which surplus labour is not extorted by direct compulsion from the producer, nor the producer himself yet formally subjected to capital. In such forms capital has not yet acquired the direct control of the labour-process. By the side of independent producers who carry on their handicrafts and agriculture in the traditional old-fashioned way, there stands the usurer or the merchant, with his usurer's capital or merchant's capital, feeding on them like a parasite. The predominance, in a society, of this form of exploitation excludes the capitalist mode of production; to which mode, however, this form may serve as a transition, as it did towards the close of the Middle Ages.[153]

Pre-capitalist, transitional forms of society constituted, in the eyes of Marx, a mosaic of many modes of production. The economic structure of English society differed from that in Italy and still more from the one in France in the immediate aftermath of the French Revolution. What all these societies had in common was that the old feudal structures had either collapsed or existed in some residual form, while the capitalist mode of production was only just developing and had not yet gained a dominant position in the economy. Yet, "Only in the period of the decline and fall of the feudal system, but where it still struggles internally – as

152 Karl Marx [1881], *Letter to Vera Zasulich: The "First" Draft*, <https://www.marxists.org/archive/marx/works/1881/zasulich/draft-1.htm> [accessed August 2017]; Karl Marx [1881], *Letter to Vera Zasulich: The "Second" Draft*, <https://www.marxists.org/archive/marx/works/1881/zasulich/draft-2.htm> [accessed August 2017]; Karl Marx [1881], *Letter to Vera Zasulich: The "Third" Draft*, <https://www.marxists.org/archive/marx/works/1881/zasulich/draft-3.htm> [accessed August 2017];

Karl Marx [1881], *Letter to Vera Zasulich: The "Fourth" Draft*, <https://www.marxists.org/archive/marx/works/1881/zasulich/draft-4.htm> [accessed August 2017].

153 Karl Marx [1867], *Capital: A Critique of Political Economy*, Volume I, <https://www.marxists.org/archive/marx/works/download/pdf/Capital-Volume-I.pdf> [accessed August 2017], 360.

in England in the fourteenth and first half of the fifteenth centuries – is there a golden age for labour in the process of becoming emancipated."[154]

The Western variant of the rise of capitalism is of particular interest for researchers of property relations because it was precisely at this time and place that, in the course of the transition, individual private ownership developed nearly universally. In Western cities, this encompassed craftsmen who increasingly broke away from the supervision of the guild; there were also new forms of small-scale manufacturing, trading, and providing of services anchored in the work of an owner and his family. In the rural countryside of the West, the usual form of cultivation was individual farms, independently managed by free peasants. Their legal status varied from possessors to lessees and tenants, to users, *ad perpetuum*; but many of them were, indeed, legal owners of their land. Key is that they were formally freemen and that, from an economic perspective, they should thus be counted as individual owners of the conditions of labor. Moreover,

> This form of free self-managing peasant proprietorship of land parcels as the prevailing, normal form constitutes, on the one hand, the economic foundation of society during the best periods of classical antiquity, and on the other hand, it is found among modern nations as one of the forms arising from the dissolution of feudal land ownership. Thus, the yeomanry in England, the peasantry in Sweden, the French and West German peasants. We do not include colonies here, since the independent peasant there develops under different conditions.[155]

This state of affairs preceded the shaping of capitalism in the majority of Western European countries. In speaking of this, Marx provides examples: the independent individual owner of a parcel of land who was already evident in the 15th-17th centuries in the English countryside ("Even in the last decade of the 17th century, the yeomanry, the class of independent peasants, were more numerous than the class of farmers"[156]); the small tenant farmer or the petty landowner who appeared in the Italian villages after the Mediterranean trading centers and trade itself had collapsed; the French peasant whom the French Revolution emancipated from feudal dependencies and who was granted title to a parcel of cultivated land; or the German peasant who, in some German lands, was a free

154 Karl Marx [1857–1861], *Grundrisse: Foundations of the Critique of Political Economy* (Rough Draft), <https://www.marxists.org/archive/marx/works/download/pdf/grundrisse.pdf> [accessed August 2017], 433–434.

155 Karl Marx [1863–1883], *Capital: A Critique of Political Economy*, Volume III, <https://www.marxists.org/archive/marx/works/download/pdf/Capital-Volume-III.pdf> [accessed August 2017], 584–585.

156 Marx, *Capital: A Critique of Political Economy*, Volume I, 512.

landowner prior to Napoleon, or who, during the Napoleonic wars, gained the same rights as his French peer had somewhat earlier.

Overall, in France, "The country folk – over two-thirds of the total French population – consist for the most part of so-called free *landowners*. The first generation, gratuitously freed by the Revolution of 1789 from its feudal burdens, had paid no price for the soil."[157] Similar was the situation in the English colonies in North America where individual ownership of land, worked independently by the farmer and his family, was widespread. In Italy, however,

> where capitalistic production developed earliest, the dissolution of serfdom also took place earlier than elsewhere. The serf was emancipated in that country before he had acquired any prescriptive right to the soil. His emancipation at once transformed him into a free proletarian, who, moreover, found his master ready waiting for him in the towns, for the most part handed down as legacies from the Roman time. When the revolution of the world-market, about the end of the 15th century, annihilated Northern Italy's commercial supremacy, a movement in the reverse direction set in. The labourers of the towns were driven *en masse* into the country, and gave an impulse, never before seen, to the *petite culture*, carried on in the form of gardening.[158]

Marx uses different terms in naming individual private ownership: the free ownership of the self-managing peasant, peasant proprietorship of land parcels, free self-managing peasant proprietorship of land parcels, petty bourgeoisie ownership, individual private ownership, the private property of the laborer in his means of production, etc. All of the abovementioned terms for "individual private ownership" reflect a completely different nature than the capitalistic, feudal, or slavery types of private ownership. As Marx notes, "Political economy confuses on principle two very different kinds of private property, of which one rests on the producers' own labour, the other on the employment of the labour of others. It forgets that the latter not only is the direct antithesis of the former, but absolutely grows on its tomb only."[159]

Marx describes how individual private ownership takes on "numberless shades":

> Private property, as the antithesis to social, collective property, exists only where the means of labour and the external conditions of labour belong to private individuals. But according as these private individuals are labourers or not labourers, private property has a different character. The numberless shades, that it at first sight presents, correspond

157 Karl Marx [1850], *The Class Struggles in France, 1848–1850*, <https://www.marxists.org/archive/marx/works/download/pdf/Class_Struggles_in_France.pdf> [accessed August 2017], 61.

158 Marx, *Capital: A Critique of Political Economy*, Volume I, 508–509.

159 Ibid., 543.

> to the intermediate stages lying between these two extremes. The private property of the labourer in his means of production is the foundation of petty industry, whether agricultural, manufacturing, or both; petty industry, again, is an essential condition for the development of social production and of the free individuality of the labourer himself. Of course, this petty mode of production exists also under slavery, serfdom, and other states of dependence. But it flourishes, it lets loose its whole energy, it attains its adequate classical form, only where the labourer is the private owner of his own means of labour set in action by himself: the peasant of the land which he cultivates, the artisan of the tool which he handles as a virtuoso.[160]

It would be worthwhile to present a few such distinctions. Firstly, the conditions of labor were diverse in nature – they could entail land or only work instruments. Secondly, the economic goals could also differ. The owner might work primarily to meet his own needs and those of his family; therefore he creates all necessary items whereas his farm constitutes an isolated, independent manufacturing organism. But it could also be the case that the owner might produce commodities for the market; thus his activity comprises a segment of the social division of labor which has been conditioned by existing trade relationships. Thirdly, some of the forms of individual private ownership became the foundation for exploitation, others were subjected to exploitation, and still others were free of exploitation.

During this transition period – from feudalism to capitalism – the class of wage laborers was not numerous. Wage labor existed primarily as an additional job for petty owners of the conditions of labor or as a job for certain members of their families. This, in fact, stymied the development of a capitalist means of production; the majority of the population was employed within the confines of its own conditions of labor. It is true that capital was developing very rapidly, but this was nonproductive capital functioning on the basis of other means of production and living off them. Here, Marx mentions usury and trade capital as the key areas of profit-making during the changeover. The post-feudal, great landowners did not constitute the dominant factor in the rural life of Western Europe; grand capitalist tenants (of land belonging to legal landlords) were to come in the near future. This was a time of small tenants of parcels of land who paid ground rent to legal landlords and acted as private individual possessors.

160 Ibid., 541.

A Case Study

Karl Marx not only criticized, but also learned from Georg Hegel. Marx perfectly adopted Hegel's skills at theoretical analysis and was subsequently capable of extracting key elements of a phenomenon from amidst its numerous and various manifestations. Moreover, Marx's theoretical approaches are also rich in empirical material, pointing to much more complexity and diversity than would appear on the basis of a model analysis. This aspect of his research is rarely highlighted in the studies of Karl Marx. This leads to the creation of rigid schemes whereas phenomena manifested a wealth of shades and tones; this can also lead to an association of such schemes with reality.

Such is also the case with ownership. The overall, Marxist model of the individual private property has already been described herein. As expected, it would be a grievous error to treat this model as the real and actual shape of the phenomenon at hand; the concrete forms taken by individual private ownership are, of course, not a precise reproduction of that model. They do differ from one another, and, in fact, certain distinctions which can appear between specific kinds of individual ownership have already been lightly sketched. But these differences go further.

Marx describes a few such concrete ownership constellations which comprise a far-reaching transformation of the general model. One of these refers to post-feudal ownership relations in the English countryside:

> In England, serfdom had practically disappeared in the last part of the 14th century. The immense majority of the population consisted then, and to a still larger extent, in the 15th century, of free peasant proprietors, whatever was the feudal title under which their right of property was hidden. In the larger seignorial domains, the old bailiff, himself a serf, was displaced by the free farmer. The wage labourers of agriculture consisted partly of peasants, who utilised their leisure time by working on the large estates, partly of an independent special class of wage labourers, relatively and absolutely few in numbers. The latter also were practically at the same time peasant farmers, since, besides their wages, they had allotted to them arable land to the extent of 4 or more acres, together with their cottages. Besides they, with the rest of the peasants, enjoyed the usufruct of the common land, which gave pasture to their cattle, furnished them with timber, firewood, turf, &c.[161]

The quote above detects a few ways of being an individual owner: (a) as a lessee or tenant of someone else's land; (b) as the possessor of a garden plot granted to a worker; or (c) as a legal, private owner of a land parcel. Additionally, an individual can have a share of the communal real estate and work as a hired laborer.

161 Ibid., 510.

Marx indicates three crucial traits of individual private ownership, common not only for those producers who are independent, legal landowners, but also pertain to the tenant, the parcel possessor, and users of community land. All these individuals: (a) are self-employed; (b) directly appropriate the product of their own work; and (c) can participate in the market exchanging this product as a commodity.

In each of these abovementioned ways of being an owner, the realization of the position of that owner is manifested differently. Among other things, the independent, legal, private owner of a land parcel is usually afforded more chances to decide for himself about the way in which he wants to utilize his land than the tenant farmer who has to take the nominal owner's interests in mind. Distinctions between specific producers manifest themselves even more clearly in the way that they appropriate the product. Even if all of them become owners of the product created on the land they possess and utilize, then they divide and distribute that product in different proportions to others. The government imposes one kind of taxes, tariffs, or duties on the legal owner, and yet others on the remaining producers. Diversified fiscal payments depend not only upon the amount of land but also the legal status of the producer. Assuming that taxes have already been paid, then other factors begin to interfere in how the product is distributed. The legal proprietor shares his product with no one else. The tenant farmer, however, transfers a portion of the product (usually in monetary form) to the nominal landowner of a large estate; the farmer thus realizes his position as an economic landowner only partially with respect to the fruits of his labors.

It would seem that the position held by the possessor of a garden plot neighboring his household – who is granted a plot of land by right of his working on someone else's property as an agricultural wage laborer – is similar to that of the independent legal owner of a parcel since the former also takes the whole of the product reaped from his plot. However, he is limited in his production due to the small size of the parcel as well as due to a lack of time to fully take advantage of this resource.

Even more different is the appropriation of the product obtained from communal land. The communality of this land does have strictly delineated boundaries. Usage of community land is, essentially, individual, but, if it is collective (e.g., a single shepherd for a collective flock), then the product is appropriated by specific households. There will be disparities based on the production potential of each household (e.g., number of sheep, number of persons in the family, etc.).

The case study elucidated above illustrates how complicated is the nature of the ownership relations found in the transitional period between feudalism and capitalism. A single person could be an individual owner in several ways; in addition, a person could appear as a hired laborer and user of communal land.

Part of a family was sometimes employed in a cottage industry. Such a situation could no longer be a simple form of individual private ownership, but a complex system of ownership encompassing the elements of diverse forms.

Many a time Karl Marx emphasizes that – during the transition, and before the preliminary accumulation of capital had gained strength – the economic conditions of life of the individual producers (as owners of the means of maintenance) was much better than that of subsequent capitalist wage workers; the former enjoyed much better living conditions than the latter.

Preliminary Accumulation as a Process in the Transformation of Property Relations

At the turn of the 18th and 19th centuries, the primitive accumulation of capital constituted a prerequisite for the nascence of capitalism as a new economic formation in society. This was, indubitably, a complicated process which, according to Marx, could be synthesized down to two crucial consequences: the expropriation of the producer and his segregation from the conditions of labor. "What does the primitive accumulation of capital, *i.e.*, its historical genesis, resolve itself into? In so far as it is not immediate transformation of slaves and serfs into wage labourers, and therefore a mere change of form, it only means the expropriation of the immediate producers, *i.e.*, the dissolution of private property based on the labour of its owner."[162]

It would be wrong, however, to claim that the accrual of the majority of the conditions of labor, financial capital, and the means of subsistence by one side – while concurrently divesting the other side of these same resources – comprises a sufficient presupposition for the establishment of capitalist ownership relations. If that were so, then already the ancient society – wherein there was both the expropriation of producers as well as accumulation of the conditions of labor (i.e., land), financial capital, and the means of survival – would have been transfigured into a society of the capitalist type. And yet capitalist ownership relations did not appear and spread. Instead, ancient societies transformed into slavery societies.

The expropriation of producers is a necessary condition, but certainly insufficient a precondition for the founding of capitalist ownership relations. For capitalist ownership relations to be formed, the expropriation of the producer should go hand in hand with a tearing him away from the conditions of labor. Additionally, the potential laborer should nominally be a free man, too. For example, a slave is dispossessed, but he is not torn from the conditions of labor since he himself is part

162 Ibid., 541.

and parcel of those conditions. Only those owners of labor power who are formally free, but are divested of both the means of survival and the means of production, will be forced to sell the only item they own – their capability of working. And only like this do circumstances arise which facilitate the establishment of capitalist relations of ownership. As Marx explains,

> The *original formation* of capital does not happen, as is sometimes imagined, with capital *heaping up* necessaries of life and instruments of labour and raw materials, in short, the *objective* conditions of labour which have already been unbound from the soil and animated by human labour. Capital does not create the objective conditions of labour. Rather, its *original formation* is that, through the historic process of the dissolution of the old mode of production, value existing as money-wealth is enabled, on one side, *to buy* the objective conditions of labour; on the other side, to exchange money for the *living labour* of the workers who have been set free.[163]

Such an opening situation did not spread on a mass scale in the early stages of development. The merchant could not purchase land from an Asiatic community since the latter was completely uninterested in depriving itself of the conditions of its labor and its very existence. For the same reasons, the medieval merchant could not purchase a craftsman's workshop. Apart from that, the merchant would not even be interested in such an acquisition since he would not find a labor force to run the workshop. Labor power was not yet an item of trade; more to the point, labor power and the conditions of labor then constituted a single entity because the producer and the owner were the same. The producer was not interested in the selling of his skills since he utilized them in his own workshop; if, however, the producer was enslaved, then it was all the more impossible for him to present his capabilities on the labor market since his expertise and dexterity belonged to someone else.

On the one hand, nonproductive capital has a chance to transform into productive capital if it finds itself in a position to segregate labor power from the conditions of labor. On the other hand, labor power should seek out capital, if the former is to be turned into work for hire. For instance, the dispossessed Greek peasant of antiquity did have his labor power, but he surrendered himself as a slave to the owners of the means of production in exchange for the means of survival for himself and his family. He sold his capability to work for his entire lifetime. Such a transaction led to permanent, direct connections between labor power and the conditions of labor. This naturally led to the evaporation of a labor market.

163 Marx, *Grundrisse: Foundations of the Critique of Political Economy*, 430.

Labor power is reshaped into wage labor, if and when it is sold for a short period. The producer should be an individual who is formally free and who will not divest himself of his freedom by some sales contract. This situation of segregation from the conditions of work should be cyclically repeated, as Marx describes in the study *Value, Price and Profit*:

> What the working man sells is not directly his *labour*, but his *labouring power*, the temporary disposal of which he makes over to the capitalist. This is so much the case that I do not know whether by the English Laws, but certainly by some Continental Laws, the *maximum time* is fixed for which a man is allowed to sell his labouring power. If allowed to do so for any indefinite period whatever, slavery would be immediately restored. Such a sale, if it comprised his lifetime, for example, would make him at once the lifelong slave of his employer.[164]

Wage laborers did appear at earlier stages of development. Still, this did not lead to the rise of a capitalist means of production – or at least it did not lead to its evident presence at earlier points in historical time. Only the emergence of the working class – hired laborers on a mass scale – constructed the base for capitalist accumulation, leading to the establishment of production capital. Primitive accumulation is thus a process of mass expropriation of producers and their subsequent transformation into hired workers. Marx points to many means by which this occurred.

The simplest way of concentrating the conditions of labor on one side and labor power on the other is the abolishment of the old feudal institutions which gave the peasant the right to utilize part of the land. Expropriation took place by way of indirect coercion which had nothing to do with legality or common law. Only with the course of time was this formalized by legal regulations in new legislation and legal norms which referred to Roman property law. Thus ensued the expropriation of small proprietors.

In another fashion, were the manor and church servants changed into hired laborers. Since they had never been possessors of land parcels, it sufficed to deprive them of their means of subsistence which had theretofore been guaranteed them by the feudal lord: now they were potential sellers of labor power.

Another universally applied means of dispossession was taxation. A peasant who could not keep up with his payments fell into debt and was forced to sell his land, in search of other means of survival. Tax systems were a rather successful means vis-à-vis the legal but small landholders who could not simply be tossed out of their homes and divested of their cultivated land like the tenant farmers.

164 Karl Marx [1865], *Value, Price and Profit*, <https://www.marxists.org/archive/marx/works/download/pdf/value-price-profit.pdf> [accessed August 2017], 17.

In addition to systems of taxation, other means of forced dispossession were systems of prices for agricultural products which favored mass, and not small-scale production; systems of credit which also did not match small-scale farming; and usury capital which, according to Marx, contributed to an exceptionally large degree to tearing peasants away from their land.

A great role in the expropriation of producers was played by trade capital. Marx demonstrates in concrete examples how trade capital is converted into productive capital, and how the individual owner of the conditions of labor is converted into a wage laborer. This process can take a rather straightforward course. For instance, some merchant orders a larger number of non-agricultural products (such as cloth, spun fiber, etc.) which previously comprised a byproduct on the peasant's farm, wholly used by his family. At first, the merchant does not prepare or provide any tools, raw materials, or means of survival; his interference in the functioning of the peasant's farmstead is limited to the fact that he limits the producer to a single kind of work. Therefore, however, the producer starts producing commodities and becomes dependent upon the market and upon the merchant. This leads to the producer working via the mediation of and on behalf of the merchant. The former byproduct is gradually transformed into a core activity – spinning and weaving for sale, production of exchange value for trade. Expropriation of individuals so habituated is much easier than that of the agricultural producer. The next step entails the merchant's delivery of any and all raw materials. All that remains is the guise of a producer selling products to a merchant: the outcome is that the former is selling his labor power to the latter. This is how the capitalist mode of outwork production arises. Even if the tools are the property of the worker, it is a superficial ownership which the capitalist has left for the worker to reduce the costs of his enterprise. Later sometimes even this superficiality vanishes since the capitalist accumulates producers "the home of collective work" whereby the appropriation of the product becomes direct and serves the capitalist's benefit. The earlier, cottage and outwork forms of productive capital are transformed into a higher form: manufacturing is the outcome.

Social Relations within the System of Capitalistic Private Property

Capitalist Relations of Ownership in the Sphere of Production

Marx often accents the fact that it is only productive capital which can truly be called capital. This thesis becomes obvious in the context of his theory of ownership. It is precisely productive capital which is the mainstay of capitalist property relations since it permits the capitalist to accrue ownership of the means of production and another's labor power (born by the wage worker). The core of capitalist property relations is the bond between the owner of productive capital, which functions in his hands as conditions of labor, and the owner of labor power, which functions in his hands as a commodity. Such is the case of the manufactural, industrial, and agricultural modes of capitalist production.

Wherever capital functions solely in nonproductive forms (e.g., trade or currency), ownership relations correspond with a non-capitalist mode of production. An example is the coexistence of merchant capital and individual private ownership. Here an ownership relationship joins the owner of trade capital with the owner of the conditions of labor who has products for sale. Such a relationship has little to do with classic capitalist property relations.

As soon as productive capital appears, all nonproductive forms of capital lose their independent existence. How is this? As of this moment, the owner of trade and financial capital initiates the process of capitalist production either through the purchase of commodities or by granting loans for productive capitalists, or by investing directly in production. Thus, nonproductive capital is transformed into productive capital. As a consequence, these owners of money capital begin to participate in the direct appropriation of surplus product already manufactured by workers and then appropriated by the owner of productive capital (to be discussed at length later). Thus mediated by money, a capitalist property relationship is established between the owners of capital (in all of its forms) and the wage laborers.

The starting point for the formation of such relationships is the separation of the producer from the conditions of his own work and to deprive him of the means of survival. On the one hand, the conditions of labor and the means of survival are both amassed in the hands of but a few owners; on the other hand, a category of people dispossessed of these resources begins to take shape. However, both sides find themselves under duress: the owner of the conditions of labor is not capable of converting them into factors of labor alone, whereas the potential producer has been divested of a workshop, but is in possession of unfettered labor power. If production is to take place, then a bond must be formed between these owners of separated factors of labor.

When individual private ownership was in place, this connection was natural since the owner of one factor was the owner of the other. In capitalism, the connection between conditions of labor and labor power is realized because of purchasing any and all necessary factors of labor (e.g., the conditions of labor and the labor power of the employee). Therefore, when capital becomes productive, the capitalist appears as the owner of the conditions of labor and as the owner of the labor power of others. Marx pointedly explains this in *Capital*:

By the purchase of labour-power, the capitalist incorporates labour, as a living ferment, with the lifeless constituents of the product. From his point of view, the labour-process is nothing more than the consumption of the commodity purchased, *i.e.*, of labour-power; but this consumption cannot be effected except by supplying the labour-power with the means of production. The labour-process is a process between things that the capitalist has purchased, things that have become his property. The product of this process belongs, therefore, to him, just as much as does the wine which is the product of a process of fermentation completed in his cellar.[165]

The capitalist as the owner of the conditions of labor is distinct from every other non-owner in that he uses forces of nature in production, applying them as he would apply the labor power of others. This is a key trait for each kind of owner of the conditions of labor. Moreover, an owner can – similarly and with similar outcomes as with the forces of nature and labor power – apply earlier advances in human thought. Among others, Stanisław Kozyr-Kowalski calls attention to these two characteristics in his work on capitalist ownership.[166]

It is worth marking unequivocally that, during his work, the employee is not an owner of labor power. He was an owner until he agreed with the capitalist for its sale; he was thus the owner of a commodity which he offloaded. However, during that work, there is a transmutation of that commodity into a factor of labor which, as such, is the property of the capitalist.

The capitalist and the worker are also connected by a power relationship. This form of power is diversified. Firstly, this pertains to the power of the owner of the conditions of labor and the means of consumption over the non-owner of the very same items. Secondly, this means the power of the owner of labor power over the bearer of that labor power. Thirdly, this is the power of the supervisor of the production process over his subjects. The extent of a capitalist's power depends upon the extent of his capital. The more he can spend on the purchase of the conditions of labor and labor power, the greater is his permanent capital. The greater his variable capital, the more he possesses as the owner of the means of subsistence, and the more workers are employed in his enterprise.

This is how the power relationship between a single capitalist and a single worker appears. Nonetheless, from a macro-social point of view, it turns out that the class of producers is dependent upon all the classes of owners of the means of

165 Marx, *Capital: A Critique of Political Economy*, Volume I, 131.

166 Stanisław Kozyr-Kowalski, "Własność jako zjawisko ekonomiczno-społeczne w świetle badań Karola Marksa i Maxa Webera", in *Własność: gospodarka a prawo – Studia o marksistowskiej teorii własności*, ed. by Stanisław Kozyr-Kowalski (Warsaw: Państwowe Wydawnictwo Naukowe, 1977), 117–119.

employment. Of course, the worker can be independent of a concrete capitalist; the worker is at least independent as long as he does not undertake employment with the capitalist. He can, of course, resign his job, but he cannot resign from the entire class of owners of the means of employment. This structural dependency has its roots in the system of ownership; this is a relationship of one social group ruling over another:

> The worker leaves the capitalist, to whom he has sold himself, as often as he chooses, and the capitalist discharges him as often as he sees fit, as soon as he no longer gets any use, or not the required use, out of him. But the worker, whose only source of income is the sale of his labour-power, cannot leave the whole class of buyers, *i.e.*, the capitalist class, unless he gives up his own existence. He does not belong to this or that capitalist, but to the capitalist class; and it is for him to find his man – *i.e.*, to find a buyer in this capitalist class.[167]

Capitalist Relations of Ownership in the Sphere of Distribution

In the capitalistic mode of production, the work process occurs between the factors which belong to the capitalist – and thus to him belongs the product created by the producer. The industrial capitalist is the owner of the conditions of labor even when he manages the monies of others since he still appropriates a product created through the application of those factors. Furthermore, he is also an owner in a legal sense. This is a necessary attribute of his position which lends him the ability to conduct an economic activity in accordance with the law.

The creditor, however, cannot be seen as the legal owner of the conditions of labor. This capitalist takes advantage of other rights and privileges stemming from a credit contract. He is, nonetheless (like the capitalist functioning in production), an owner in the socioeconomic sense. He, too, appropriates a part of the product created by the hired laborer via the interest on the capital. Whereas the capitalist functioning in production appropriates directly, the creditor participates in the distribution of product indirectly – by way of the financial capital.

Under the circumstances of capitalist production, money and goods do not constitute some autonomous kinds of capital, but rather specific forms that industrial capital can take. The same money, depending upon the moment in the circulation of capital in which it appears, fulfills different functions, including the function of purchased factors of labor. So it is nothing strange that, by way of money, one can appropriate the labors of others and, in this indirect

---

167 Karl Marx [1847], *Wage Labour and Capital*, <https://www.marxists.org/archive/marx/works/download/pdf/wage-labour-capital.pdf> [accessed August 2017], 9.

manner, confirm the economic position of an owner of the conditions of labor. As Marx explains, "Money-capital, commodity-capital and productive capital, do not therefore designate independent kinds of capital whose functions form the content of likewise independent branches of industry separated from one another. They denote here only special functional forms of industrial capital, which assumes all three of them one after the other."[168]

All the above has considered things from the point of view of the capitalist; however, things look quite the opposite for the hired worker. He is unable to appropriate the product of his own work since he is part of the conditions of labor belonging to someone else. That part of the product which he receives in distribution represents a portion of his work but is not its direct and full product. The worker purchases goods already created in the form of wages. In other words, "Wages, therefore, are not a share of the worker in the commodities produced by himself. Wages are that part of already existing commodities with which the capitalist buys a certain amount of productive labour-power."[169]

The product received by the worker represents only a portion of his work which he delivers to the capitalist. The capitalist, in turn, applies the labor power he has procured to produce more than the value of the worker's wages. This difference constitutes the surplus value in which exploitation is realized on behalf of the capitalist. By expropriating the surplus value, the capitalist functioning in production – followed by the financial capitalist, the capitalist functioning in trade, the landowner, and other participants in this relationship – affirms his position as an owner of the conditions of labor. Since the capitalist functioning in production (e.g., the owner of an industrial enterprise, a manufacturer, or a capitalist land leaser) realizes his title both in the realm of production as well as in the realm of distribution, all others realize their position only in the sphere of distribution.

Here a need arises for a separate discussion of a Marxist analysis of capitalist relationships in agriculture. In the epoch of feudalism, large estates were divided into small parcels among tenant-peasants who directly possessed and utilized the soil. The process of primitive accumulation let to the expropriation of small-scale possessors. Under the new set of circumstances, nominal landlords lease out their land to large-scale capitalist tenants; the last of these did not cultivate the land themselves but employed agricultural wage laborers who had just recently been peasants. Thus were capitalist relationships of ownership established in agriculture.

---

168 Karl Marx [1863–1878], *Capital: A Critique of Political Economy*, Volume II, <https://www.marxists.org/archive/marx/works/download/pdf/Capital-Volume-II.pdf> [accessed August 2017], 29.

169 Marx, *Wage Labour and Capital*, 9.

Capitalist Relations of Ownership in the Sphere of Exchange

In no other form of ownership is being an owner so contingent upon the proper functioning of the exchange system as is the case in capitalist ownership. There are such modes of production in which persons operating within do not need to address others as the owners of the means of exchange to confirm their positions as owners in other areas of social life. In the case of capitalist ownership, however, this is obligatory. Those who fail in selling their commodities cease to be owners in the socioeconomic sense because no commodity is a use value for the owner. In fact, his labor power is also not a use value for the wage laborer. But for the potential capitalist, the resources he has accrued in the form of exchange capital are a use value because all commodities comprise such a value for their non-owners. Therefore, non-owners of certain goods appear before others as owners of yet other goods. These capitalists sell or trade to divest themselves of resources useless to them, subsequently acquiring products loaded with use value in their eyes.

Parties to capitalist ownership relations are owners of the means of exchange (commodities or money). The worker is an owner of labor power as a commodity which he bears until he agrees with a capitalist for its sale. In turn, the capitalist is an owner of manufactured products which are, for him, merely goods (or capital in the form of monies received in payment for those goods).

The first stage of exchange relies upon the worker's sale of his labor power to the capitalist, in exchange for which the former receives the means of subsistence (usually in monetary form). In turn, the capitalist becomes an owner of someone else's labor power as a factor of production. Thanks to this, the resources obtained become a use value for the worker whereas the labor power is a use value for the capitalist:

> The seller of labour-power, like the seller of any other commodity, realises its exchange-value, and parts with its use-value. He cannot take the one without giving the other. The use-value of labour-power, or in other words, labour, belongs just as little to its seller, as the use-value of oil after it has been sold belongs to the dealer who has sold it. The owner of the money has paid the value of a day's labour-power; his, therefore, is the use of it for a day; a day's labour belongs to him.[170]

Thanks to that first transaction initiated between the capitalist and the hired worker, capital is transformed into an effective economic means of employment and means of appropriation of the product of someone else's work. In production, the purchased labor power creates a new product for the capitalist. This product does not only reproduce the now-depleted means of production as well as the

170 Marx, *Capital: A Critique of Political Economy*, Volume I, 136.

expended (by the capitalist) means of subsistence which has been exchanged for labor power; this is not a matter of mere reproduction of spent constant or variable capital. It is also a reproduction with a surplus value since the worker provides the capitalist with unpaid surplus labor. Although the exchange of labor power for the means of survival appears to be an exchange of equivalents, this is essentially not the case since the capitalist has paid for only part of the time of the labor offered by the worker. The product appropriated by the capitalist is loaded with surplus value as the effect of unpaid surplus work.

Noteworthy here is that appropriation of the surplus product by the capitalist will not mean the realization of his position as the capitalist owner of the conditions of labor until the product is, in fact, sold. This might be adequate regarding the owner functioning in the slavery or feudal types of ownership – wherein appropriation of the fruits of other people's labor directly serves the consumption needs of the owner, his family, and his retinue – but it is inadequate with reference to capitalist ownership. Looking at the latter, the appropriation of the surplus product should take on a specific and unique form of completion.

The capitalist must sell the appropriated product. And this is the second important stage of participation in the exchange system by the owner of productive capital. During production, the worker has been exploited. Nevertheless, this exploitation has not come to fruition on behalf of the capitalist since the appropriated product does not constitute any use value for him. For the capitalist to win a profit, he must sell the product; otherwise, he will have nothing as a capitalist. It is only when he sells that commodity that he will obtain the means necessary for the renewal of the conditions of labor and the purchase of labor power. Then and only then will his position as the owner of capital be confirmed; only then will reproduction of capitalist relations of ownership occur:

> The creation of this surplus-value makes up the direct process of production, which, as we have said, has no other limits but those mentioned above. As soon as all the surplus-labour it was possible to squeeze out has been embodied in commodities, surplus-value has been produced. But this production of surplus-value completes but the first act of the capitalist process of production – the direct production process. Capital has absorbed so and so much unpaid labour. With the development of the process, which expresses itself in a drop in the rate of profit, the mass of surplus-value thus produced swells to immense dimensions. Now comes the second act of the process. The entire mass of commodities, *i.e.*, the total product, including the portion which replaces the constant and variable capital, and that representing surplus-value, must be sold.[171]

171 Marx, *Capital: A Critique of Political Economy*, Volume III, 172.

Surplus value is not the same as profit. The surplus value is included within the surplus product which is created by the laborer in the surplus, unpaid work time which has been wrung out of him by the capitalist. Profit is, however, equal to the difference between the price of the sold product and the costs of its production. All in all, it is equal to the difference between the amount of money which enters circulation and the amount of money drawn out. The surplus value arises in the process of production; the profit arises in the process of exchange. Any forms of profit stem from the derivative distribution of surplus value (already appropriated by the production capitalist) which takes place during the process of an exchange and – more generally – the process of the circulation of capital.

It can, therefore, happen that a capitalist goes bankrupt despite his appropriation of the surplus product. This can occur when he does not sell or sells the product below the profit line. In the first case, the product is wasted; in the second, its value is captured by other participants in the exchange. Hence only such appropriation of surplus value which is realized in the form of monetary profit leads to reproduction of the capitalist's position as an owner of capital.

In the process of circulation, capital takes on various forms – money capital, productive capital, commodity capital, commercial capital, merchant capital, money-dealing capital, or financial capital. Therefore, at different stages of exchange, the capitalist is the owner of capital manifesting itself in different functions – either as a function of the factors of labor, commodities, or money. Regardless of the above, it remains the same capital even if someone else is the owner of each form since production capital comprises a surplus value for the owner of capital in all the remaining forms.

For instance, the monetary capitalist can grant a loan to the industrial capitalist; the former surrenders to the latter the use value of the funds. This is because, by using the money, the industrial capitalist can buy all manner of factors of production, while the monetary capitalist preserves the exchange value of the money which will return to him with interest. Hence more money returns to the monetary capitalist than he disbursed in the loan. Lending money is thus a unique kind of inequivalent exchange during which economic titles of ownership to the product which will be created in the future are realized. Thus, the same funds "work" – for both the monetary and industrialist capitalists – as a factor of production: this results in a surplus value for both, which they subsequently divide amongst themselves. Both capitalists are economic owners of that value and therefore owners of the conditions of labor.

During the process of exchange, a realization of the title of ownership also transpires for the trade capitalist who is rewarded by the capital functioning in production. The goods which he manages are already laden with a surplus value which has been appropriated by the capitalist functioning in production. The merchant also appropriates a portion of the surplus value created by the wage laborers.

The significance of the exchange for the position of the parties to capitalist ownership relations becomes evident when the process of the circulation of capital succumbs to a crisis. If monetary capital does not function in production in the form of purchased factors of labor, then it turns into a treasure. Its use value as capital disappears and it ceases to be a means of appropriation of surplus value. If on the one hand, labor power is not sold, then the owner is no longer the economic owner of its exchange value; on the other hand, the means of production fall into disuse. If capital gets stuck at the stage of produced goods, then the capitalist is not capable of renewing the factors of production, and the unsold product is wasted. Economic crises are, among other things, an outcome of the collapse of the circulation of capital. For each capitalist, such a situation can mean partial dispossession or loss of his position as an owner of capital; for the worker, this means an incapability of realizing his title of ownership to labor power.

Capitalist Relations of Ownership in the Sphere of Consumption

One of the more general assertions of the Marxist theory of ownership states that, to maintain the position of owner of the conditions of labor, one must be the owner of the means of subsistence (owner of the means of consumption) before and for the whole duration of production undertaken within the framework of those conditions – until new means of subsistence are created. The same refers to an owner of productive capital. He can maintain the position of the owner of the means of production, since he possesses the necessities of life for himself, his family, and his hired laborers for the period preceding the completion of the product. In Marx's words, "The employer, by commanding the means of employment, commands the means of subsistence of the worker, *i.e.*, the latter's life depends on him; just as the worker himself degrades his life activity to a mere means of existence."[172]

This also pertains to the owner of nonproductive forms of capital. If for example, a rentier lacks the means of survival, then he will need to withdraw his monetary capital from the bank and will, therefore, lose the possibility of earning interest. The means of survival takes on a monetary form which functions as exchange capital. If, however, a potential capitalist lacks such resources, then he will not find a hired laborer: "However, the money-capital converted into variable

172 Karl Marx [1846], "Wages", in *Marx and Engels, Collected Works* (Moscow: Progress Publishers, 1976), Volume VI, 423.

capital, *i.e.*, the money advanced for wages, plays a prominent role in the circulation of money itself, since the labourers must live from hand to mouth and cannot give the industrial capitalists credit for any length of time."[173] The worker hands over labor power solely in exchange for the means of survival.

Thus, it turns out that, for the capitalist, no less important than the position he occupies as owner of the conditions of labor is the position he occupies as the owner of the means of survival. This might sound tautological when considering the fact that production capital exists in both constant and variable form. The first form represents the conditions of labor; the second represents the means of subsistence for the worker, meaning wages for the wage workers.[174]

Ownership of the means of survival comprises a presupposition for the realization of the capitalist's title as owner of the conditions of labor as long as he finds a free laborer who possesses neither the means of production nor the means of subsistence. In such an economic situation, the latter is enforced to sell his labor power. In the case of the free wage laborer, this is the only way of acquiring the means of consumption.

In fact, Marx proposes that employees accumulate reserve supplies to avoid being under the thumb of employers. Marx does not preclude the possibility that a worker could sell his skills so profitably that both he and his family would attain a high living standard: in fact, in his times, a segment of the working class (the so-called labor aristocracy) had won significant earnings. But the majority lived in poverty with wages so low as to lead to physical and intellectual degradation.

Marx and Engels devote much attention to the issue of the price of labor power. They do not express an opinion about the level of fair wages because capitalist property relations are unfair in and of themselves. According to Marx and Engels, the lowest pay for labor power constitutes the necessary means of existence: "The average price of wage-labour is the minimum wage, *i.e.*, that quantum of the means of subsistence which is absolutely requisite to keep the labourer in bare existence as a labourer– meaning necessary to keep the worker and his family alive. What, therefore, the wage-labourer appropriates by means of his labour, merely suffices to prolong and reproduce a bare existence."[175] This limit depends upon physical and historical factors; the limit stretches since capital develops just as well at the price of poorly fed persons with a shorter lifespan and a rapid succession of generations or at the price of healthy workers living longer and

---

173 Marx, *Capital: A Critique of Political Economy*, Volume II, 253.

174 Marx, *Capital: A Critique of Political Economy*, Volume I, 146–147.

175 Karl Marx, Friedrich Engels [1847], *Manifesto of the Communist Party*, <https://www.marxists.org/archive/marx/works/download/pdf/Manifesto.pdf> [accessed August 2017], 23.

under good conditions. Justifying such a conclusion was the miserable situation of hired workers in 19th-century Europe.

The wage worker receives in the form of paying such a quantity of resources as will suffice for the period of employment alone. Consumption, however, means the destruction of the object of ownership. From the moment he stops working, he ceases to be an owner in that sense and, hence, will be forced to sell his labor power anew. At one point, Marx claims that even if workers, in general, reach a pay level which would assure them of good living conditions, there will always be a relationship of exploitation between the capitalist and the worker since the sole source of the means of survival for the worker is the sale of his labor power. There can also be such a situation that, to limit consumption, the worker will set aside and amass a portion of his income, subsequently transforming it into capital. Nonetheless, such cases do not signify a change in the crucial content of capitalist ownership relations. The worker simply becomes yet another capitalist: this is merely a personal, individual shift and not a structural one.

The Theory of Exploitation

General Characteristics of Exploitation

Two preconditions are necessary for exploitation to appear. Firstly, the producer can create the surplus product, and, secondly, that product is afterward appropriated by someone other than the producer himself. But these two elements are not the only ones. Accordingly, Marx provides several examples of appropriation of surplus product (meaning portions thereof) which cannot be qualified as exploitation.

This problem is thoroughly deliberated in his critique of the social-democratic concept of "the undiminished proceeds of labor."[176] The appropriation of the entire product by direct producers is an illusion. A share of the social product must be set aside for the reconstruction of the conditions of labor, for their expanded reproduction, and for a reserve fund. Also coming into play are the costs of supporting nonproductive employees as well as persons of nonproductive age cohorts (i.e., those who cannot yet work or who can no longer support themselves by working). Only the remainder of the product is subject to division among the direct producers. From the individual's point of view, it appears that each producer has granted a part of the surplus product on behalf of other

---

176 Karl Marx [1875], *Critique of the Gotha Programme*, <https://www.marxists.org/archive/marx/works/download/Marx_Critque_of_the_Gotha_Programme.pdf> [accessed August 2017], 8–10.

persons and that each has been expropriated of a portion of his labor. In the opinion of Karl Marx, however, this does not yet constitute exploitation.

If so, then how great a part of the surplus value must be transferred into the hands of others before one can speak of exploitation? Marx never sets a threshold as of which exploitation ensues. This is a practical problem for every society to assess: the social labor productivity, the costs of the reproduction of labor power, the living standard, tradition, and the natural environment which the producers inhabit. Still, any principle for the division and distribution of the social product is, essentially, a principle of inequality. Even the ostensibly just principle of "each according to his work" accepts an unequal division of abilities and allows for inequality. Nonetheless, Marx does answer the question of why the partial dispossession of a producer of the fruits of his labors does not comprise exploitation: whatever the individual loses as a private person, he regains. In other words, "The 'undiminished' proceeds of labor have already unnoticeably become converted into the 'diminished' proceeds, although what the producer is deprived of in his capacity as a private individual benefits him directly or indirectly in his capacity as a member of society."[177]

Such compensation can take on diverse forms. A society fulfills a protective function with respect to an individual. The producer, should he cease to be one, can count on similar benefits and payments; the producer saves time and, because of the increased labor productivity, he appropriates the greater mass of the use value than he would have, if not for the cooperation of others. From this point of view, exploitation transpires if and only if a producer who is dispossessed of surplus value loses more as an individual than he gains as a member of society.

Marx projects such a situation in which exploitation is nonexistent. This would be at a higher stage of development of the communist society in which his illustrious principle – "From each according to his ability, to each according to his needs!"[178] – is in place. A requirement for this to be brought to fruition is an abundance of goods to distribute. Thus, no one is excluded from the distribution of the social product; the appropriation of the product by one person does not result in the loss of use value by another – even if the product of the work of others is consumed. That is, exploitation assumes a shortage of goods. This is a specific kind of scarcity which Karl Marx describes in *The Poverty of Philosophy*. Exploitation exists wherever a scarcity of goods runs alongside the production of luxury and overconsumption.

---

177 Ibid., 10.

178 Ibid., 11.

Preliminary conclusions are made evident. Exploitation assumes: (a) the creation of surplus product; (b) such an expropriation of the producer from the surplus product as would result in his loss of more as an individual than he would gain as a member of the collective; and (c) the production of luxury and excess consumption under the conditions of a paucity of fundamental goods, under the conditions of impoverishment. This is not a very precise delineation of exploitation, but one more precise than this cannot be found in Karl Marx.

In his *Contribution to the Critique of Political Economy*, under the heading of "Production and Distribution," Marx writes: "It is a long-established view that over certain epochs people lived by plunder. But to be able to plunder, there must be something to be plundered, and this implies production. Moreover, the manner of plunder depends itself on the manner of production, e.g., a stock-jobbing nation cannot be robbed in the same way as a nation of cowherds."[179]

A few of the matters found herein are worth underscoring. Exploitation can take on many historical forms. Diverse types of owners can be exploited. The onset of exploitation is the moment when the proportions (to which producers and other human categories participate in the distribution of product) are disturbed. Exploitation is always, at its deepest core, an exploitation of the producer. In any case, this is the origin of the source, this is where it begins, and only subsequently do its further stages fall into succession. The exploiter becomes the exploited. All complex forms of movement of an item through which exploitation is realized can be reduced to this most fundamental one. For example, a stock market speculator can be subjected to exploitation as the next owner of the product of someone else's labor. In turn, whoever expropriates the speculator ultimately participates in the exploitation of the original producer. This is the vital content of exploitation, regardless of its historical form.

The Feudal Relationship of Exploitation – A Case of Explicit and Visible Exploitation

In feudalism, exploitation takes on an explicit tangible form. It can be recognized through the senses. As Marx explains this, surplus labor has an "an independent and palpable form."[180] This materializes in the specific and historical form of ground rent – specifically feudal rent. If profiteering takes on the form of rent in

179 Karl Marx [1859], *A Contribution to the Critique of Political Economy*, <https://www.marxists.org/archive/marx/works/download/Marx_Contribution_to_the_Critique_of_Political_Economy.pdf> [accessed August 2017], 121.

180 Marx, *Capital: A Critique of Political Economy*, Volume I, 164.

kind (e.g., serfdom), then work one performs on one's field is detached – in time and space – from work performed on behalf of an expropriator. The situation is similar with rent in kind versus rent in money: here, too, surplus value is transferred to the feudal lord in a form both autonomous and material.[181]

The producer – regardless of the legal characteristics of his position – is the economic possessor of land and is hence equipped with funds of consumption for the duration of the labor period. He is, therefore, economically independent of the exploiting party. Therefore, necessary for exploitation are non-economic instruments. In the case of serfdom, this is direct coercion applied during servile work; in the case of other forms of rent, the coercion can take on a very mild, indirect form. The regulators will be tradition along with common or written law; coercion is unnecessary when servitude and rents are an obvious and non-debatable cultural norm. In all these situations, profit constitutes the economic realization of estate privilege. More importantly, this relationship is one of personal dependency: the exploiter and the exploitee are known by name.

The perceptibility of feudal exploitation depends upon three factors: (a) in certain cases, work performed on one's own behalf and on behalf of an exploiting party are manifestly distinct from one another; (b) the volume of the surplus product to be exploited can be tangibly quantified; and (c) the parties on both sides are personally identifiable.

The Capitalist Relationship of Exploitation – A Case of Implicit and Invisible Exploitation

Quite different is exploitation in capitalism, in the relationship between the industrial capitalist and the wage laborer. Here the exploitation has latent form. It cannot be recognized through the senses. To identify this exploitation, one needs to apply the theoretical analysis of real processes.

Looking at the bottom layer, it is evident that the wage laborer (who is the producer) possesses neither his own workshop nor funds of consumption. Non-economic means of coercion are redundant as the economic position held by the wage laborer forces him to undertake employment on behalf of someone else. A relationship appears between the capitalist and the laborer, in which the latter sells his labor power to the former, in exchange for which the laborer receives the means of subsistence. This is how it appears from the outside. The exchange of commodities (wage labor for labor power) disguises the exploitative relationship thus created.

---

181 Marx, *Capital: A Critique of Political Economy*, Volume III, 571–583.

The capitalist would not be interested in establishing such an exchange if he were to remit to the laborer just as much as the former extracted from the latter in the form of labor and its effects. If that were the situation, then the capitalist would be an ordinary organizer of the process of production and would have to put himself to work in order to obtain anything. Exploitation would, therefore, be precluded – yet this is not the outcome here. Only a part of the worker's labors – that which is indispensable – is compensated by wages, so he works on behalf of the capitalist. This is surplus labor and herein lies capitalist exploitation. Work performed for himself and work performed for someone else is neither separated by time nor space. On the surface, it seems as if the laborer's work was remunerated. Camouflaging the exploitation relationship are the wages which blur the workday boundaries between paid and unpaid work. Wage makes the actual relationship of exploitation invisible:

> The wage form thus extinguishes every trace of the division of the working day into necessary labour and surplus labour, into paid and unpaid labour. All labour appears as paid labour. In the corvée, the labour of the worker for himself, and his compulsory labour for his lord, differ in space and time in the clearest possible way. In slave labour, even that part of the working day in which the slave is only replacing the value of his own means of existence, in which, therefore, in fact, he works for himself alone, appears as labour for his master. All the slave's labour appears as unpaid labour. In wage labour, on the contrary, even surplus labour, or unpaid labour, appears as paid. There the property-relation conceals the labour of the slave for himself; here the money-relation conceals the unrequited labour of the wage labourer.[182]

In feudalism, the flow of labor and its products was unidirectional hence profit was something one could touch and see. In capitalism, however, the flow is bidirectional; moreover, the exchange appears equivalent, so it is only in the analysis of the economic facts that exploitation can be identified. As Marx notes,

> Firstly. The *value or price of the labouring power* takes the semblance of the *price or value of labour itself*, although, strictly speaking, value and price of labour are senseless terms. / Secondly. Although one part only of the workman's daily labour is *paid*, while the other part is *unpaid*, and while that unpaid or surplus labour constitutes exactly the fund out of which *surplus value* or *profit* is formed, it seems as if the aggregate labour was paid labour. / This false appearance distinguishes *wages labour* from other *historical* forms of labour. On the basis of the wages system even the *unpaid* labour seems to be *paid* labour. With the *slave*, on the contrary, even that part of his labour which is paid appears to be unpaid. Of course, in order to work the slave must live, and one part of his working day goes to replace the value of his own maintenance. But since no bargain is struck between

---

182 Marx, *Capital: A Critique of Political Economy*, Volume I, 381.

him and his master, and no acts of selling and buying are going on between the two parties, all his labour seems to be given away for nothing.[183]

If a capitalist operates with his capital, then it is possible to identify the exploiting party rather precisely. Of course, this identification is feasible only to a certain degree because the capitalist appears on the market with his goods and there he shares a part of the expropriated surplus value with other participants in an exchange. Nonetheless, under the conditions of functioning financial capital, the infeasibility of demarcating the participating sides in the profit-making rises. Profits are then realized in interest, in dividends, in rents of various ilk as well as in other forms. Thus, are camouflaged the social facts of profit, its magnitude, the paths expropriation of the product takes, and the persons who are partaking thereof.

The Parties in Relationships of Exploitation and the Means of Exploitation

Marx identifies a specific kind of incomplete forms of exploitation. For instance, sometimes exploitation is only realized to the detriment of the producers, as they are expropriated of surplus product. But the same exploitation is not realized at an advantage to the appropriators. There is a lack of economic effectivity in the appropriation of this product because an appropriator gains no profit or another benefit from it. For exploitation to be realized to the benefit of the capitalist, he must change the appropriated surplus product into a commodity which he must sell. Otherwise, he appropriates nothing as a capitalist (as the economic owner of capital), even though he has become the legal owner of the appropriated product. To complete the process of exploitation, the capitalist must convert appropriated surplus value into profit that takes on the form of currency:

> The entire mass of commodities, *i.e.*, the total product, including the portion which replaces the constant and variable capital, and that representing surplus-value, must be sold. If this is not done, or done only in part, or only at prices below the prices of production, the labourer has been indeed exploited, but his exploitation is not realised as such for the capitalist, and this can be bound up with a total or partial failure to realise the surplus-value pressed out of him, indeed even with the partial or total loss of the capital. The conditions of direct exploitation, and those of realising it, are not identical.[184]

One of the most known of Marx's theorems states that the owners of the means of production exploit the producers who are deprived of the means of production and survival. However, this is not a simple, automatic assumption. It is worth

183 Marx, *Value, Price and Profit*, 20.

184 Marx, *Capital: A Critique of Political Economy*, Volume III, 172–173.

looking at a Marxist example which unsettles certain stereotypical thinking about exploitation: it is possible for a wage laborer to be the exploiting side. This occurs when the laborer does not work effectively enough to earn his wages during the time in which he has submitted his labor power to the capitalist. Marx describes this situation as follows: "Capital is dead labour, that, vampire-like, only lives by sucking living labour, and lives the more, the more labour it sucks. The time during which the labourer works, is the time during which the capitalist consumes the labour-power he has purchased of him. If the labourer consumes his disposable time for himself, he robs the capitalist."[185]

Therefore, concerning the same funds, exploitation can go in either direction. Directly, it could seem that this is a capitalist exploitation executed by a worker, but this would merely be a description of the surface level of this relationship. In truth, in this case, one worker is exploiting another via the capitalist (who is not, after all, the producer of the surplus value). This form of exploitation comprises for Marx the basis for distinguishing the so-called labor aristocracy. It is with this social group that the capitalist shares a portion of the expropriated surplus value.

The exploiting parties can be even more difficult to identify if the exploitation depends upon a transfer of some product created from one form to another form of ownership. This is a relationship much more complicated than that previously discussed. In *Capital*, Marx expands upon this:

> The high rate of profit in the Middle Ages is not entirely due to the low composition of capital, in which the variable component invested in wages predominates. It is due to swindling on the land, the appropriation of a portion of the landlord's rent and of the income of his vassals. If the country-side exploits the town politically in the Middle Ages, wherever feudalism has not been broken down by exceptional urban development – as in Italy, the town, on the other hand, exploits the land economically everywhere and without exception, through its monopoly prices, its system of taxation, its guild organisation, its direct commercial fraudulence and its usury.[186]

In the description just cited an entire spectrum of instruments of exploitation – both economic and non-economic – is presented. Privilege and the system of taxation appear alongside means less visible. The non-economic means of exploitation only complement the fundamental means which is the exchange of market goods. Nonequivalent exchange based on a monopoly system of prices is one rudimentary means of exploitation and, simultaneously, a means by which exploitation is camouflaged.

185 Marx, *Capital: A Critique of Political Economy*, Volume I, 163.

186 Marx, *Capital: A Critique of Political Economy*, Volume III, 581.

Worthy of special attention is who exploits whom because a claim that the city exploits the villages is far too general. The party directly exploited by the city is the feudal lord. Nonetheless, beneath the exchange between the feudal lord and the merchant or craftsman lies the exploitation of the peasant. This aspect of exploitation is difficult to discern because the feudal lord mediates in this relationship: it is through him that the surplus product is transferred to the town. The peasant farmstead also participates in exchanges with the town, and is thus subject to direct exploitation, too.

The urban locality is not homogenous in its composition, and only certain categories of the population expropriate the surplus product of the rural areas. Here the exploiters are, above all, the owner of trade capital and usury capital. But setting the owners of capital aside here, the focus will be on the workshop of a master craftsman associated with a guild. Precisely this workshop can be a center of exploitation.

At first glance, it would appear that there is no relationship of exploitation in this case because this is a form of ownership entailing a working producer. However, since the production of the workshop is assigned to the market, the goods sold by the master become a means by which a product which is the fruit of other people's labors is expropriated. Via exchange, the master obtains such an amount of product or currency which represents much more labor than is contained in the product he is selling. An indicator of this exploitation is, among other things, the standard of living enjoyed by the master craftsman. Through his own labors as well as that of his apprentices and journeymen he would not be able to guarantee himself such a high living standard, especially since the productivity of his work is not very high. His workshop thus fulfills two functions. In the first order, this is a means by which he can employ himself which also grants him the possibility of expropriating the product of his own labors. But, secondly, this is also a means of exploitation – yet not so much of the journeyman and apprentice, but that of the peasant. This is an apparently paradoxical conclusion, especially since the master is not linked to the peasant by any direct bond. Yet, exploitation does transpire. This is particularly made possible when the master's products are encompassed by monopoly prices, or when there is a longer period of imbalance between supply and demand.

Individual private ownership can become a basis for exploitation but is more often its subject. Exploitation of the peasant of ancient times led to his transformation into a Roman proletariat or a slave. Exploitation of the individual peasant working within the Germanic form of ownership led to the establishment of feudal dependencies. Exploitation of individual owners in the interim period between feudalism and capitalism led to the expropriation of people working within various forms of individual ownership of the conditions of labor and to the emergence of the working class, of wage laborers.

Different forms of exploitation were used with regard to these forms of ownership: means of non-economic coercion (e.g., privileges, taxation, prices dictated by the state, etc.) and means of economic coercion (e.g., nonequivalent exchange, a credit system inappropriate for small ownership, drawing small owners into the system of a market economy, etc.). Marx illustrates the exploitation relations whose victim was the 19th-century French peasant:

> The roots that small-holding property struck in French soil deprived feudalism of all nourishment. The landmarks of this property formed the natural fortification of the bourgeoisie against any surprise attack by its old overlords. But in the course of the nineteenth century the urban usurer replaced the feudal one, the mortgage replaced the feudal obligation, bourgeois capital replaced aristocratic landed property. The peasant's small holding is now only the pretext that allows the capitalist to draw profits, interest, and rent from the soil, while leaving it to the agriculturist himself to see to it how he can extract his wages. The mortgage debt burdening the soil of France imposes on the French peasantry an amount of interest equal to the annual interest on the entire British national debt. Small-holding property, in this enslavement by capital toward which its development pushes it unavoidably, has transformed the mass of the French nation into troglodytes.[187]

In this case, because the exploited party is easy to identify, it is not always clear who exactly benefits from the exploitation. One can only ascertain that the exploiting side encompasses owners of capital in their diverse, nonproductive forms (e.g., owners of trade capital, usury capital, loan capital, etc.). This type of exploitation does not require the existence of direct links between the expropriator of product and its producer (as was the case of production capital rooted in wage labor).

Based on the deliberations presented thus far, it could seem that those subject to being exploited are, above all, producers employed in the production of material goods. Nevertheless, it turns out that each wage laborer who executes some socially useful work of a nonproductive nature – in the sphere of services, culture, politics, education, healthcare, or administration – can also be exploited. Each of these is the owner of labor power which, during the work process, is utilized for various social aims. If a person does not obtain appropriate wage

187 Karl Marx [1851–1852], *The Eighteenth Brumaire of Louis Bonaparte*, https://www.marxists.org/archive/marx/works/download/pdf/18th-Brumaire.pdf> [accessed August 2017], 64.

compensation for his labors, then the worker is divested of a portion of his talents, skills, and capabilities. His toils free representatives of other social groups of the obligation to pay for achievement of those goals. These issues are discussed by Marx when investigating the transformations in state administration which took place because of the Paris Commune.[188] It was not for naught that Marx devoted so much time to discussing the issue of wages which he perceived not only as a source of income but, above all, as a social relationship. Wages comprise a social bond of a depersonalized nature, and so discernment of the exploitation concealed by forms of payment is hampered here, too.

In Marx's concept, the means of ownership fulfills various functions – among them, the means of production, means of exchange, or means of subsistence. Under certain circumstances, the means of ownership are transformed into means of exploitation. Still, the individuals who participate in these relationships as the exploiting party do gain – regardless of their legal situation – the economic status of owners of the conditions of labor and someone else's labor power.

188 Karl Marx [1870–1871], *The Civil War in France*, <https://www.marxists.org/archive/marx/works/download/pdf/civil_war_france.pdf> [accessed August 2017].

Chapter IV: Social Property – Shades of Privatization and Socialization of Property

Sketching Out the Problem

Karl Marx claims that property manifests itself more rarely in pure, extreme forms – be it private or social property – than in mixed or transitional forms. Property assumes an endless number of shades and tones. Certain aspects of specific forms of property can be socialized, while others cannot. The purpose here will be to analyze and extract those aspects of property which were taken under consideration by Marx when he spoke of the level of socialization of some form, or when he openly categorized some form as private or social.

In his eyes, each form of property is, in fact, a system of social relationships. The crux of socialization, therefore, is found in transformations of interpersonal relationships: this is what submits to socialization.

Presented here, too, will be Marxist sketches of select forms of property which he studied in particular. The guideline will be to identify relationships closer to pure private or social property. Reconstructed here, too, will be Marx's model of socialization via components of property distinguished earlier and via application of previously identified criteria of socialization. This model can be understood in various ways:

1) as a set of relationships manifest in real, historical modes of ownership described by Marx as common, communal, collective, or social (even if they never occurred simultaneously in any one form);
2) as a set of axiological assessments underlying critiques of existing forms of ownership;
3) as a set of classificatory criteria;
4) as a program for communist socialization; and
5) as a sort of utopia.

Many a sociologist, economist, or lawyer has held a view that the socialization of property is the same as the liquidation of property. For instance, in the very title of their article, Krzysztof Brozi and Lech Winiarski pose the question straight out: "Is collective property still property?" They claim that application of the category of property should be abandoned and substituted by another. Their proposal for amended terminology is defended by such far-reaching changes in the content of the phenomenon itself that property relations *per se* are made null and void.[189] Other thinkers conclude that, since the state and law will be rescinded in communism, then so, too, will the right to property. For example, the well-known Soviet economist, Anatoly Venediktov writes: "It is understood that one can only speak of the right to property with respect to such formations in which the state and law exist at all. For that reason, there is no need to deal with the problem of property in the tribal society or in the communist one (once the state and law have died out)."[190]

According to Marx, socialization means the appropriation – by a group of individuals as well as by each alone – of the whole of the conditions of their existence. It does not mean the expropriation of all members of society. Each revolutionary transformation of property relations has reached for the essence. Still, the lifting of slave property did not entail the lifting of property in its entirety, but the introduction of a new kind of relationship. Similar was the case with the revocation of feudal property relations; similar would be the case with the communist stage of socialization. Dissolution of the capitalist property would mean ushering in a new historical form of property relations. This issue was unambiguously addressed by Marx and Engels in *Manifesto*:

> The abolition of existing property relations is not at all a distinctive feature of communism. All property relations in the past have continually been subject to historical change consequent upon the change in historical conditions. The French Revolution, for example, abolished feudal property in favour of bourgeois property. The distinguishing feature of Communism is not the abolition of property generally, but the abolition of bourgeois property.[191]

Thus, the structure of the Marxist category of property is such that no stage of socialization is associated with obliteration of property. Social property is also a sort of property and people who function economically within its framework are, indeed, owners.

---

189 Krzysztof Brozi, Lech Winiarski, "Czy 'własność ogólnospołeczna' jest 'własnością'?", *Studia Filozoficzne*, 176/7 (1980), 19–32.

190 Anatoly W. Wieniediktow [Vieniediktov], *Państwowa własność socjalistyczna* (Warsaw: Wydawnictwo Prawnicze, 1952), 18.

191 Karl Marx, Friedrich Engels [1847], *Manifesto of the Communist Party*, <https://www.marxists.org/archive/marx/works/download/pdf/Manifesto.pdf> [accessed August 2017], 22.

Property and Social Development

Formulating one of the key theorems in this theory of social development, Marx writes in *Contribution to the Critique of Political Economy*:

> At a certain stage of development, the material productive forces of society come into conflict with the existing relations of production or – this merely expresses the same thing in legal terms – with the property relations within the framework of which they have operated hitherto. From forms of development of the productive forces these relations turn into their fetters. Then begins an era of social revolution. The changes in the economic foundation lead sooner or later to the transformation of the whole immense superstructure.[192]

In comparable versions, this theorem appears in *German Ideology*, *Poverty of Philosophy*, *Capital*, and other works. Often met are also other versions. The material productive forces are set in contrast to relationships of various appellations: social relationships, social forms of work, social forms of interpersonal relations, the whole of social relationships, economic relationships, or economic property relations. The growth of the productive forces leads to the transformation of property relations which, in turn, influence the pace and directions of change taken by material productive forces. The theorem describing reciprocal dependencies between productive forces and property relations was dubbed by the Polish Marxist sociologist, Jerzy J. Wiatr as the theorem of the development of the mode of production.[193]

Each form of property determines its own specific economic goals, and the development of the productive forces depends upon the primary one. Certain kinds of property facilitate prudence and economic growth while others do not. There are such kinds whose structure hampers or even prevents the development of the forces of productivity. For example, societies of the Asian formation reproduced themselves for centuries in nearly unaltered shape while the development of the forces of productivity was very slow. The cause of this state of affairs should be sought in the binding system of property. The goal of activities undertaken within the basic economic unit (the commune) was the reproduction of social ties within it and reproduction of the position of each of its members.

---

192 Karl Marx [1859], *A Contribution to the Critique of Political Economy*, <https://www.marxists.org/archive/marx/works/download/Marx_Contribution_to_the_Critique_of_Political_Economy.pdf> [accessed August 2017], 4.

193 Jerzy J. Wiatr, *Marksistowska teoria rozwoju społecznego* (Warsaw: Książka i Wiedza, 1973), 101.

Yet, the goal of activities undertaken within the system of state property was the reproduction of political and economic dependencies in the institutional shape typical for a specific state of the Asiatic type. Not facilitating the development of the forces of productivity were also property relations typical for the majority of ancient societies. Endeavors undertaken within most of these forms of property are directed not so much towards growing economic effectiveness as towards reproduction of pre-existing interpersonal dependencies, preservation of positions in the power structure, maintenance of quality of life and consumption, etc. Such is the logic behind the action of owners:

> The individual is placed in such conditions of earning his living as to make not the acquiring of wealth his object, but self-sustenance, his own reproduction as a member of the community; the reproduction of himself as proprietor of the parcel of ground, and, in that quality, as a member of the commune. The survival of the commune is the reproduction of all of its members as self-sustaining peasants, whose surplus time belongs precisely to the commune, the work of war etc.[194]

Also, not facilitating the development of forces of productivity is the property system characteristic for the feudal formation society. The surplus product of the rural areas is neither directed towards the reproduction of the expanding latifundium of serfdom nor the development of the peasant economy, but rather consumption by both the feudal manor and its retinue as well as the more well-to-do peasants. Likewise, in the city in the framework of the guilds and other professional corporations, the individual craftsmen's ownership delineated the upper limits of production and even the methods of production. Here, too, the product serves personal consumption by the master, his family, and the workshop staff; this supports simple reproduction of existing interdependencies:

> With the urban crafts, although they rest essentially on exchange and on the creation of exchange values, the direct and chief aim of this production is *subsistence as craftsmen*, as *master-journeymen*, hence use value; not *wealth*, not *exchange value as exchange value*. Production is therefore always subordinated to a given consumption, supply to demand, and expands only slowly.[195]

In the opinion of Marx, capitalist private property facilitates to a great degree the development of the forces of productivity (albeit up to a point). This is the fundamental goal of economic activity: the striving to achieve a profit which, in

---

194 Karl Marx [1857–1861], *Grundrisse: Foundations of the Critique of Political Economy* (Rough Draft), <https://www.marxists.org/archive/marx/works/download/pdf/grundrisse.pdf> [accessed August 2017], 402–403.

195 Ibid., 436.

turn, stimulates the dynamic reproduction of the expanding forces of productivity. The capitalist has a few pathways by which to increase his profits. He can:

1) lower the real wages;
2) increase the workday;
3) introduce new methods for the organization of production and save on resources; and
4) improve the applied tools, instruments, and technology.

The first two of these (most readily harnessed) meet with resistance by the workers (e.g., strikes and other forms of battle); hence the capitalist also reaches for the last two means for profit-gaining. First, he introduces the least costly new methods in organizing production, then he will bring in new technologies and technical solutions which will increase the productivity of his workforce. Since he is not allowed by wage laborers to lengthen their physical workday, he lengthens the so-called relative day of labor. Therefore, the class battle, which arises out of capitalistic property relations, becomes a factor for the rapid growth of the forces of productivity. The fundamental goal of the capitalist's actions – profits – can be attained above all by developing those very forces.

Finally and ultimately, there is the communist property anticipated and promoted by Karl Marx. Herein will be created the best conditions for the development of material forces of productivity and an all-embracing development of human capabilities. The aim of production becomes the versatile man characterized by a wealth of needs accompanied by a wealth of ways to meet them – and not wealth as an end unto itself.[196]

The dialectics of the relationship between the two categories, productive forces of society and property, is also expressed in a reverse dependency – meaning that the development of the productive forces causes the transformation of property relations. A certain phase in the development of the forces of productivity leads to the disintegration of most forms of property in common because these hinder individuals in their economic or political activity. Marx observes, "In the last analysis, their community, as well as the property based on it, resolves itself into a specific stage in the development of the productive forces of working subjects – to which correspond their specific relations amongst one another and towards nature. Until a certain point, reproduction. Then turns into dissolution."[197] And those forms of property, which can survive in a relict form in a milieu dominated

196 Marx, Engels [1847], Manifesto of the Communist Party.
197 Marx, *Grundrisse: Foundations of the Critique of Political Economy*, 419.

by private property, assume new historical forms appropriate to a higher level of development of the forces of productivity (e.g., the Russian *obshchina* or *artel*, the German mark, etc.).[198]

Another stage in the development of the forces of production leads to the transformation of diverse types of individual private property and feudal land property into the property of the capitalistic type. Marx especially accents the transformation of the means of labor into such means as befit collective application. Finally, there is the reshaping of capitalist property relations into the communist type of property. The socialization of property will be possible, according to Marx, only when such production forces are created which are decelerated and hindered by the capitalist property. The prerequisites for revolutionary action are generated en route to the centralization of the means of production, the socialization of the very process of production, and the concentration of producers (e.g., wage laborers).

In this property transformation process, Marx assigns great significance to changes taking place in social consciousness. It is worth accenting this activist theme in his theory of development, especially since commentators most often underscore the determinist theme. They frequently take into consideration this overused quotation:

> In the social production of their existence, men inevitably enter into definite relations, which are independent of their will, namely relations of production appropriate to a given stage in the development of their material forces of production. The totality of these relations of production constitutes the economic structure of society, the real foundation, on which arises a legal and political superstructure and to which correspond definite forms of social consciousness. The mode of production of material life conditions the general process of social, political and intellectual life. It is not the consciousness of men that determines their existence, but their social existence that determines their consciousness.[199]

Commentators forget about a dialectic dependency between the mode of production and superstructure – between economic relations and human activity which is stimulated by human consciousness and which can change economic conditions of life. The process by which property would be socialized is expected to go hand in hand with radical changes in social consciousness. In the eyes of Marx, the process was foreseen as taking the following course:

---

198 Karl Marx [1881], *Letter to Vera Zasulich: The "First" Draft*, <https://www.marxists.org/archive/marx/works/1881/zasulich/draft-1.htm> [accessed August 2017]; Karl Marx [1881], *Letter to Vera Zasulich: The "Second" Draft*, <https://www.marxists.org/archive/marx/works/1881/zasulich/draft-2.htm> [accessed August 2017].

199 Marx, *A Contribution to the Critique of Political Economy*, 4.

> In order to abolish the *idea* of private property, the *idea* of communism is quite sufficient. It takes *actual* communist action to abolish actual private property. History will lead to it; and this movement, *which in theory* we already know to be a self-transcending movement, will constitute in actual fact a very rough and protracted process. But we must regard it as a real advance to have at the outset gained a consciousness of the limited character as well as of the goal of this historical movement – and a consciousness which reaches out beyond it.[200]

The socialization of property will become possible, according to Marx, when people unfetter themselves from old habits, convictions, and aims, and when the idea of communist property becomes a component in the consciousness of acting individuals and collectives. Communist socialization, therefore, entails something more than changes in property relations. It is a process both objective and subjective: "The transcendence of private property is therefore the complete *emancipation* of all human *senses* and qualities, but it is this emancipation precisely because these senses and attributes have become, subjectively and objectively, *human*."[201] This is a process which pertains to the personality of the owners as well as their imaginings of the social world. It is, above all, a process which transpires by way of individual and collective action within the framework of an organized social movement or by way of other mass action. Hence, the principles described earlier (concerning the place of property in general social development) are not enacted without the participation of human beings. In and of themselves, these principles do not constitute any threat to any property – until some individual or collective activity enters the scene and changes the existing state of affairs.

Privatization and Socialization of Property in the Sphere of Production

The Dualism of Private and Collective Elements in Historical Forms of Common Property

The property which Marx describes as common, communal, collective or social has taken on many a historical form. Firstly, this could be a commonality in the process of production. Work often does entail teamwork with people performing the most important tasks together. The basic object of property here is the land which is not subject to parceling. Moreover, the most important tools are

200 Karl Marx [1844], *Economic & Philosophic Manuscripts of 1844*, <https://www.marxists.org/archive/marx/works/download/pdf/Economic-Philosophic-Manuscripts-1844.pdf> [accessed August 2017], 53.

201 Ibid., 46.

not permanently and exclusively ascribed to specific users. Secondly, in younger forms, the community is the only presupposition for the appropriation of land. As a union of people, the community takes possession of a demarcated territory; with the help of all of its members, it defends that land from other communities; and next, it divides and distributes the land amongst individual producers who are self-employed and cultivate it on their own:

> Finally, although the arable land remained communal property, it was periodically divided among the members of the agricultural commune, so that each farmer tilled on his own behalf the various fields allocated to him and individually appropriated their fruits. In the more archaic communities, by contrast, production was a common activity, and only the final produce was distributed among individual members.[202]

In this variant of common property, work no longer has a direct, social nature. This category applies to most of the developmental variations in the Asian type of community, the early ancient type, and certain Slavic communities (including such forms as the Russian *obshchina* contemporary to Marx). Max strongly stresses the dualism of these younger forms which manifest both commonality and privacy in property relations between members of the community. Sometimes it allows people to develop their personality and skills but, at the same time, it is dangerous for the integrity of the community. He writes: "It is just as evident, however, that the very same dualism may eventually become a source of disintegration."[203]

Thirdly, in yet other forms, common property exists as a complementary form of individual property. Each producer is an individual owner of the land, irrespective of the community. Furthermore, a part of the territory belonging to the community is not divided into parcels but is used in common. This land is defended by the community, and each of its inhabitants uses the whole of the land they share. Even so, work performed within the scope of the common conditions of labor is already of an individual nature – as in the case of the German type of communities: "The new commune – in which cultivable land is *privately owned* by the producers, while the forests, pastures, waste ground, etc., still remain *communal property* was introduced by the Germans to all the countries they conquered."[204] Here, the individual households are the presupposition for the existence of a community which manifests itself as an association of independent families and groups.

202 Marx, *Letter to Vera Zasulich: The "First" Draft.*

203 Ibid.

204 Ibid.

In the case above, individual property and common property begin to separate and become distinct from one another, although people themselves are not divided into those who will function solely in one or the other form of property. However, fourthly, in societies of the classical formation at its peak, this was what happened. Persons who are free private owners of small parcels of land cannot be possessors of state or commune land. At this point, the land belongs to a union which functions as an independent entity and is represented by the functionaries and bureaucrats of state institutions. The latter are the possessors (tenants) of the common land.[205]

The differences among the forms of common property presented above are significant, and hence a question arises: What premises underlying Marx's delineations of all these forms can be identified as integral to common property? The kind of object of ownership is not such a criterion since there are such types of common property in which the conditions of labor are concentrated, and others in which they have been divided. The kind of work is also not this type of criterion since the socialization of property does not go hand in hand with collective labor. There are such types in which work is of an individual nature and, despite that, are qualified by Karl Marx as forms of common property. There are other types of property wherein the conditions of labor are concentrated and the work itself bears a directly social nature, and yet these should be counted as private property (e.g., slavery type property). Therefore, neither a concentration of the conditions of labor nor any teamwork suffices as a criterion for classifying the abovementioned forms of property as common property. The criteria are situated elsewhere. They refer to the problem of access to the conditions of labor.

Surfacing in many places in Marx's works is an assertion that common property assumes belonging to a community. Each member can thank a community for his affinity with the conditions of labor. Such an affinity is anchored in the fact that each member of the community finds employment on the territory inhabited by his community. Either the person must be self-employed or he is employed by the community of which he is a member; no one can be barred access to the conditions of labor and barred from the possibilities to apply his own labor power. The commonality of this ownership lies in the fact that each member of the community actively realizes the right to work which is owed to him (looking at this from a legal perspective) simply because he is a member of the community. It is less important if he finds employment on the plot of communal land allotted him or somewhere else on the whole of the territory.

205 Marx, *Grundrisse: Foundations of the Critique of Political Economy*, 397–438.

The commonality here means access to the land which is in the hands of the community. Still, the historical formation within which everyone participates in this relationship with employment can differ – from direct access to the whole of the conditions of labor to access solely to some portion thereof.

The commonality in the conditions of labor displays many shades. In the tribal community, its range is broad because all members have equal and unlimited access to the conditions of labor. As members of a community they employ themselves, employ other people, or are employed by the community. Only the onset of complications in kinship relations leads to specific individuals gaining differentiated opportunities to apply their talents and skills on the land constituting community territory.

In certain of the developmental variants found among Asiatic formation societies, there is even a manner of compulsion to work in accordance with the plan imposed by the institutionalized patriarchal authorities or other communal functionaries. For some this means significant privilege, for others, this entails a handicap when it comes to accessing communal conditions of labor. At any rate, no member finds himself without employment within the realm of his community's property. On the one hand, he is subjugated; on the other hand, he is a co-possessor of the communal property.

In still other cases, such as the German community, members have universal access only to a part of the territory inhabited by their community; other parts are the exclusive domain of specific families. Moreover, each family has different prospects for utilization of communal land, depending upon the labor power, the tools and instruments, and the livestock resources at the disposal of a given farmstead. And it is precisely access to communal lands – however varied this may be – which suffices (for Marx) to categorize this form as the common property of individual owners.

An extreme situation is that of communal property in classical antiquity wherein members of the community do not have access to state lands. This is the land belonging to a union – not to its citizens – and hence is utilized solely by functionaries of the state. Nonetheless, the very fact that someone possesses citizenship does authorize him to gain the title of ownership to an individual parcel of land. It is worth emphasizing here that persons without citizenship are cut off from this relationship – the collectivity is of strictly delineated objective and subjective limits.

In some forms of private property, circumstances can arise in which the producer is not able to find employment. Hampering the initiation of an employer-laborer relationship can be the owner of the conditions of labor; the commune itself is incapable of hampering this process (unless it previously excludes the producer from its membership). The commune can only create more or less beneficial conditions of employment for particular members. Most importantly, no one within the commune will employ a producer as a private person independent of the commune. One can be an employer only as a representative of the commune – as its functionary or personification.

What does this mean from the viewpoint of the conceptual model of property which Karl Marx uses? No one is an owner of labor power born by another member of the commune. No man possesses the power of an owner of someone else's labor power with respect to his compatriots.

In such cases as private property in the slavery, feudal (the serfdom variant) or capitalistic type there is a separation and distinction between the position of the owner of the conditions of labor and the means of subsistence, and that of the laborer who possesses nothing more than his work capability. Hence, the laborer finds employment inasmuch as his labor power becomes the property of an owner of the conditions of labor – and thus the owner holds power (i.e., as an owner of someone else's labor power) over the producer.[206] Appearing here is the phenomenon of an identicality between the owner and the producer. For this reason, this sort of power relationship does not take root among members of the community. If that were to happen, it would signify the emergence of privatization processes within the realm of common property.

In the primitive, tribal community, power is of a non-economic nature. It does not spring from the property relations but rather from personal traits and kinship relations. In the Asiatic type community, the situation becomes more complicated. On the one hand, the power relations arise out of supra-economic factors (e.g., caste privilege, kinship relations, or the delegation of some state rights to functionaries living within the community, etc.). On the other hand, this relationship succumbs to transformation into a permanent, institutionalized possibility of hiring other people. In the case of community functionaries, the boundary between the sphere of privacy and the commonality of interests is not engraved and is difficult to identify. The community authorities – as the collective owner of the capabilities of its members – becomes a private functionary and powerholder. The political function goes hand in hand with a more advantageous position in the structure of ownership relations. The following statement by Engels illustrates this:

206 Karl Marx [1865], *Value, Price and Profit*, <https://www.marxists.org/archive/marx/works/download/pdf/value-price-profit.pdf> [accessed August 2017], 17–18.

> But to whom did this new wealth belong? Originally to the gens, without a doubt. Private property in herds must have already started at an early period, however. It is difficult to say whether the author of the so-called first book of Moses regarded the patriarch Abraham as the owner of his herds in his own right as head of a family community or by right of his position as actual hereditary head of a gens. What is certain is that we must not think of him as a property owner in the modern sense of the word. And it is also certain that at the threshold of authentic history we already find the herds everywhere separately owned by heads of families, as are the artistic products of barbarism – metal implements, luxury articles and, finally, the human cattle – the slaves.[207]

Communal property of the Asian type is therefore dualistic, encompassing elements of the common and the private. This is the case within the commune; however, within state property of the Asian type, the phenomenon of privatization goes still further. This is a form of property within which certain individuals become the private owners of the labor power of others. It is likewise with state property of the ancient type wherein state functionaries also possess power as an owner of someone else's labor power. This sort of power does not, however, link or bind the members of the ancient community's citizenry, nor the members of the Germanic commune.

The Lower Phase of Communist Socialization of Property as Confirmation of Private Property

In *Economic & Philosophic Manuscripts of 1844*, in *German Ideology*, in *Manifesto*, and in *Critique of the Gotha Programme* – in all these works, Karl Marx speaks of the two stages of communist socialization of property relations (and also about a multi-stage theoretical reflection regarding communist socialization). The first stage entails the dissolution of capitalist private property and, for this reason, the new form of property relations inherits many traits of its predecessor. It is only during the second stage that the process of full socialization is initiated. Questionable is whether one can speak of a specific moment of development, since communism (as Marx and Engels write) is not a state which can be introduced: it is rather a movement nullifying private property, and a process of socialization: "Communism is for us not a *state of affairs* which is to be established, an *ideal* to which reality [will] have to adjust itself. We call communism the *real* movement which abolishes the present state of things."[208]

---

207 Friedrich Engels [1884], *Origin of the Family, Private Property, and the State*, <https://www.marxists.org/archive/marx/works/download/pdf/origin_family.pdf> [accessed August 2017], 29.

208 Karl Marx, Friedrich Engels [1845–1846], *The German Ideology*, <https://www.marxists.org/archive/marx/works/download/Marx_The_German_Ideology.pdf> [accessed August 2017], 14.

The process of privatization entailed the tearing asunder of the original unity between producers and their conditions of labor. This process undergoes (very generally speaking) a few phases of which the two most important are: (a) the transformation of various forms of common property into individual private property; and, subsequently, (b) the expropriation of individual owners. It was especially the period of the capitalist economy which contributed to the mass expropriation of direct producers and concentration of the conditions of labor and the means of subsistence in the hands of a few people.

Accompanying capitalist privatization of property was the socialization of the process of labor. On the scale of capitalist enterprises, this work took on the nature of teamwork. However, on a broader scale, this socialization of work was expressed in its distribution and the exchange of goods and currency. Thus, were created the presuppositions for the dispossession of capitalists and a restoration of social property based on the already concentrated conditions of labor.

Communist socialization of property is a process which reinstates the original unity between the producers and the conditions of labor – but in a new historical form. Crucial in the first stage is the dispossession of the capitalists. As Marx puts it, this is not communism which starts from itself, but rather from private property. In denying the latter, the former must refer to it. Property thus takes on the traits of a dualistic ownership which connects both private and social elements. Crucial here is a discussion of how the socialization of this form is expressed and how privacy is expressed.

The first stage of socialization restores a social nature to ownership in the sense that each person, as a member of the communist community, finds employment within the conditions of labor belonging to the community; the power of capital over the workers is erased. Nonetheless, this is, first, labor performed under coercion by the communist community (an obligation to work) whereas the measure of this labor which each person executes on behalf of the community is of a nature matching private property. Everyone takes care not to expend more energy than other people and treats his own capabilities as his very own property (in danger of being taken). Second, the power of capital is replaced by a dictatorship of the proletariat – more precisely, the power held by functionaries of the community.[209]

209 Karl Marx [1875], *Critique of the Gotha Programme*, <https://www.marxists.org/archive/marx/works/download/Marx_Critque_of_the_Gotha_Programme.pdf> [accessed August 2017].

In this superficial equality in access to work (which is the very subject of Marx's deliberations), the key is the eradication of relationships befitting capitalist property: namely, to make null and void such situations in which someone is incapable of finding employment or somebody employs others, yet does not work himself. Indeed, these traits of capitalist property are lifted, but the communist society of this type is merely a community with regards to the conditions of labor. Each member acts like a private owner who aims to curb the possibilities of the labors of others, and who aims to rise above them (or at least bring them down to his level). This is the logic of private owners:

> This type of communism – since it negates the *personality* of man in every sphere – is but the logical expression of private property, which is this negation. General *envy* constituting itself as a power is the disguise in which *greed* re-establishes itself and satisfies itself, only in *another* way. The thought of every piece of private property as such is *at least* turned against *wealthier* private property in the form of envy and the urge to reduce things to a common level, so that this envy and urge even constitute the essence of competition. [….] The community is only a community of *labor*, and of equality of *wages* paid out by communal capital – by the *community* as the universal capitalist. Both sides of the relationship are raised to an *imagined* universality – *labor* as the category in which every person is placed, and *capital* as the acknowledged universality and power of the community.[210]

This form of property is one proper to a specific kind of union of citizens, i.e., a state, in which communists assume political power: "The immediate aim of the Communists is the same as that of all other proletarian parties: formation of the proletariat into a class, overthrow of the bourgeois supremacy, conquest of political power by the proletariat."[211] The state is an organism somewhat independent and sovereign with regards to its members. Communism is still (in the words of Marx) political: state power is realized in the form of the dictatorship of the proletariat.[212] This is to avoid the return of privatization processes. Producers are no longer subjected to the power of the capitalist but the power of the functionaries of the state. Those representatives of the working class who represent the state to a greater degree than others also hold more beneficial positions in the ownership system: this is because they realize the power of the state – the employers and the organizers of production who decide on the ways by which the capabilities, talents, and skills of their members will be utilized.

---

210 Marx, *Economic & Philosophic Manuscripts of 1844*, 42–43.

211 Marx, Engels [1847], Manifesto of the Communist Party, 22.

212 Karl Marx [1870–1871], *The Civil War in France*, <https://www.marxists.org/archive/marx/works/download/pdf/civil_war_france.pdf> [accessed August 2017].

Therefore, the above-discussed type of socialization still constitutes a socialization within a form of alienation, within the context of widespread private property. Progressively returned to one and all is the status of the owner of the conditions of labor; additionally, one and all are employed which is an indicator of this socialization. Nonetheless, everybody is connected by mutual relations typical of private ownership: competition in a new historical form, and power relations dominated by representatives of a community organized as a state. As Marx explains,

> The first positive annulment of private property – *crude* communism – is thus merely one *form* in which the vileness of private property, which wants to set itself up as the *positive community system, comes to the surface.* / (2) Communism (a) still political in nature – democratic or despotic; (ß) with the abolition of the state, yet still incomplete, and being still affected by private property, i.e., by the estrangement of man. In both forms communism already is aware of being reintegration or return of man to himself, the transcendence of human self-estrangement; but since it has not yet grasped the positive essence of private property, and just as little the *human* nature of need, it remains captive to it and infected by it. It has, indeed, grasped its concept, but not its essence.[213]

Concentration of the Conditions of Labor versus Association of Producers

From the moment in which the vision of the communist society is formulated, there have been debates about whether the socialization of property requires concentration of the conditions of labor, or not. Marx's position on this is not univocal; he expresses theses which could serve to illustrate both prospects. For example, in *Capital*, he asserts that communism restores individual property:

> The capitalist mode of appropriation, the result of the capitalist mode of production, produces capitalist private property. This is the first negation of individual private property, as founded on the labour of the proprietor. But capitalist production begets, with the inexorability of a law of Nature, its own negation. It is the negation of negation. This does not re-establish private property for the producer, but gives him individual property based on the acquisition of the capitalist era: *i.e.*, on co-operation and the possession in common of the land and of the means of production.[214]

Engels recollects the controversies concerning the just-cited opinion, stating that this is a conundrum which Marx left for his followers to solve. Still, Engels does provide his own interpretation:

---

213 Marx, *Economic & Philosophic Manuscripts of 1844*, 43.

214 Karl Marx [1867], *Capital: A Critique of Political Economy*, Volume I, <https://www.marxists.org/archive/marx/works/download/pdf/Capital-Volume-I.pdf> [accessed August 2017], 542.

> The state of things brought about by the expropriation of the expropriators is therefore characterised as the re-establishment of individual property, but *on the basis* of the social ownership of the land and of the means of production produced by labour itself. To anyone who understands plain talk this means that social ownership extends to the land and the other means of production, and individual ownership to the products, that is, the articles of consumption.[215]

On many an occasion Marx speaks positively about individual private ownership, pointing to the fact that, in this form, there is no direct exploitation of the labor power of others. This is a form of ownership of working owners who create conditions for the development of the unrestricted personality of the producer. During performing his work, the producer is not subject to the power of anyone else. Furthermore, within the realm of this form of ownership, processes of alienation do not necessarily have to take place. The positive characteristics of individual private ownership now surface, especially positive when compared to such forms of private ownership which are anchored in the labor of producers who are not owners of the conditions of labor.

Nonetheless, Marx does also identify such traits of individual ownership which could encumber the process of socialization. In certain situations, this form could be subject to exploitation which leads to the physical and intellectual degradation of the producers and, subsequently, to their dispossession. Therefore, Marx determines that this model of socialization is unrealistic since universalization of individual ownership would have to lead to the re-expropriation of the producers. Further, Marx notes that the communist movement cannot also emerge from the middle class (the class of individual owners) since conditions leading to association and organization against private ownership would be inauspicious for this group. Representatives of this class produce in mutual isolation and live dispersed from one another.

However, in capitalism, the work of hired laborers already entails teamwork as the laborers toil under circumstances of concentrated conditions of labor. Interpersonal contact amongst many workers facilitates their organization and armed protest; the concentration of the conditions of labor shape conditions which facilitate the revoking of capitalistic private property. From this point of view, the concentration (and not division) of the conditions of labor constitutes a means leading to the socialization of property.

---

215 Friedrich Engels [1876–1878], *Anti-Dühring: Herr Eugen Dühring's Revolution in Science*, <https://www.marxists.org/archive/marx/works/download/pdf/anti_duhring.pdf> [accessed August 2017], 81.

Marx arrives at the conclusions noted above upon investigation of the Western version of capitalism. Yet when he analyzes ownership relations typical for rural Russian communes, he deduces that communist socialization is possible without obliterating the separate communes. It would suffice to (by way of revolutionary protest) get rid of the despotic institutions rising above these communes, and to introduce agencies of local government whose representatives (organized nationwide) would come to an agreement on economic cooperation. For example, "All that is necessary is to replace the *volost,* a government institution, with a peasant assembly chosen by the communes themselves – an economic and administrative body serving their own interests."[216] In this way, the activity of specific communes would comprise fragments of a general social plan whereas work performed within all the communities is re-endowed with a direct social nature, without a need for the concentration of the conditions of labor.

In this variant of socialization, it is not the concentration of the conditions of labor, but the association of producers which matters. Interpersonal bonds are what become socialized. This is one of the possible implications of controlling the conditions of labor together. Labor takes on a direct social nature, not because the conditions of labor are concentrated, but because the presuppositions of its execution are the gathering of producers. Classical, ancient communities are a historical case in point since producers herein achieve access to the conditions of labor via their belonging to a specific association. In ancient communities, associations encompassed a rather small number of persons; in modernity, the associations encompass the whole of society.

Deliberating upon the subject of an optimal path to the revolutionary movement in Russia, he muses in *Drafts of Letter to Vera Zasulich* that the very probable path of changes in Russia is this expropriation of agriculture communes and then expropriation of capitalists. Yet in that brief letter, he writes: "The 'historical inevitability' of this course is therefore *expressly* restricted to *the countries of Western Europe*."[217] Together with Engels, Marx expresses a similar line of thinking in the preface to the second Russian edition of *Manifesto of the Communist Party*:

> The Communist Manifesto had, as its object, the proclamation of the inevitable impending dissolution of modern bourgeois property. But in Russia we find, face-to-face with the rapidly flowering capitalist swindle and bourgeois property, just beginning to develop, more than half the land owned in common by the peasants. Now the question is: can the Russian obshchina, though greatly undermined, yet a form of primeval

216 Marx, *Letter to Vera Zasulich: The "First" Draft.*

217 Karl Marx [1881], *The Reply to Zasulich*, 8 March 1881, <https://www.marxists.org/archive/marx/works/1881/zasulich/reply.htm> [accessed August 2017].

common ownership of land, pass directly to the higher form of Communist common ownership? Or, on the contrary, must it first pass through the same process of dissolution such as constitutes the historical evolution of the West? / The only answer to that possible today is this: If the Russian Revolution becomes the signal for a proletarian revolution in the West, so that both complement each other, the present Russian common ownership of land may serve as the starting point for a communist development.[218]

The Higher Phase of Communist Socialization of Property

The higher phase of communist socialization commences as a negation of the first stage of "crude communism" – as Marx calls it. He characterizes the second stage of socialization as "communism itself because of its character as a negation of the negation, as the appropriation of the human essence through the intermediary of the negation of private property – as being not yet the true, self-originating position but rather a position originating from private property."[219] This comes with the rescinding of all manner of restrictions in access to conditions of work shared in common as well as restrictions in the possibility of utilizing a person's skills and talents. Above all, forced labor will cease to exist – including forced execution of certain tasks – and no one will be limited by the rigors of the distribution of labor. Work itself will not crush the producer but will become, instead, a means of comprehensive development of his talents and his personality. The human being will begin to treat work as a primary need as well as a means of his own personal development – not as an absolute necessity or a means by which to meet his own needs. He will not worry about whether he did more work than others or if others do not think he is living off their labor. He will feel that he is working for himself and for his community while his community works for him. This comprises a full dis-alienation of the human being in the process of labor.

As part of this type of ownership, nobody (neither as a private individual nor as a representative of a community) bears power over other members of the community (neither as owner of someone else's labor power nor as an employer of someone who bears labor power but whose access to the means of production can be hampered). This idea is formulated in different variants by Marx and Engels. In their *Manifesto*, for instance, they write: "Communism deprives no

---

218 Marx Karl, Engels Friedrich [1882], *Preface to The 1882 Russian Edition*, <https://www.marxists.org/archive/marx/works/download/pdf/Manifesto.pdf> [accessed August 2017], 5.

219 Marx, *Economic & Philosophic Manuscripts of 1844*, 53.

man of the power to appropriate the products of society; all that it does is to deprive him of the power to subjugate the labour of others by means of such appropriations."[220] Marx expresses this even more emphatically this in a speech he made on the law of inheritance:

> Our efforts must be directed to the end that no instruments of production should be private property. The private property in these things was a fiction, since the proprietors could not use them themselves; they only gave them dominion over them, by which they compelled other people to work for them. In a semi-barbarous state, this might have been necessary, but it was no longer so. All the means of labor must be socialized, so that every man had a right and the means to exercise his labor power. If we had such a state of things, the right of inheritance would be of no use.[221]

Can it be therefore stated that, during their work, no power relationship is established between the producers? Indeed it does, but its roots extend completely elsewhere. In *Capital*, Karl Marx presents a general rule which is quite applicable in this case: all collective work requires leadership. In fact, the nature of work in the communist society is the same: certain individual tasks must be agreed upon so that a supervisory power does exist. However, Friedrich Engels asserts in *Anti-Dühring* that management of people becomes replaced by the management of things.[222]

Neither Marx nor Engels perceives a threat to the communist community stemming from the fact that select members of the community direct teams of subordinates or control community resources. Neither of them caught sight of this even though in Eastern Europe the transformation of the German and the Slavic types of communities into feudal societies stemmed therefrom. In their opinion, the process would no longer lead to the alienation of labor since management personnel will not constitute a fixed group because the individual will have freed himself from limitations rooted in the distribution of labor; subjugation to the decisions of managers will depend solely upon the producers themselves. Eventually, such transformations of social consciousness will take place that enticements to stabilize principles of domination and inequality will vanish.

220 Marx, Engels [1847], *Manifesto of the Communist Party*, 24.

221 Karl Marx [1869], *The Right of Inheritance: Report of the General Council.* Written by Marx on August 2–3, 1869, Endorsed by General Council of The International Workingmen's Association on August 3, 1869. <https://www.marxists.org/archive/marx/iwma/documents/1869/inheritance-report.htm> [accessed August 2017].

222 Engels, *Anti-Dühring: Herr Eugen Dühring's Revolution in Science.*

Privatization and Socialization of Property in the Sphere of Product Distribution

The Dualism of Private and Collective Elements in Historical Forms of Common Property

In the tribal community, the individual directly appropriates the product of his individual labor through its direct consumption – or he gains goods mediated by his commune. As time goes by, differences in specific member access to the resources stored by the commune become fixed and permanent. Those persons who guard the supplies held in common appropriate a greater portion of that product than the rest of the group. Initially, this does not lead to the shaping of stabilized dependencies upon things since no one appropriates so great an amount of the product gained by working together that some other member of the community is excluded from participating in consumption. The place of specific persons in the hierarchy of power depends upon the kinship structure, personal characteristics, or tradition – and not on individually possessed commodities.

In the Asian type community, fixed relationships of domination appear which are of an objective, material nature and at the roots of which is the private appropriation of the product of one's own or someone else's labor. Although it is the non-economic factors (e.g., position in the kinship structure, personality traits, tradition, state intervention through its functionaries, etc.) which continue to generate power within the commune, that power is economically affirmed in the way that product created by communal members is arrogated. In earlier forms of common property, the unequal distribution of product did not contribute to the emergence of material interdependencies. Here, a quantitative sort of phenomenon is subjected to a qualitative transformation as functionaries amass surplus at the expense of the producers. Nonetheless, this power remains secondary with respect to non-economic power. To control the product of the labor of others, one must be a group functionary (e.g., patriarch, clerk, etc.). Subsequently, the direct producers are assured the minimum means of consumption by the very fact of membership in the community.

Under the ancient type of property, everyone appropriates product, irrespective of the community of which he is a member (i.e., citizen). He is a private owner of a distinct parcel and appropriates the fruits of his labors. There appear, nonetheless, vast disproportions in the possibilities for the appropriation of the product by separate families and households because this depends upon the quality of the land, the workforce resources, the time which the owner can devote to land cultivation, and other factors. The producer functioning within this form of property can easily fall into a material dependency upon other people if he does not obtain a fitting amount of product. If he produces things for sale, then he can be subject to exploitation in an indirect form as a consequence of nonequivalent exchange. He himself does participate in an indirect exploitation of those working on state land (*ager publicus*): although a significant portion of the product generated from that land is appropriated by state functionaries, the remainder goes towards maintenance of the state institutions of whose services he, as a citizen, takes advantage.

In the German type of community, everyone has the chance to appropriate product produced on communal lands under the condition that he is already an individual landowner, meaning that he already possesses the means to utilize the community lands (e.g., tools, livestock, etc.). Quite the opposite takes place in the Rumanian variant wherein owners transfer a part of their product for community purposes. Marx points to the transformation of this type of communal sharing of product into private appropriation of the product by representatives of the community who become the exploiting party. According to Marx, out of this latter group would emerge the feudal lords (i.e., the eastern variant of the rise of feudalism):

> This is what took place in the Roumanian provinces. Their original mode of production was based on community of the soil, but not in the Slavonic or Indian form. Part of the land was cultivated in severalty as freehold by the members of the community, another part – *ager publicus* – was cultivated by them in common. The products of this common labour served partly as a reserve fund against bad harvests and other accidents, partly as a public store for providing the costs of war, religion, and other common expenses. In course of time military and clerical dignitaries usurped, along with the common land, the labour spent upon it. The labour of the free peasants on their common land was transformed into corvée for the thieves of the common land. This corvée soon developed into a servile relationship existing in point of fact, not in point of law, until Russia, the liberator of the world, made it legal under presence of abolishing serfdom.[223]

Upon analyzing the historical forms of common ownership, Karl Marx claims that inequalities in product distribution are universal, but these infringe upon the shared nature of ownership only when they lead to exploitation and are expressed in material intercourse among members of a community. It is at this point that those who exploit and, therefore, rule over others come to function as private owners. Engels concurs:

223 Marx, *Capital: A Critique of Political Economy*, Volume I, 165.

> In the first place the wealth of the ancient tribal and village communities was in no sense a domination over men. And secondly, even in societies moving in class antagonisms, wealth, in so far as it includes domination over men, is mainly and almost exclusively a domination over men exercised *by virtue of*, and *through the agency of*, the domination over things.[224]

Common property differs from extreme forms of private property in the absence of exploitation and material rule by the owners of product over its producers. But what differentiates common from individual private property? The key lies in the fact that, in common ownership, nobody as a private person (i.e., independent of the community) can accrue reserve supplies. The more a process of supply accumulation (by specific units, regardless of the community) intensifies in a specific form of reserves, the more elements of privatization that form entails. Moreover,

> It is just as evident, however, that the very same dualism may eventually become a source of disintegration. Apart from the influence of a hostile environment, the mere accumulation over time of movable property, beginning with wealth in livestock and even extending to wealth in serfs, combines with the ever more prominent role played by movables in agriculture itself and with a host of other circumstances, inseparable from such accumulation, which would take me too far from the central theme. All these factors, then, serve to dissolve economic and social equality, generating within the commune itself a conflict of interests which leads, first, to the conversion of arable land into private property, and ultimately to the private appropriation of forests, pastures, waste ground, etc., already no more than communal appendages of private property.[225]

This is the essence of the private growth of wealth – meaning here such reserves at the disposal of families or individuals which – even with maximum consumption – exceed those resources necessary for the survival of a production cycle. This wealth does not constitute a surplus plain and simple, but rather the potential economic power of certain private individuals over those who do not personally possess such material goods.

Communist Socialization of Property as the Process of Dis-Alienation

In his *Capital*, Karl Marx describes a situation illustrating a thesis crucial to his vision of communism:

> Let us now picture to ourselves, by way of change, a community of free individuals, carrying on their work with the means of production in common, in which the labour power of all the different individuals is consciously applied as the combined labour

224 Engels, *Anti-Dühring: Herr Eugen Dühring's Revolution in Science*, 113–114.
225 Marx, *Letter to Vera Zasulich: The "First" Draft.*

power of the community. (...). The total product of our community is a social product. One portion serves as fresh means of production and remains social. But another portion is consumed by the members as means of subsistence. A distribution of this portion amongst them is consequently necessary. The mode of this distribution will vary with the productive organisation of the community, and the degree of historical development attained by the producers.[226]

Thus, product distribution in the communist society is conducted in such a way as to dedicate a portion to the reproduction of the conditions of joint labor. Moreover, no one can appropriate any of this portion as a private individual, and only the remainder is shared by the members of the society.

Yet this gives rise to a question: how should this latter part of the product be distributed to endow property relations with a socialist nature? The answer has a deep theoretical sense since, according to Marx, the means of production belong to whoever appropriates the product produced thereby.

The socialization of this component in property relations (entered by people in the sphere of production) does not necessarily accompany the socialization of property relations which arise in the sphere of distribution. Therefore, Marx often points to a need for transformation of the principles for participation in product distribution. He writes of this outright, offering his own proposal for the regulation of relations taking shape in the sphere of distribution. Less overtly, he also writes of this when he underscores the convergence of the processes of socialization and dis-alienation.

Under the circumstances of extreme forms of private property, exploitation is found as well as power relations whose roots lie in the appropriation of surplus product. This is how private property makes itself known in the sphere of distribution. Both these relations taken together – relations of exploitation and the associated relations of power – are captured perfectly by Marx by way of the category of human alienation in the process of labor. In *Economic & Philosophic Manuscripts of 1844*, Marx reasons that,

If the product of labor does not belong to the worker, if it confronts him as an alien power, then this can only be because it belongs to some *other man than the worker*. If the worker's activity is a torment to him, to another it must give *satisfaction* and pleasure. Not the gods, not nature, but only man himself can be this alien power over man.[227]

226 Marx, *Capital: A Critique of Political Economy*, Volume I, 51.
227 Marx, *Economic & Philosophic Manuscripts of 1844*, 53.

Furthermore,

> Through *estranged, alienated labor*, then, the worker produces the relationship to this labor of a man alien to labor and standing outside it. The relationship of the worker to labor creates the relationship to it of the capitalist (or whatever one chooses to call the master of labor). *Private property* is thus the product, the result, the necessary consequence, of *alienated labor*, of the external relation of the worker to nature and to himself. *Private property* thus results by analysis from the concept of *alienated labor*, i.e., of *alienated man*, of estranged labor, of estranged life, of *estranged* man.[228]

Therefore, it is not the product which confines the producer but his fellow man who appropriated the product of the producer. This is the primary issue in the marking out of alienation, but this aspect of Marx's theory of alienation requires a more unequivocal exposition. The alienation of man in the process of labor and in the product is, in other words, a relationship of exploitation and the power that comes with that – the power of someone who appropriates the product of someone else's labors, power over the producer. The socialization of property relations depends, therefore, upon the elimination of relationships of exploitation and power between the exploited and the exploiters. More precisely, socialization is a movement revoking alienation.

Marx stresses that people confirm their positions as the economic owners of the labor conditions by appropriation of products. "*The direct relationship of labor to its products is the relationship of the worker to the objects of his production*. The relationship of the man of means to the objects of production and to production itself is only a *consequence* of this first relationship – and confirms it."[229] Nevertheless, he does not propose an exact and explicit recipe for the socialization of property by a relevant distribution of the product. In *Capital*, Marx writes that "the share of each individual producer in the means of subsistence is determined by his labour time,"[230] whereas in *Economic & Philosophic Manuscripts of 1844* he speaks of distribution in line with the principle of each according to "his work."[231] Further, in *Critique of the Gotha Programme* he emphasizes that this principle is applicable only to that portion of the product which remains after setting aside a portion dedicated to the renewal of the conditions of labor as well as to the upkeep of people who are of a non-productive age or who perform non-productive work.

228 Ibid.

229 Ibid., 30.

230 Marx, *Capital: A Critique of Political Economy*, Volume I, 51.

231 Marx, *Economic & Philosophic Manuscripts of 1844*.

Employment of the first principle restores to the producers the position of an owner of the conditions of labor, but it does not yet eliminate exploitation since the productivity of various individual tasks varies. Consequently, this means that those who produced more than others in the same amount of time are dispossessed of some of their product. Employment of the second principle does eliminate exploitation but contributes to another kind of inequality. This is because each human being enjoys different skills and capabilities; he thus produces a different mass of goods and participates differently in the appropriated product. Essentially this entails the principle of "each according to his ability." Communism, however, does not (in Marx's opinion) realize a principle of equality in the distribution of goods. After all, such a principle would also be one of inequality. Ultimately, it would posit inequality in other areas of life such as in the labor, put in by specific individuals, or in the chances to meet one's own needs. Everyone has different needs and so the same means would satisfy each person differently and would create different chances for personal development.

In effect, Marx quite often criticizes the just-mentioned principles of product distribution as ones supporting alienation and unceasingly referring back to private property. In a later, higher phase of the communist society, a new principle would be introduced:

> In a higher phase of communist society, after the enslaving subordination of the individual to the division of labor, and therewith also the antithesis between mental and physical labor, has vanished; after labor has become not only a means of life but life's prime want; after the productive forces have also increased with the all-around development of the individual, and all the springs of co-operative wealth flow more abundantly -- only then then can the narrow horizon of bourgeois right be crossed in its entirety and society inscribe on its banners: From each according to his ability, to each according to his needs![232]

Yet the introduction of this will be possible only when labor power develops to such a degree that no one will be cut off from participating in the distribution of goods he simply desires because others are also aspiring to the same.

Even if a person were to appropriate the fruits of someone else's labors, he cannot dispossess the producer of the things he needs since the society will offer an abundance of means by which to gratify human needs. Nobody will be building such power over others which could facilitate the usurpation of the product of others because such power can only exist in a situation where there is a dearth of goods, wherein the individual must guarantee himself the possibility of appropriating goods in the future. In the communist society, nobody will be

232 Marx, *Critique of the Gotha Programme*, 11.

accumulating reserves in amounts exceeding his ad hoc needs; uncertainty about the future will vanish.

Here, Marx affirms that this does not refer to some program for a moral metamorphosis. Indubitably there would also be a transformation of the personality of owners and, therefore, of their moral attitudes and worldviews – but underlying these changes would be favorable economic conditions. In this context, it is easier to comprehend the statement by Marx and Engels that communism is grounded neither in principles of altruism nor egoism:

> Within Communist society, the only society in which the genuine and free development of individuals ceases to be a mere phrase, this development is determined precisely by the connection of individuals, a connection which consists partly in the economic prerequisites and partly in the necessary solidarity of the free development of all, and finally, in the universal character of the activity of individuals on the basis of the existing productive forces. We are, therefore, here concerned with individuals at a definite historical stage of development and by no means merely with individuals chosen at random, even disregarding the indispensable Communist revolution, which itself is a general condition for their free development. The individuals' consciousness of their mutual relations will, of course, likewise be completely changed, and, therefore, will no more be the 'principal of love' or *devoument* than it will be egoism.[233]

Privatization and Socialization of Property and the Issue of Exchange

The Sociological Aspect of Exchange

The term common property in Marx encompasses both such forms in which there is absolutely no exchange as well as some forms in which commodity or commodity-currency relations do exist. In communities of the oldest type, where work is of a directly social nature, there is no product exchange. Product there is common property to be directly consumed or, at most, distributed for later consumption.

When exchange does appear, it is first conducted between communities as a means by which they reduce surplus movable property and acquire things which are necessary. Over the course of time, the exchange becomes fixed within communities as well since certain households also begin to accrue reserve supplies. And it is precisely this kind of movable wealth that is exchangeable if other households perceive a need for it and, concurrently, have something else to offer in exchange.

A surplus, exclusive reserve in the hands of individuals or families becomes the initial basis for the privatization of ownership relations within various types of

233 Marx, Engels, *The German Ideology*, 465.

communities. In communities of the Asian type, it is, above all, movable property which is exchanged. However, in the ancient society, tools and land become an additional object of exchange. Gradually, the range of the use value increases to such a degree that a means of exchange which evolves is the human himself – meaning his labor power.

Marx treats the spreading of private property and commodity exchange (later including commodity-currency exchange) as two aspects of the same process of privatization. On the one hand, the exchange takes place thanks to the existence of private property. On the other hand, private property becomes more strongly embedded thanks to exchange.

For private owners, their goods have an exchange value, but not a use value which is attached to goods held by other private owners. For this reason, the two meet on the market and exchange goods between themselves. At some point, the owners will also begin to use a specific instrument of exchange – currency.

It is exchange which restores usefulness (use value) to products which are socially useful only inasmuch as they find a buyer. Yet another important function of exchange is that it restores a social nature – verifying the social distribution of labor – to specific individual tasks performed by the private owners. If a product cannot be sold, then it is superfluous – as is the work which went into its creation. Thanks to exchange, via a circuitous route, specific endeavors become a component in the social distribution of labor: individual endeavors complement and match one another and thus become social in character.

Means of exchange in the hands of their owners are resources serving the execution of power over other human beings. Money, too, is something more than just a means of exchange; it is a means of gaining influence over those who are in need of money:

> By possessing the *property* of buying everything, by possessing the property of appropriating all objects, *money* is thus the *object* of eminent possession. The universality of its *property* is the omnipotence of its being. It is therefore regarded as an omnipotent being. Money is the *procurer* between man's need and the object, between his life and his means of life. But *that which* mediates *my* life for me, also *mediates* the existence of other people for me. For me it is the *other* person.[234]

Exchange in its essence is not only a process in which products circulate amongst people. Aside from this strictly economic aspect, there is also the sociological one. Exchange of currency constitutes a certain kind of objective bond connecting humans, too:

---

234 Marx, *Economic & Philosophic Manuscripts of 1844*, 59.

> If *money* is the bond binding me to *human* life, binding society to me, connecting me with nature and man, is not money the bond of all *bonds*? Can it not dissolve and bind all ties? Is it not, therefore, also the universal *agent of separation*? It is the *coin* that really *separates* as well as the real *binding agent* – the … *chemical* power of society.[235]

The very act of exchange is linked to an extortion of desirable human behavior. Who possesses the means of exchange, possesses an ability to use the labors of others as well as the products of their labors.

Still, as long as the exchange is more or less on par, then mutual interactions between people are mediated by various goods. However, from the moment in which exchange ceases to be equivalent, unilateral dependencies are formed; relationships of dominance and exploitation arise. The cornerstone for this exploitation is the foregoing possession of the means of exchange. Thanks to these means – which personify a smaller amount of socially indispensable labor – products are acquired which are loaded with a larger amount of already objectified labor, or labor power is acquired which will produce a surplus product.

Communist Socialization of Property as a Process for the Elimination of Commodity Exchange

Alongside assertions about the strict connections between commodity exchange and private property, just as often in the works of Karl Marx appear assertions that the socialization of property is strictly connected with the elimination of commodity exchange. For instance, "In order for labour to relate to its objective conditions as its property again, another system must take the place of the system of private exchange, which, as we saw, posits the exchange of objectified labour for labour capacity, and therefore the appropriation of living labour without exchange."[236]

In the first phase of the communist society, principles befitting the exchange of goods still reign: a delimited amount of the means of subsistence is exchanged for a delimited amount of labor. As Marx elaborates,

> Here, obviously, the same principle prevails as that which regulates the exchange of commodities, as far as this is exchange of equal values. Content and form are changed, because under the altered circumstances no one can give anything except his labor, and because, on the other hand, nothing can pass to the ownership of individuals, except individual means of consumption. But as far as the distribution of the latter among the

---

235 Ibid., 61.

236 Marx, *Grundrisse: Foundations of the Critique of Political Economy*, 434.

individual producers is concerned, the same principle prevails as in the exchange of commodity equivalents: a given amount of labor in one form is exchanged for an equal amount of labor in another form.[237]

However, in the subsequent phase of the developed communist society, the quantitative measure fades away. At this point, each human being secures such an amount of product as he needs for personal development. Further, the labor he offers on behalf of the society ceases to be a means of product appropriation (because, as a member of the community, he is an owner of product) and becomes a means for his personal development. Thus, in the communist society, exchange of commodities is replaced by another economic system. Commodity exchange vanishes, but not any and all exchange. How should this be understood? The eradication of commodity exchange assumes such a transformation of property relations that no individual can use previously produced things in order to gain power over another individual. The power of the owner of the means of exchange – typical for various forms of private property – is lifted.

In the communist society, no one is the owner of means which would be a use value for someone else but would be useless to him. It would be unreasonable to seize a surplus of which the individual could make no use. He would be incapable of transforming such means into a commodity since everybody would already be an owner of necessary means. Since each member of the community draws upon the common reserves, any product taken by one member would not be desired by another.

Hence this does not pertain to the liquidation of product circulation, but rather the liquidation of such a form of their turnover which could lead product to be a means for the transmission of power. This pertains solely to the liquidation of commodity exchange. The process of mutual sharing of the use values of product and labor power not only ceases to flow from material dependencies but, simultaneously, precludes formation thereof. As Friedrich Engels wrote: "With the seizing of the means of production by society, production of commodities is done away with, and, simultaneously, the mastery of the product over the producer."[238]

237 Marx, *Critique of the Gotha Programme*, 10–11.

238 Friedrich Engels [1880], *Socialism: Utopian and Scientific*, <https://www.marxists.org/archive/marx/works/download/Engels_Socialism_Utopian_and_Scientific.pdf> [accessed August 2017], 10.

Privatization and Socialization of Property in the Sphere of Consumption

In the tribal community, there is, basically, no personal ownership of the means of consumption. Therefore, individual consumption of resources leads to the obliteration of that object of possession. Nonetheless, any relatively permanent objects (such as a residential structure) are never divided among individuals (or among smaller groups within the community) but are used in common. This also pertains to products which need to be stored: they are in the hands of the community, not specific individuals.

In comparison, in the Asian community, the group holds and stores a certain portion of the means of subsistence. However, the remainder is divided amongst the families by community functionaries. The means of subsistence is thus put in storage and consumed by individual households; the home also becomes personal (familial) property. Nevertheless, the community functionaries can intervene in the state of ownership; they can dispossess any family of a portion of the product belonging to it. This might occur, for example, when the community's existence is threatened or when the state burdens the community with excessively high taxes.

As for the ancient and Germanic types of community, the appropriation of the product takes on a completely individualized nature. Units (families) appropriate product independent of the community. Each family ensures itself of the means of subsistence and decides what part can be allotted for personal consumption and what part can be allotted for support of production.

In their *Communist Manifesto*, Karl Marx and Friedrich Engels shed light on the communist socialization of property:

> When, therefore, capital is converted into common property, into the property of all members of society, personal property is not thereby transformed into social property. It is only the social character of the property that is changed. It loses its class character. [….] We by no means intend to abolish this personal appropriation of the products of labour, an appropriation that is made for the maintenance and reproduction of human life, and that leaves no surplus wherewith to command the labour of others. All that we want to do away with is the miserable character of this appropriation, under which the labourer lives merely to increase capital, and is allowed to live only in so far as the interest of the ruling class requires it.[239]

Thus, they bluntly state that communism does not eliminate personal ownership of the means of consumption which continues to be, to a significant degree, personal property. Yet this is a different sort of appropriation than under the conditions of

239 Marx, Engels [1847], *Manifesto of the Communist Party*, 23.

the private property. No one takes more than is necessary to satisfy his needs; he appropriates neither to render other members of the community dependent upon him nor to insure himself before others. The shaping of relations is characterized by the fact that nobody appropriates the means of subsistence in excess of some reasonable reserves. This is one of the conditions for communist socialization.

In its first phase, the magnitude of acquired means depends upon the labor of the producer; in the second phase, what matters is the magnitude of his needs. With reference to this, Gabriel Temkin writes that Marx is inconsistent in identifying phases of communism. Although Marx sees the issue of the distribution of the means of consumption as subordinated by the issue of the distribution of the means of production, he seems to consider the former to be crucial to the periodization of communism, rather than the latter.[240] Temkin's interpretation assumes that ownership of the conditions of labor is realized solely in production. Yet ownership as a social relationship also comes to fruition in other spheres of human activity – including consumption. To be an owner of the means of production, a person must manifest himself as an owner of the means of subsistence – and must do so in a very specific manner. Namely, he must be an owner of the means of subsistence prior to undertaking work and must continue to be an owner for the whole period of the new production cycle. Therefore, his participation in consumption is not only a mode of being an owner of the means of consumption, but also a mode of realizing his ownership of the conditions of labor.

Both phases of communist socialization can be described, too, from the point of view of varying economic goals. What is key in the first phase is the reproduction of a new type of community and preclusion of a return to relationships emblematic of earlier forms of property. For this reason, the communist society continues to function in the form of a state which organizes itself as a dictatorship of the proletariat. Taking up the role of a collective owner of a significant segment of the means of subsistence, the state prevents (by the weight of its power) individual households from enriching themselves. The second phase is characterized by the fact that the direct economic goal becomes the universal and comprehensive personal development of each member of the communist society. Fulfillment of this aim is assured by a plentitude of means by which to satisfy needs. The means of individual consumption continues. Even so, this – in and of itself – does not constitute the quintessence of socialization. The core of the matter concentrates on the nature of interpersonal bonds. As Marx puts it, the nature of property relations succumbs to socialization.

---

240 Gabriel Temkin, *Marks i idea pieniądza pracy* (Warsaw: Książka i Wiedza, 1965), 101–102.

In Summary

Marx describes the socialization of property in a twofold manner. From the negative side, he does so by pointing out relationships uniquely proper to the various forms of private property and not to be found in the socialist property. From the positive side, he does so by pointing out relationships which people establish within various forms of socialist property. According to Marx, this line of reasoning is reflected in the real processes of socialization. The first stage of communism is a process of elimination of private property. In the second, higher stage of communism, this process takes on the form of a "positive socialization." Socialization stops being a process in critical reference to private property; it starts self-perpetuating as a positive, everyday confirmation of social property.

From Marx's perspective, the positive side of communist socialization is marked by the features of utopian thinking. Yet Marx does not fall in step with representatives of utopian socialism and forecasts the creation of scientific socialism. Nonetheless, Marx does create a utopia in the sense of a cognitive construct which presents an alternative to the current state of affairs. This is an ideal society worth launching, but also a sort of cognitive experiment relying upon the extraction of theoretical investigations and practical implications from Marx's theories of property and of social development.

Marx does not leave behind a tested recipe for the building of a communist society. The task he sets before himself comprises a critique of capitalism and a striving towards eradication of private property in its capitalist form. The program indications which he articulated in the positive sense are rather modest, closer to the philosophical than the economic. On more than one occasion he affirmed that the starting conditions for transformation in each society would vary, and, hence, the interim forms that property relations would assume en route to building a communist society would vary, too.

Marx's ideas about the socialization of property have been utilized in various ways by social-democratic and revolutionary movements. Moreover, many an academic trend has been inspired by his conceptions. In the 20th century, one of the numerous feasible interpretations did come to fruition – the one dubbed "Soviet Marxism" by Leszek Kołakowski.[241] This was not the path which Marx most emphatically delineated in his vision of communism. That said, his intellectual agency in this historical circumstance is obvious: many an allegation built into his vision directly facilitated such a development of Marx's utopia.

---

241 Leszek Kolakowski, *Main Currents of Marxism*, Volumes I-III (Oxford: Oxford University Press, 1978).

Chapter V: Property and Social Structure

Introduction

The convictions held by Karl Marx about social structure can be analyzed with reference to three aspects: class-forming factors, social differences, and social groups. The first of these can be considered the deep structure, meaning factors which contribute to the ascension of social and especially class differences. The second encompasses differences in conditions of life and lifestyles between classes or between individuals belonging to certain classes. The last one pertains to the class structure seen as a configuration of social groups as well as the collective activities they undertake. The chapter at hand constitutes an analysis of Marx's assertions on the topic of these three levels. The line of thinking here will be conducted in such a way as to illustrate the connections between his concept of ownership and the concept of class structure.

Class Relations as Property Relations

Karl Marx, in fact, never provided an exhaustive, comprehensive definition of social class – meaning one which would encompass all the referents of the concept which appear in his analyses of concrete social classes. His writings only reveal many partial definitions thereof. Yet, there is more than one way to reconstruct the Marxist concept of class: (a) by collecting and analyzing the fragmentary descriptors; (b) by identifying the premises of his contentions regarding class structure; and (c) by referring to his concept of ownership. And it is in the last of these that, it seems, the key to an understanding of his concept of class structure is found.

Many a sociologist or economist has built a definition of social class on the cornerstone of Marxism. One of the most well-known was penned by Lenin:

> Classes are large groups of people differing from each other by the place they occupy in a historically determined system of social production, by their relation (in most cases fixed and formulated in law) to the means of production, by their role in the social organisation of labour, and, consequently, by the dimensions of the share of social wealth of which they dispose and the mode of acquiring it. Classes are groups of people one of which can appropriate the labour of another owing to the different places they occupy in a definite system of social economy.[242]

242 Vladimir I. Lenin, "A Great Beginning: Heroism of the Workers in the Rear 'Communist Subbotniks'", in *Collected Works*, ed. by Vladimir I. Lenin (Moscow: Progress Publishers, 1974), Volume XXIX.

This definition has been interpreted in a variety of ways, but, for the purposes of this study, the stance taken by Mikhail Rutkievich is a good start. Rutkievich claims that the first part of the definition constitutes a brief, general outline of class whereas the second part comprises its detailing.[243] Such a construal finds its justification elsewhere in Lenin's works wherein he writes that,

> The fundamental criterion by which classes are distinguished is the place they occupy in social production, and, consequently, the relation in which they stand to the means of production. Appropriation of one part or another of the social means of production and its application to private enterprise, to undertakings organised for the sale of the product, is the fundamental distinction of one class in present-day society (the bourgeoisie) from the proletariat, which is deprived of the means of production and sells its labour-power.[244]

Applying his definition quite literally, one can identify a few social classes which display a relationship to the means of production. However, if recognizing only its latter half, then it is possible to distinguish only two classes: the exploited and the exploiters. Yet for Vladimir Lenin, it was obvious that the structure of the capitalist society is much more complicated than the above characterization indicates. This is evident in, among others, his book, *The Development of Capitalism in Russia*.[245] Investigating the transformation of Russian society, Lenin spots many classes within that system whose detection would be at least hampered by the employment of his above-cited definition. For instance, he sees different classes among the peasant population itself. Thus, it is clear that Lenin's study assumes a more detailed definition, containing yet other criteria for class membership.

This particular definition takes into consideration two crucial traits which are also typical of a Marx's approach to the issue of class. Firstly, the criteria for class belonging (or traits reflecting conditions of class existence) are part and parcel of the system of social production. Secondly, class relations have a polarizing tendency. Nonetheless, in a literal sense, the definition constitutes an exaggerated simplification – not only with relation to the concept of class which Lenin's own study assumes, but also to a concept which lies in the assumptions of Marx's theory of social classes. For example, in their *Manifesto*, Marx and Engels provide

---

243 Mikhail N. Rutkievich, *Tiendientsii rozvitiya* sotsialnoy struktury sovietskogo obshchiestva (Moscow: [no publisher given], 1957), 5.

244 Vladimir I. Lenin, "Vulgar Socialism and Narodism as Resurrected by the Socialist-Revolutionaries", in *Collected Works*, ed. by Vladimir I. Lenin (Moscow: Progress Publishers, 1974), Volume VI, 263–270.

245 Vladimir I. Lenin, "The Development of Capitalism in Russia", in *Collected Works*, ed. by Vladimir I. Lenin (Moscow: Progress Publishers, 1974), Volume III.

a much more complex picture of the class structure found in pre-capitalist societies:

> In the earlier epochs of history, we find almost everywhere a complicated arrangement of society into various orders, a manifold gradation of social rank. In ancient Rome we have patricians, knights, plebeians, slaves; in the Middle Ages, feudal lords, vassals, guild-masters, journeymen, apprentices, serfs; in almost all of these classes, again, subordinate gradations. / The modern bourgeois society that has sprouted from the ruins of feudal society has not done away with class antagonisms. It has but established new classes, new conditions of oppression, new forms of struggle in place of the old ones. / Our epoch, the epoch of the bourgeoisie, possesses, however, this distinct feature: it has simplified class antagonisms. Society as a whole is more and more splitting up into two great hostile camps, into two great classes directly facing each other – Bourgeoisie and Proletariat.[246]

In closer affiliation with Marxist analyses is a reconstruction of this concept proposed by Stanisław Kozyr-Kowalski. It incorporates more criteria of class status, including ownership of labor:

> If, however, we take into consideration Marx's theoretical research in practice – as objectified in *Capital* as well as in his economic manuscripts penned earlier – then we will be able to label as a social class such groups of individuals which are elements of different types of material production and which, in these means of production, occupy an identical or nearly identical economic ownership position. That is, they remain in identical or nearly identical relations with reference to the means of material production as well as to the labor power of others or themselves.[247]

Property relations cannot play a part in the segmentation of society into separate classes if all units are owners in a similar fashion. This is the case in some forms of common ownership as well as in societies in which individual private ownership is widespread. In truth, this last situation rarely transpired in history, albeit present in the German form of ownership. Nevertheless, differentiation of ownership positions does lead to class differences. This happens (among other things) when many forms of ownership are concurrent within a single economic system, or when large-scale private ownership appears within a single formation. As Engels explains,

246 Karl Marx, Friedrich Engels [1847], *Manifesto of the Communist Party*, <https://www.marxists.org/archive/marx/works/download/pdf/Manifesto.pdf> [accessed August 2017], 14–15.

247 Stanisław Kozyr-Kowalski, "Klasy społeczeństwa a ekonomiczne-socjologiczne pojmowanie własności, Część pierwsza", *Kultura i Społeczeństwo*, 1 (1984), 15.

> But it is obvious that large-scale farming always gives rise to a distribution which is quite different from that of small-scale farming; that large-scale agriculture presupposes or creates a class antagonism – slave-owners and slaves, feudal lords and serfs, capitalists and wage-workers – while small-scale agriculture does not necessarily involve class differences between the individuals engaged in agricultural production, and that on the contrary the mere existence of such differences indicates the incipient dissolution of smallholding economy.[248]

Classes are such human groups as can be distinguished by: (a) a form of ownership in which they conduct their socioeconomic activity and (b) a mode of being an owner within the bounds of that form. Individuals of a similar class position are, in similar ways, owners of the conditions of labor, the labor power, the means of consumption, and the means of exchange; individuals of different classes differ from one another with respect to the same. Yet there are such classes whose members are not at all owners in at least some of the abovementioned categories; in the case of specific classes, these means of being owners manifest themselves in various configurations.

The unfinished, final chapter of the third volume of *Capital* – which was to have dealt with social classes – contains the following sketch: "The owners merely of labour-power, owners of capital, and land-owners, whose respective sources of income are wages, profit and ground rent, in other words, wage-labourers, capitalists and landowners, constitute then three big classes of modern society based upon the capitalist mode of production."[249]

Somewhat further on, there is more:

> The first question to be answered is this: What constitutes a class? – and the reply to this follows naturally from the reply to another question, namely: What makes wage-labourers, capitalists and landlords constitute the three great social classes? / At first glance – the identity of revenues and sources of revenue. There are three great social groups whose members, the individuals forming them, live on wages, profit and ground-rent respectively, on the realisation of their labour-power, their capital, and their landed property.[250]

---

248 Friedrich Engels [1876–1878], *Anti-Dühring: Herr Eugen Dühring's Revolution in Science*, <https://www.marxists.org/archive/marx/works/download/pdf/anti_duhring.pdf> [accessed August 2017], 90.

249 Karl Marx [1863–1883], *Capital: A Critique of Political Economy*, Volume III, <https://www.marxists.org/archive/marx/works/download/pdf/Capital-Volume-III.pdf> [accessed August 2017], 633.

250 Ibid.

The above-cited depictions of social classes refer to the ownership of the conditions of labor (land and capital), ownership of labor power, and ownership of the means of subsistence. Different sources of profit mean different ways of realizing one's position as owner. Furthermore, classes gradually come to be embedded in strictly delineated forms of ownership; there are capitalist private ownership and its corresponding capitalist mode of industrial as well as agricultural production.

A basis for belonging to the class of wage workers is being the non-owner of the conditions of production and, at the same time, being the owner of the exchange value of labor power. In other words, "The existence of a class which possesses nothing but the ability to work is a necessary presupposition of capital."[251] Marx identifies a few social classes according to the different ways in which someone is an owner of labor power as a commodity. For instance, a criterion for distinguishing wage laborers working in trade – as a class distinct from among all other workers – is the higher value of their labor power, as well as their chance to appropriate the surplus value of other workers. It sometimes happens that one worker exploits another via their employer. When that employer pays one worker a higher wage for lower output, and, at the same time, pays another worker a wage clearly lower for higher output, then the first worker expropriates surplus value produced by this last worker. Marx recognized such a class in the economic structure of 19th-century England: "The commercial worker, in the strict sense of the term, belongs to the better-paid class of wage-workers – to those whose labour is classed as skilled and stands above average labour."[252]

Nonetheless, taking up the position of an owner of the use value of labor power is characteristic of completely different social classes whose members are working owners of the means of production. Applying this criterion, Marx outlines (among others) the peasant and the petty bourgeois classes which were annihilated by the capitalist mode of production in his time:

> The lower strata of the middle class – the small tradespeople, shopkeepers, and retired tradesmen generally, the handicraftsmen and peasants – all these sink gradually into the proletariat, partly because their diminutive capital does not suffice for the scale on which Modern Industry is carried on, and is swamped in the competition with the large capitalists, partly because their specialised skill is rendered worthless by new methods of production.[253]

251 Karl Marx [1847], *Wage Labour and Capital*, <https://www.marxists.org/archive/marx/works/download/pdf/wage-labour-capital.pdf> [accessed August 2017], 14.

252 Marx, *Capital: A Critique of Political Economy*, Volume III, 206.

253 Marx, Engels [1847], *Manifesto of the Communist Party*, 18.

According to the just-cited, the object of ownership for representatives of the middle class comprises their very skills and capacities which they apply in their own workshops or on their plots of land.

Nevertheless, an important characterization of class position is ownership of one's own means of manufacture. Marx and Engels describe, for example, the bourgeoisie as a class which possesses a monopoly on all tools of production and means of survival. Yet regarding the differences between slaves and wage laborers with reference to ownership of the means of subsistence, Marx phrases this in as follows:

> The slave receives a permanent and fixed amount of maintenance; the wage-labourer does not. He must try to get a rise of wages in the one instance, if only to compensate for a fall of wages in the other. If he resigned himself to accept the will, the dictates of the capitalist as a permanent economical law, he would share in all the miseries of the slave, without the security of the slave.[254]

Of quite a different character are class differences between workers, capitalists, and, for example, landholders when looking at the way in which they are owners of the means of consumption.

At this point, there is the problem of how to delineate social classes with respect to ownership of the means of exchange. In *The German Ideology*, Marx and Engels write: "The next extension of the division of labour was the separation of production and commerce, the formation of a special class of merchants…."[255] Here they extricate the class of those who own the means of trade, yet Engels claims that, in the case of the merchant class, there is a distinct way of being an owner of the means of exchange. By appearing before others as an owner of commodities, these owners usurp the product of someone else's work – they participate in the exploitation of other human beings:

> Civilization … creates a class which no longer concerns itself with production, but only with the exchange of the products – the merchants. Hitherto whenever classes had begun to form, it had always been exclusively in the field of production; the persons engaged in production were separated into those who directed and those who executed, or else into large-scale and small-scale producers. Now for the first time a class appears which, without in any way participating in production, captures the direction of production as a

254 Karl Marx [1865], *Value, Price and Profit*, <https://www.marxists.org/archive/marx/works/download/pdf/value-price-profit.pdf> [accessed August 2017], 26.

255 Karl Marx, Friedrich Engels [1845–1846], *The German Ideology*, <https://www.marxists.org/archive/marx/works/download/Marx_The_German_Ideology.pdf> [accessed August 2017], 26.

> whole and economically subjugates the producers; which makes itself into an indispensable middleman between any two producers and exploits them both.[256]

Finally, there is the issue of forms of ownership as a criterion for distinguishing social classes. It can happen that individuals are owners in a similar fashion. Their positions in the sphere of property relations are characterized by comparable ways of being an owner, but these individuals function within different forms of ownership. It is through different types of activity and benefits that they realize their positions as owners. Yet Marx does differentiate these classes from one another which is justified by their economic activity within varied forms of ownership. The Polish Marxist, Julian Hochfeld claims that, in the writings of Marx, one can discover a few models of class structure, including one of the multi-branched class structures. The keystone supporting the materialization of many classes is, according to his interpretation, the existence of many different means of production which form the economic system of a concrete society. Each of these ways of production creates conditions of existence predetermining one or more social classes which, therefore, leads to a complex class structure.[257]

Worth examining at this point is the 19th-century French society as described in the works of Marx – *The Class Struggles in France*,[258] *The Civil War in France*,[259] and *The Eighteenth Brumaire of Louis Bonaparte*.[260] Therein, Karl Marx identifies many a social class: (a) the great landholders; (b) the bourgeoisie which he further divides into the great financiers, industrialists, and wholesalers; (c) the middle class to which he assigns, among others, the small tradespeople, shopkeepers, and retired tradesmen, the handicraftsmen, petty bourgeoisie,

---

256 Friedrich Engels [1884], *Origin of the Family, Private Property, and the State*, <https://www.marxists.org/archive/marx/works/download/pdf/origin_family.pdf> [accessed August 2017], 889–890.

257 Julian Hochfeld, "Studia o marksowskiej teorii społeczeństwa", in *Marksizm, socjologia, socjalizm: Wybór pism*, ed. by Julian Hochfeld (Warsaw: Państwowe Wydawnictwo Naukowe, 1982), 574–579.

258 Karl Marx [1850], *The Class Struggles in France, 1848–1850*, <https://www.marxists.org/archive/marx/works/download/pdf/Class_Struggles_in_France.pdf> [accessed August 2017].

259 Karl Marx [1870–1871], *The Civil War in France*, <https://www.marxists.org/archive/marx/works/download/pdf/civil_war_france.pdf> [accessed August 2017].

260 Karl Marx [1851–1852], *The Eighteenth Brumaire of Louis Bonaparte*, https://www.marxists.org/archive/marx/works/download/pdf/18th-Brumaire.pdf> [accessed Au gust 2017].

peasants, and owners of other small service businesses; and (d) the working class and lumpenproletariat. Listed above, almost literally, are but a few (albeit the most frequently noted) of the social classes discussed in these three treatises. This reflects the complexity of the social class structure in France in this period. In fact, these classes are also mentioned in the *Manifesto* as well as in other works. For example, in *Capital*, Marx bestows the term "social class" upon a few factions of the capitalist class; there, he speaks openly of the class of industrial capitalists, merchant capitalists, and monetary capitalists.

The owners of capital take up analogous positions of ownership – and this allows Marx to count them as part of a single class. Nevertheless, they differ so fundamentally from one another in the ways they fulfill their roles as owners that Marx identifies still further, distinct capitalist classes from among them. For example, the class of industrial capitalists affirms its ownership position in all spheres of reproduction. But the class of owners of trade capital generally affirms its position in exchange, in distribution, and in consumption, while the class of owners of monetary capital accomplishes this only in distribution (by usurping the surplus product in the form of interest and dividends) and in consumption.

Noteworthy is also Marx's sketch of the class of grand, legal landowners in the capitalist formation of society. The uniqueness of their class status is affixed in the specific way that they are owners of the conditions of labor (possessors of land) and the means of existence. On the one hand, in the sphere of production, they realize their positions as landowners only to the extent that they make the land available to capitalist lessees. On the other hand, in the sphere of distribution, they realize their position through their appropriation of surplus product in the form of ground rent, mediated by the agricultural capitalists as middlemen. However, as owners of the means of survival, these landholders assume a much more advantageous position than the owners of capital who function in agriculture as tenants of large estates. The legal owners of grand estates allocate appropriated surplus value solely to consumption since the economic situation in which they find themselves does not force them to accumulate or reproduce capital. While the great capitalist tenants of land must pay ground rent to the legal landlords, the former also invest a part of the appropriated product, employ agriculture workers, and run tenant farms.[261]

261 Marx, *Capital: A Critique of Political Economy*, Volume III, 571–589.

Class Relations and Class Differences in Material Conditions of Existence

Marx's classes do not constitute social categories, extricated according to logical criteria of the "rich man-poor man" sort. These are, instead, collectivities of human beings who occupy varying positions in the structure of property relations. Therefore, as owners, they behave differently in socially meaningful situations and remain in unique relations with each other.

Marx does not execute a stratification; he only identifies the real relations existent amongst people. A similar manner of acting and entrance into similar kinds of social relations portend inclusion into a single class, while dissimilarities in this regard portend assignment to different classes. Social classes actually exist since the ties between various types of owners and non-owners actually exist, too. Therefore, social classes are groups of humans who are distinguished by the fact that they enter into distinctive dependencies, fulfilling the roles of owners.

In *The German Ideology*, Marx and Engels declare:

> The fact is, therefore, that definite individuals who are productively active in a definite way enter into these definite social and political relations. Empirical observation must in each separate instance bring out empirically, and without any mystification and speculation, the connection of the social and political structure with production. The social structure and the State are continually evolving out of the life-process of definite individuals, but of individuals, not as they may appear in their own or other people's imagination, but as they really are; i.e. as they operate, produce materially, and hence as they work under definite material limits, presuppositions and conditions independent of their will.[262]

Testifying to their class belonging are deep features which tally with the sphere of property relations. However, the observable variances between the classes with respect to the material conditions of existence, lifestyle, standard of living, etc. only occasionally correspond with the factors of structuralization situated in ownership relations.

In his treatise, *Wage Labour and Capital*, Marx writes,

> We have thus seen that even the most favorable situation for the working class, namely, the most rapid growth of capital, however much it may improve the material life of the worker, does not abolish the antagonism between his interests and the interests of the capitalist. Profit and wages remain as before, in inverse proportion. / If capital grows rapidly, wages may rise, but the profit of capital rises disproportionately faster.

262 Marx, Engels, *The German Ideology*, 8.

> The material position of the worker has improved, but at the cost of his social position. The social chasm that separates him from the capitalist has widened.[263]

This fragment is cited most often when speaking of the relative pauperization of the working class. But it can also illustrate the Marxist stance with reference to relations between the deep and the surface levels of class structure. Here Marx clearly differentiates the social from the material position of the working class. Decisive in the social position of the workers (and hence their class belonging) are the ownership relations between them and the capitalists, and not the level of earnings. In the above-cited quotation, Marx points to employment relationships that take on the form of wage and relationship exploitation. This relationship joins the capitalist with the wage laborers.

Belonging to the working class does not always mean poverty, illiteracy, or being underfed and poorly dressed. Truth be told, this did often (e.g., in 19th-century England) go hand in hand with the position of a laborer for hire. An exceptional analysis of precisely this situation of the working class is presented by Engels in his *Condition of the Working Class in England*.[264] A comparable description of the living conditions of the working class is also provided by Marx in *Capital*. Yet this situation can come across otherwise. One segment of workers lives under horrid circumstances while another lives in good ones, or the same set of workers lives in better or worse conditions depending upon the time period. And yet, despite this fact, they are qualified as the same class. Marx expresses this thesis emphatically in *Capital*:

> Finally, the labourer in the capacity of owner and seller of his individual labour-power receives a portion of the product under the label of wages, in which that portion of his labour appears which we call necessary labour, i.e., that required for the maintenance and reproduction of this labour-power, be the conditions of this maintenance and reproduction scanty or bountiful, favourable or unfavourable. / Whatever may be the disparity of these relations in other respects, they all have this in common: Capital yields a profit year after year to the capitalist, land a ground-rent to the landlord, and labour-power, under normal conditions and so long as it remains useful labour-power, a wage to the labourer.[265]

The employed laborer – regardless of his earnings – belongs to the working class because he participates in the following relations: he sells his labor, lives off a

---

263 Marx, *Wage Labour and Capital*, 19.

264 Friedrich Engels [1844–1845], *Condition of the Working Class in England*, <https://www.marxists.org/archive/marx/works/download/pdf/condition-working-class-england.pdf> [accessed August 2017].

265 Marx, *Capital: A Critique of Political Economy*, Volume III, 594.

worker's wages, is subject to the authority of the employer, and is exploited by that employer. The fact that he is poor, hungry, and survives in miserable living conditions is a result of specific ownership relations. Still, it does transpire that the worker is wealthy, has good housing, and takes intense advantage of cultural goods. Despite such a state of affairs, he will continue to be a representative of the working class since the position which he occupies in the ownership system is similar to that occupied by other workers.

This is the way it is with the wretched Irish laborer, the better prospering English one, and the superbly situated, highly skilled laborer performing some rare occupation at a time of prosperity. Any quantitative differences between them do not lead to some new quality of life; this does not cause qualitatively new economic relations to emerge.

Engels describes this aspect of the phenomenon using workers as an example – specifically those who at a time of prosperity enjoy a lavish lifestyle. Irrespective of that, the amount of goods appropriated by them is still insufficient for a change in their class position. They do not capitalize their income, but earmark these funds for an extemporaneous increase in their living standard:

> To save is unavailing, for at the utmost he cannot save more than suffices to sustain life for a short time, while if he falls out of work, it is for no brief period. To accumulate lasting property for himself is impossible; and if it were not, he would only cease to be a working-man and another would take his place. What better thing can he do, then, when he gets high wages, than live well upon them? The English bourgeoisie is violently scandalised at the extravagant living of the workers when wages are high; yet it is not only very natural but very sensible of them to enjoy life when they can, instead of laying up treasures which are of no lasting use to them, and which in the end moth and rust (*i.e.*, the bourgeoisie) get possession of.[266]

Marx and Engels do sometimes apply, too, a quantitative criterion (e.g., wealth) in the identification or description of social classes. Illustrating this is a statement by Engels about the "splitting up of society into a small class, immoderately rich, and a large class of wage-labourers devoid of all property."[267] In line with this thinking, Stanisław Ossowski claims that, in Marx's conception, one can indeed detect (among other things) a gradated class structure scheme, characterized by a criterion delineating class membership and discerning social classes according

266 Engels, *Condition of the Working Class in England*, 119.

267 Friedrich Engels [1891], *Introduction to Karl Marx's "Wage Labour and Capital"*, <https://www.marxists.org/archive/marx/works/download/pdf/wage-labour-capital.pdf> [accessed August 2017], 6.

to the level of wealth.[268] Certain statements by Marx and Engels actually do build a foundation for the reconstruction of such a model – yet still of marginal significance. Most often such declarations serve in describing the living conditions of predetermined social classes identified based on relational characteristics – i.e., based on ownership relations.

The description of living conditions in Marx and Engels performs a few functions. Firstly, it facilitates the enhancement of the sketches of already identified classes and the verification of previous generalizations about class structure. For example,

> Having now investigated, somewhat in detail, the conditions under which the English working-class lives, it is time to draw some further inferences from the facts presented, and then to compare our inferences with the actual state of things. Let us see what the workers themselves have become under the given circumstances, what sort of people they are, what their physical, mental, and moral status.[269]

Secondly, it also allows a conclusion to be drawn about the existence of a specific kind of ownership relations between persons because living conditions might go hand in hand with the class position. For example, in analyzing the conditions of existence of 19th-century French peasants, Marx claims that their ownership position differs completely from their status at the end of the 18th century. He saw the peasants of his day as exploited by owners of capital and the state, but not in such relations with other classes during the Napoleonic wars. If so, then these are two completely distinct social classes, even if one stems from the other.[270]

Thus, the poor person can be either a peasant, a craftsman, a hired laborer, or even a capitalist. After all, the consumption funds of the last of these are reversely proportionate to capitalization funds. For this reason, some capitalists preserve their class membership at the expense of their families' living conditions; in the 19th-century Puritan England this was none too rare. Yet, keeping ownership in mind, it would be difficult to count all these impoverished people as part of a single class.

On the one hand, class position is a characteristic of individuals and collectives in the system of property relations. On the other hand, the class conditions are characteristic of the entire context of the life of large collectivities which have already been differentiated according to the traits of their class position. The first type pertains to the deep structure and factors of structuralization whose

268 Stanisław Ossowski, "Struktura klasowa w społecznej świadomości", in *O strukturze społecznej*, ed. by Stanisław Ossowski (Warsaw: Państwowe Wydawnictwo Naukowe, 1982), 184–185.

269 Engels, *Condition of the Working Class in England*, 106.

270 Marx, *The Civil War in France*; Marx, *The Eighteenth Brumaire of Louis Bonaparte*.

identification requires theoretical analysis of dependencies between people. The second type pertains to superficial descriptions of directly observable living conditions.

Class Structure as a System of Social Groups

When a large mass or set of people finds itself in similar ownership positions and relations, then it constitutes a social class in the economic sense – a "class itself." Further, when such a class exists for some time, certain group-forming processes take place, and it transforms itself into a political "class for itself." As Marx notes, the same refers to the working class:

> Economic conditions had first transformed the mass of the people of the country into workers. The combination of capital has created for this mass a common situation, common interests. This mass is thus already a class as against capital, but not yet for itself. In the struggle, of which we have noted only a few phases, this mass becomes united, and constitutes itself as a class for itself. The interests it defends become class interests. But the struggle of class against class is a political struggle.[271]

The concept encompasses a specific type of social phenomena. A "class for itself" is a group of people of similar or like ownership positions which displays the following traits:

1) Supra-local (on the scale of the territorial state) ties appear among members of the class;
2) The group is organized on a nationwide or countrywide scale and possesses a system of formalized political institutions which ensure its permanence and development;
3) In their individual activities, members of the class submit to the expectations of their own milieu and its leaders;
4) The actions of the members of a class can be described as collective activity, as a social movement (e.g., members fight together against other classes);
5) The class creates its very own culture;
6) Members of the class have a sense of belonging to a single community and a sense of separateness from other communities; and
7) The spiritual activity of the members of the class takes the form of class consciousness (i.e., group consciousness).

---

271 Karl Marx [1847], *The Poverty of Philosophy: Answer to the "Philosophy of Poverty" by M. Proudhon*, <https://www.marxists.org/archive/marx/works/download/pdf/Poverty-Philosophy.pdf> [accessed August 2017], 79.

Depending upon whether the class is only nascent, in full bloom, or in decline, these traits manifest themselves to different degrees.

Many a scholar has pointed out this multidimensionality in the concept of class as found in the writings of Marx and Engels. Among the more renowned Polish commentators, Julian Hochfeld writes that "relations between classes seen as social aggregates are a condition and presupposition for the shaping of classes understood as social groups, actively participating in the historical process."[272] Hochfeld claims here that the reasons behind the formation of classes into social groups should be sought in the antagonistic positions of large groups – displaying a degree of permanent contacts among members with the awareness of a common situation, shared goals, and an organization – in the means of production.[273] In turn, Stanisław Ossowski accents the shaping of class consciousness as a trait of the Marxist class for itself.[274]

Marx's writings reveal many declarations which manifestly encompass both above-noted aspects of class. Returning to the 19th-century French peasants, his analysis of their class position documents the duality of this concept:

> The small-holding peasants form an enormous mass whose members live in similar conditions but without entering into manifold relations with each other. Their mode of production isolates them from one another instead of bringing them into mutual intercourse. The isolation is furthered by France's poor means of communication and the poverty of the peasants. [....] A small holding, the peasant and his family; beside it another small holding, another peasant and another family. A few score of these constitute a village, and a few score villages constitute a department. Thus the great mass of the French nation is formed by the simple addition of homologous magnitudes, much as potatoes in a sack form a sack of potatoes. Insofar as millions of families live under conditions of existence that separate their mode of life, their interests, and their culture from those of the other classes, and put them in hostile opposition to the latter, they form a class. Insofar as there is merely a local interconnection among these small-holding peasants, and the identity of their interests forms no community, no national bond, and no political organization among them, they do not constitute a class. They are therefore incapable of asserting their class interest in their own name, whether through a parliament or a convention. They cannot represent themselves, they must be represented.[275]

On the one hand, Marx calls the French peasants a class many times. The above-cited treatise is littered with such a label, the basis for which is a similarity in their position within the system of property relations. On the other hand, precisely in

272 Hochfeld, *Studia o marksowskiej teorii społeczeństwa*, 610.
273 Ibid., 609–610.
274 Ossowski, *Struktura klasowa w społecznej świadomości*, 180–181.
275 Marx, *The Eighteenth Brumaire of Louis Bonaparte* 62.

the quoted section, he denies the peasants such a designation since they do not comprise a conscious community. Here he lists the following requirements of class communities: similar conditions of existence, mutual contacts which take on the form of supra-local bonds, political organizations, a distinct culture, and a brothers-in-arms battle in defense of their common interests. These are traits of a class for itself.

A related description of a social class can also be read in *The German Ideology*:

> Out of the many local corporations of burghers there arose only gradually the burgher class. The conditions of life of the individual burghers became, on account of their contradiction to the existing relationships and of the mode of labour determined by these, conditions which were common to them all and independent of each individual. The burghers had created the conditions insofar as they had torn themselves free from feudal ties, and were created by them insofar as they were determined by their antagonism to the feudal system which they found in existence. When the individual towns began to enter into associations, these common conditions developed into class conditions. The same conditions, the same contradiction, the same interests necessarily called forth on the whole similar customs everywhere…. The separate individuals form a class only insofar as they have to carry on a common battle against another class; otherwise they are on hostile terms with each other as competitors.[276]

A mutual battle against another class goes through several stages, constituting part of the group-formation processes within the class. This can be traced, for instance, by looking at the workers' movement. In the first phase, when the class still exists only as a group of people of a similar economic position, the class battle is of an individual nature. Each person by himself opposes a concrete representative of another class to whom he is connected by a conflict in property relations. For example, in the case of the 19th-century working class, there were various forms of individual rebellion, theft, and sabotage. The next phase in this battle relates to the rise of more or less permanent local associations (e.g., in one factory or city) and collective encounters against specific representatives of the antagonistic class. At this stage, too, a phenomenon of a new type appears: it is at this point that the class fight takes on the form of a social movement. People subordinate themselves in their activities to the goals of the movement in which they participate. The subsequent phase is a nationwide organization, the creation of various kinds of coalitions between separate factions of workers, and the selection of union and political representatives. The last of these can refer to labor unions, political parties, or representatives of the class in government. At this point, the class community fights not only for the concrete economic interests of specific

276 Marx, Engels, *The German Ideology*, 34.

members but also for its very own existence as a community. It strives to achieve a more advantageous position in the political system of a concrete society and only then, by way of realizing this goal, strives for a more advantageous position for its members in the economic system.

At some point, the actions of the class community entity become, for its members, a goal surpassing any struggle on behalf of the individual interests which gave rise to the movement. Thus, the class fight becomes a collective political fight. Inasmuch as the laborer, at earlier stages, discerned his class enemy as a concrete capitalist and stood up against that individual; at this stage, the laborer stands up against the entire antagonistic class, in solidarity with his own. When the class battle enters the phase of political battle – a fight aiming to protect its own community and concurrently destroy or subordinate another one – then we are dealing with a fully shaped class for itself.

From the point of view of these phases of battle – from the individual economic through to the collective political behavior – it is possible to analyze the group-forming processes within different social classes. A similar description of the transformation of the class battle can be found in *Condition of the Working Class in England* (e.g., the chapter *Labour Movements*) as well as in the first volume of *Capital* and in the *Manifesto*. In all these works, Marx and Engels claim that the group-forming processes are accompanied by a transformation of the form of class battle from individual to group action, from directionless protest to programmed activities, and from a spontaneous fight to one that takes advantage of formalized class institutions.

That is the case with the revolutionary class. However, the counter-revolutionary class which has much earlier organized as a class in and of itself aims to attain quite the opposite result: it strives to maintain the *status quo* or cause the disintegration of that class community which wants to supplant it.

The interpersonal relations within one and the same class change as the group-forming processes intensify. Individuals initially compete with one another. For example, workers compete with one another on the labor market to find a job; capitalists compete for better sales for their goods. But, together with the development of a class community, this type of competition decreases whereas the members of the class begin to cooperate with one another. They give up their individual goals on behalf of those realized by the community. They subordinate their actions – even those associated with an effective fulfillment of their ownership roles – to the expectations of the class. Their behavior can no longer be explained by reference solely to their position in the system of ownership.

To comprehend the logic behind this, it is necessary to refer to their membership in a specific class community. It does happen that the second factor, the political one, supersedes the economic one. Members of a class group get so involved in the striving for collective objectives and in collective action that they are incapable of realizing their direct interests, directly connected with their position in the ownership system. For instance, the wage laborer, in solidarity with his class during the course of a strike, does not even consider a well-paying job and hence does not work to realize the exchange value of his own labor. In individual behavior, the economic and political elements thus merge together; a crossover occurs from actions solely conditioned by economic position to actions designated, too, by belonging to a community. The class becomes independent with reference to the individual; the former subordinates the latter, delineating the individual's fate, way of life, way of thinking, and social position.

The Composition of the Class for Itself

A description of the composition of the class itself which has not yet transformed into a large social group is obvious: the components are people of a comparable or similar position in the system of property relations. But in the case of the class for itself, this can appear otherwise.

The simplest and most frequent situation found in the history of societies is one in which group-forming processes encompass human collectives of a uniform ownership status. This was sometimes the case of some merchant classes present in pre-capitalist societies which manifested themselves before other classes as a class community.

Not infrequently representatives of a few different classes "for itself" organize themselves in a large single class community. This takes place on the basis of some fundamental similarity in ownership position; even if specific members of this class hold various ownership positions, these are, in a sense, close positions. For instance, the class of industrial workers links to that of trade workers and farm workers. Or the class of individual owners can join together in a single, organized petty bourgeoisie class. Or different kinds of owners of capital can combine into a single class community. The integration of different economic classes into one political class for itself does not mean the disappearance of the distinct traits of the class positions of its members. In connection with this, Marx occasionally uses the concept of class factions.

Sometimes even a few, already-formed classes "for itself" join together in one, larger class for itself. An example of such a process can be the outcomes of class battles in France. A separate class community there was the grand landholders;

another class community was that of owners of monetary capital. Furthermore, there were the classes of the owners of industrial and trade capital. Up to a moment, these classes conducted organized battles amongst each other. They each had their own parties, political institutions, and representatives in government institutions. Each of these classes created its separate culture and separate ideology. Some of them, each at a different time, held power and ruled in France. For instance, in the period of the Restoration, the landowners reigned, whereas, during the Orleans monarchy, it was the great financiers who did so:

> Under the Bourbons, big landed property had governed, with its priests and lackeys; under Orleans, high finance, large-scale industry, large-scale trade, that is, capital, with its retinue of lawyers, professors, and smooth-tongued orators. The Legitimate Monarchy was merely the political expression of the hereditary rule of the lords of the soil, as the July Monarchy was only the political expression of the usurped rule of the bourgeois parvenus. What kept the two factions apart, therefore, was not any so-called principles, it was their material conditions of existence, two different kinds of property; it was the old contrast between town and country, the rivalry between capital and landed property. That at the same time old memories, personal enmities, fears and hopes, prejudices and illusions, sympathies and antipathies, convictions, articles of faith and principles bound them to one or the other royal house, who denies this? Upon the different forms of property, upon the social conditions of existence, rises an entire superstructure of distinct and peculiarly formed sentiments, illusions, modes of thought, and views of life. The entire class creates and forms them out of its material foundations and out of the corresponding social relations.[277]

Yet in the newer economic and political conditions, they united with each other into a single class community.

Yet another type of connection between economic and political class is that the group-forming processes encompass only part of an economic class whereas the rest of its representatives do not participate in the life of the community. Such was the case, for instance, with the wage laborer class during the 19th-century French upheavals. This class organized as a class for itself only in Paris; in the provinces outside the capital, workers functioned as individuals in mutual isolation.

Most frequently, the political classes "for itself" include two categories of members: the core composed of persons of similar or close ownership positions, and those persons who stem from fundamentally different economic classes. The two categories combine in the class community, even if their place in the system of ownership would predestine them for life as part of quite a different class community. For various reasons – political, ideological, moral, or other – they

---

277 Marx, *The Eighteenth Brumaire of Louis Bonaparte*, 22.

change their class membership. An example here would be that, in the times of Karl Marx, many of the petty bourgeoisie, and sometimes even owners of capital, toiled within the ranks of the working class:

> Finally, in times when the class struggle nears the decisive hour, the progress of dissolution going on within the ruling class, in fact within the whole range of old society, assumes such a violent, glaring character, that a small section of the ruling class cuts itself adrift, and joins the revolutionary class, the class that holds the future in its hands. Just as, therefore, at an earlier period, a section of the nobility went over to the bourgeoisie, so now a portion of the bourgeoisie goes over to the proletariat, and in particular, a portion of the bourgeois ideologists, who have raised themselves to the level of comprehending theoretically the historical movement as a whole.[278]

The Category of Interest and Class-Forming Processes

In the final, incomplete volume of *Capital*, after providing an introductory definition of social classes which refer to ownership categories, Marx asserts that, if one were to stop at the stage of research, conclusions would suggest the existence of a much more complicated class structure than is the case. In each society of a capitalist formation, it would behoove the researcher to distinguish a high number of social classes since people do differ (even if slightly) in the ownership positions they occupy.[279] Yet that is not the case: class communities which emerge out of collectivities of a similar ownership position take the form of sizeable social groups.

A question as to why this happens Marx and Engels already pose in *The German Ideology*:

> How is it that personal interests always develop, against the will of individuals, into class interests, into common interests which acquire independent existence in relation to the individual persons, and in their independence assume the form of *general* interests? How is it that as such they come into contradiction with the actual individuals and in this contradiction, by which they are defined as *general* interests, they can be conceived by consciousness as *ideal* and even as religious, holy interests? How is it that in this process of private interests acquiring independent existence as class interests the personal behavior of the individual is bound to be objectified [*sich versachlichen*], estranged [*sich entfremden*], and at the same time exists as a power independent of him and without him, created by intercourse, and is transformed into social relations, into a series of powers which determined and subordinate the individual, in which, therefore, appear in the imagination as 'holy' powers?[280]

278 Marx, Engels [1847], *Manifesto of the Communist Party*, 19–20.
279 Marx, *Capital: A Critique of Political Economy*, Volume III, 633.
280 Marx, Engels, *The German Ideology*, 262–263.

And it is precisely therein that the categories of personal interest and class interest appear. Marx and Engels employ these categories in other places as well when elucidating the processes of the social becoming of the class for itself.

In *The Holy Family*, Marx and Engels describe individual interest as a need (or even necessity) in establishing bonds with these individuals – via such relationships the means can be attained to meet material and spiritual needs. Only the entrance into mutual dependencies permits individuals to satisfy their needs, especially since the means are found in the hands of others. Because individuals are not isolated atoms, the necessity for establishing reciprocal dependencies becomes a fixed element in the realization of individual needs, becoming an interest of the individual. Each person lives together with others, and his individual life depends on others. This leads to the development of various types of social groups, including classes or estates. Rather than mutual altruism, it is egoism (the compulsion to meet needs) which conjoins human beings in different kinds of communities and causes individual interests to take on the form of their counterpart – group interests which stabilize as such. This new sort of interest – group interest, political interest – is expressed in a need to protect and reproduce the interwoven group ties and the group as a whole.[281]

Class communities and class interests arise as a consequence of the clash of different individual interests – all of which is linked to the ownership positions of the members of a class. Marx and Engels develop this thesis numerous times in their explanations with reference to the development of the classes of capitalists, of workers, and of the petty bourgeoisie as classes "for itself."

Owners of capital compete with one another. Nonetheless, they decide to cooperate with each other to achieve their common class interests. Marx deals with this matter in *Capital*, summarizing his explications about the diverse ways by which the profit margin can be increased: "Here, then, we have a mathematically precise proof why capitalists form a veritable freemason society vis-à-vis the whole working-class, while there is little love lost between them in competition among themselves."[282]

Here, too, discrete workers have contrary interests since they compete for jobs or for higher earnings. But, in the face of a threat to their individual interests on the part of the capitalists, contrasts become secondary, and the workers organize. Defense of their unions, which attempt to thwart exploitation from the side of

281 Karl Marx, Friedrich Engels, *The Holy Family or Critique of Critical Critique* (Moscow: Foreign Languages Publishing House, 1936), 105–192.

282 Marx, *Capital: A Critique of Political Economy*, Volume III, 144.

the capitalists, becomes more important than money. An alignment of political and class interests is shaped among the workers:

> Large-scale industry concentrates in one place a crowd of people unknown to one another. Competition divides their interests. But the maintenance of wages, this common interest which they have against their boss, unites them in a common thought of resistance – *combination*. Thus combination always has a double aim, that of stopping competition among the workers, so that they can carry on general competition with the capitalist. If the first aim of resistance was merely the maintenance of wages, combinations, at first isolated, constitute themselves into groups as the capitalists in their turn unite for the purpose of repression, and in the face of always united capital, the maintenance of the association becomes more necessary to them than that of wages.[283]

Interests also exist subjectively – as diagnoses and explanations of reality, as ideologies, and as programs of action. The emergence of class groups takes place not only in connection with similar living circumstances but also in connection with the social imagination of those circumstances. The ideological interpretation of interests (on an individual and group scale) is no less a factor in this than the objective interests. Among other things, this factor means that the composition of classes "for itself" is not always homogenous with regards to ownership; that collective actions by specific classes do not always correspond with their objective interests; and, that group-forming processes are subject to acceleration or deceleration. In analyzing transformations within the working class, Marx claims that this class – when shifting through specific stages of battle and suffering certain losses – sheds its false image of its place in the society; only via the acquisition of a consciousness of its objective interests can the working class realize its class interests.

Representatives of the ruling class are aware of the class-forming functions of subjective interests; for this reason, they impose their own worldview and their own ideology upon other classes. Marx underscores many times the fact that the originators of ideologies themselves begin to share the delusions which they create for others. Subjective interests play a significant role, especially in the case of classes holding an ambiguous position in the system of ownership. A case study can be the petty bourgeoisie of France in 1848 whose collective actions – especially vis-à-vis other social classes – had little to do with their real interests, stemming above all from ideological indications.

283 Marx, *The Poverty of Philosophy*, 79.

From the perspective of the deliberations herein, one could ascertain that Marx's classes were vast interest groups anchored in collectives whose members hold similar (in some way) positions in the ownership system.

Class Communities and Property Relations

In addition to an assertion declaring that ownership relations presuppose class relations, Marxist theory also contains claims regarding reverse dependencies: ownership relations are shaped by class communities. Firstly, it is possible to establish property relations via membership in class communities. Secondly, class communities bear an impact upon reproduction of and changes in property relations.

In sociological theories of ownership, a common contention is that a social class cannot be a subject of property. Many a representative of the social sciences has made such a declaration. For instance, Etienne Balibar writes, "But a class cannot be the *subject* of property in the sense in which – legally – the individual is the subject of *his* property, nor a *partner*, nor 'third party', of a contract."[284] Balibar denies social classes the status of a party to ownership relations; although he claims the application of a socioeconomic concept of ownership, he is, in fact, using a legal category which precludes the possibility of such a status.

Yet Marx provides many examples of how a class community can be party to property relations. Although this is more frequently a veiled relationship, it is discernible. The first such illustration concerns the community of the classical, ancient type. Citizens of antiquity were organized as a class community and exploited non-citizens via institutions of the state. Although the citizens did not directly exploit persons working on state-owned land, they did – as a class – participate in this exploitation. The surplus product which is a yield of the state-owned land is allocated to the maintenance of the state which provides various services on behalf of the citizens. The profit of the class community is thus obvious. Nevertheless, in the case of individual citizens, the effect is that, in the first order, they take advantage of state services, and, in the second order, they themselves do not have to provide services or pay taxes to sustain the state institutions.

A second illustration concerns the class of capitalists. If this class – by way of state institutions – burdens representatives of other social classes (e.g., peasants, petty bourgeoisie, etc.) with excess taxes, then it does not need to pay into the state whose institutions serve in the realization of its class interests. In this case, membership in the class of capitalists permits the usurpation and hoarding of a

284 Étienne Balibar, "The Basic Concepts of Historical Materialism", in *Reading Capital*, ed. by Louis Althusser, Étienne Balibar (London: New Left Books, 1970).

greater amount of the society's product than would be possible, if the remaining classes were not encumbered by such taxes and duties. Via its class community, members participate in the relations of exploitation even if they do not establish direct connections with representatives of the other classes. With reference to this form of class community participation in ownership relations, Marx writes in *Theories of Surplus Value* (Part III, Chapter XXIV), "Capital cannot abolish landed property. But by converting it into rent [which is paid to the State] the capitalists as a *class* appropriate it and use it to defray their State expenses, thus appropriating in a roundabout way what cannot be retained directly."[285]

Class communities either strive to maintain the *status quo* in the system of ownership or they strive to change it. To achieve its objective, the class community takes advantage of state institutions. Therefore, the battle over the nature of ownership relations takes on a political form. Although its roots and its results are found in the economic sphere, the fight is played out within a state and its institutions. The state is its own arena and the medium in this battle.

In the second half of the 19th century, capitalists strove to maintain the *ancien régime*, the *status quo* while workers started organizing as class for itself and striving towards revolution. The latter wanted to take power in the state, to expropriate the owners of capital, and to implement the socialization of property. In *Capital*, Karl Marx predicts that the transformation of conditions of an economic nature – including competition and mutual expropriation by capitalists – will lead to a situation in which workers will be able to expropriate a few of the expropriators. As Marx notes in *Capital*,

> The transformation of scattered private property, arising from individual labour, into capitalist private property is, naturally, a process, incomparably more protracted, violent, and difficult, than the transformation of capitalistic private property, already practically resting on socialised production, into socialised property. In the former case, we had the expropriation of the mass of the people by a few usurpers; in the latter, we have the expropriation of a few usurpers by the mass of the people.[286]

Nonetheless, in the West in his own lifetime, this process began to slow down. Hence, if one were to treat literally Marx's arguments (constructed on the basis of solely economic phenomena) about the inevitable fall of capitalism, then his

---

285 Karl Marx [1861–1863], *Theories of Surplus Value*, <https://www.marxists.org/archive/marx/works/1863/theories-surplus-value/add3.htm> [accessed August 2017], 22.

286 Karl Marx [1867], *Capital: A Critique of Political Economy*, Volume I, <https://www.marxists.org/archive/marx/works/download/pdf/Capital-Volume-I.pdf> [accessed August 2017], 542.

theory would be faced with an insoluble conundrum. Paradoxically, an explanation for this fact is found in statements by Marx about class domination. What escapes his attention is that capitalists, organized as a political class for itself, are also capable of backing down from particular interests in order to defend a strategic class interest. Among other things, this leads to an improvement in the position of the working class and a reduction of interclass tensions. Marx did not develop this explanatory, prognostic possibility which lies at the heart of his conception of class domination. Perhaps he did not want to use this line of argumentation due to his engagement in the revolutionary movement whose program had set its sights on a confrontation between the classes.

Chapter VI: Conclusions

The oeuvre of Karl Marx is like a splintered mirror in which two visages manifest themselves simultaneously: Marx the theorist versus Marx the ideologue. This metaphor takes on special meaning in the context of his thoughts about property and ownership.

First, Marx is persistently modern and up-to-date. He elaborated a theory which continues to meet the standards of contemporary paradigms in the social sciences. In contrast, most 19th-century concepts have become anachronistic; although inspiring, rarely can they be directly applied in the modeling or explaining of existing reality. The grand schemes of Ferdinand Tönnies and Georg Simmel have grown stale and hackneyed. An air of modernity, freshness, and innovation has endured only with regards to two theories of ownership: that of Max Weber and that of Karl Marx. It is about this side of Marx that this volume speaks.

In his analysis of ownership, Marx concurrently employed three main, theoretical perspectives of sociology (even if he did not see himself as a sociologist). This trio of viewpoints includes:

1) treatment of ownership as a social system;
2) perception of ownership through the prism of individuals acting as owners; and
3) treatment of ownership as a configuration of social relationships between various types of owners and non-owners, relations established by individuals through the mediation of diverse objects of property.

The last of these includes currency as one of the possible objects mediating ownership. Marx did see money in and of itself as a sort of vehicle for social relations. This perspective is especially prolific in a cognitive sense because it permits identification of a rich network of interpersonal relations palpitant under the membrane of the ownership of capital.

Second, Marx is critical – this is one of the key merits of his legacy. His analytical and methodical approach sensitized him to key social problems and processes. Furthermore, it enabled him to enter a tighter intellectual contact with reality as well as theories pertaining thereto. Therefore, Karl Marx constructed exceptional instruments for the description and explication of societal phenomena. It was his cogent and cutting line of attack with regards to the social reality and theories of his time which made possible the formation of a new cognitive apparatus which, in effect, laid bare the oppressive economic relations of the 19th century.

This was not a simple task since Marx had to tear through the veil of what civil society had seemingly achieved: at the end of the 18th century, the French Revolution had declared the victory of freedom, equality, fraternity, and democracy which had become more rooted with every decade.

To tackle this situation Marx built a conceptual model in which key roles are played by the following categories: value, surplus labor, surplus value, and a fundamental distinction between surplus value and profit. It was this model which unveiled the exploitative relationships present in capitalistic private ownership – as well as in feudal land ownership and certain other forms of individual private ownership; even more noteworthy, it also unveiled the exploitative relationships found in many forms of communal ownership.

But Marx's model met with mass criticism from the side of classic and liberal economists who emphasized its natural weaknesses while diminishing its usefulness in the detection of exploitation. It is a matter of course that any theory or theoretical tool will obscure or overlook one thing while bringing something else to light. What is notable about Marx (and underscored in Chapter III of the book at hand) is precisely his exposure of the exploitation which manifests itself in relations between the owners of capital and the owners of labor power. Other theories, including the most contemporary, have ignored surplus value. In focusing on profit and added value, they shroud the core of the relationship between capital and wage labor and are thus incapable of identifying the sources of revenue appropriated by the owners of capital.

Rousing his censure were the undignified and inhuman living conditions of the peasants and wage laborers – the material conditions of existence accompanying the rise of capitalism in Western Europe. In the eyes of Karl Marx, however, contempt and critique, incisive diagnoses of capitalist society and explications did not suffice. And hence he sought a way out of this situation. Most concisely he articulated his aims in a single, terse sentence which rounds off his *Theses on Feuerbach*: "The philosophers have only *interpreted* the world, in various ways; the point, however, is to *change* it."[287]

In fact, his *Theses on Feuerbach* are often cited as a program for unifying theory and practice – and yet they also forecast Marx's oscillation between the two. An illustration of this fork in the road is his theory of ownership vis-à-vis his doctrine of ownership. His scorn for what he witnessed gave rise to a theory which proposes an accurate and multilevel diagnosis of capitalist property

287 Karl Marx [1845], "Theses on Feuerbach", in *Marx/Engels, Selected Works* (Moscow: Progress Publishers, 1968), 30.

relations; it also provoked a doctrine which heralds a simple, albeit risky program for the socialization of ownership.

What inspired Karl Marx were possibilities anchored in a vision of a whole new society, a whole new world – one better than the one which he inhabited. He formulated a utopia: a communist society based upon communal ownership. He joined in the creation of a revolutionary movement which, as he prescribed, would first abolish the current state of affairs, characterized by financial enslavement and exploitation. Next, it would build a society of free men and women with an unlimited fund of the means of production and the means of existence at their disposal.

Both Marxist theory and doctrine on ownership are affixed to the premise that property relations are a crucial element delineating the framework of social activity and behavior. Such a positioning of ownership in the social system underpinned Karl Marx's momentous proposition. Among others, Steve Pejovich, one of the leaders of the Property Rights School and apologists for private ownership, recognizes its value: "I conjecture that Karl Marx was the first social scientist to have a theory of property rights."[288] Pejovich then accents the fact that Marx in the 19th century – just like the Property Rights School in the 20th century – asserted that pre-existing ownership structures shape economic behavior. So, too, the resolution of social problems necessitates more than just ordinary intellectual musing: it will be a process of social changes which will encompass the whole of the social system and will entail the appropriate reshaping of property rights.

Nonetheless, Pejovich does not (in this author's opinion) fully grasp the particulars of Marx's approach. For Karl Marx, the law – including property rights – is derived from (but not a consequence of) economic relationships. That stated, property relations – defined by Marx as socioeconomic relations, by Pejovich and his school as legal relations – bear an impact on many other aspects of collective life. In any case, the robust status held by the category of ownership in Marx's theory constitutes a premise for an equally strong position of property issues in the program for the building of a communist society. Karl Marx felt that the battle against the evil which was part and parcel of 19th-century capitalism, and the struggle to build a better society in the future required the abolition of capitalist property rights and the enforcement of common ownership.

288 Steve Pejovich, "Karl Marx, Property Rights School and the Process of Social Change", *Kyklos*, 3/35 (1982), 383.

Under the circumstances of capitalist private ownership, any purported achievements of civil society were, in the opinion of Marx, a legal delusion. Economic relations led to an economic coercion which forced men, women, and children into twelve-hour workdays and a destitute life. Moreover, this also incorporated the political sphere of guaranteed freedoms because their living conditions prevented laborers from taking advantage of their civil rights. Karl Marx did not intend to undermine democracy, liberty, and equality, but rather to complete this tour de force by transforming a legal fiction into a legal reality. True democracy demanded the taking of the next step – the proletarian revolution and the abolition of private property and ownership.

Raymond Aron synthesized this Marxist conviction: "To create a society in which *all* men would be capable, *throughout* their lives, of *effectively* fulfilling the democratic ideal: this was certainly the Utopia toward which the thought of the young Marx tended."[289] Aron nonetheless described Marx's determination to socialize ownership as a cardinal mistake. Marx did not foresee that, after the revolution, the workers – still living in poverty, just like their 19th-century predecessors – would be incapable of attaining economic freedom and would succumb to complete servitude before the functionaries of the communist state.

Building his doctrine, Karl Marx made only partial use of the possibilities embedded in his theory of ownership. Some of them he rejected; others he simply ignored. Additionally, many directives found in his doctrine were formulated in such a fashion as to suggest that he wanted to diminish the meaning of his discoveries with regards to the diverse historical forms of private and communal property. Worth examining more closely are the presuppositions triggering such a clear choice and its consequences.

Firstly, Marx stated that a real and permanent improvement of the living conditions of laborers is impossible within capitalism; therefore, this system must be liquidated by eradicating any and all private ownership. Marx criticized capitalist relations as fundamentally wrong and derogatory. This is, in his eyes, a system aimed at inhuman goals: the affluence of a few accompanied by the exploitation of many. Capitalism results in the degradation of not only workers but also the alienation of capitalists. For this reason, Karl Marx resolutely criticized ideas for the enhancement of the situation of wage laborers which were alternatives to his own vision.

He debated, for instance, with advocates for a proliferation of individual ownership based upon the labor of petty owners – even while himself indicating

---

289 Raymond Aron, *An Essay on Freedom* (New York: World Publishing Company, 1970), 26.

many a positive characteristic of this form. In his opinion, such a plan could not ever succeed. Individual property of producers had been a widespread state of affairs: from ancient to Germanic communities, as well as for a rather long period between feudalism and capitalism in certain Western European countries. In each and every case, this entailed dispossession of the majority of producers and the installation of large-scale ownership of the conditions of labor anchored in the work of others (e.g., ownership on the basis of slave labor, ownership on the basis of serfdom or feudal rent in kind or in money, capitalist ownership based upon wage labor, etc.).

Karl Marx also butted heads with leaders of workers movements – primarily social democrats and union activists whose goal was some form of coexistence and understanding between laborers and capitalists through wage increases, shorter workdays, improvements in workplace safety and hygiene, etc. In his opinion, even a radical improvement of the situation of workers could not purge capitalism of its fundamentally inhuman nature. He noted with approval the ideas of Russian communists on how to universalize communal ownership by way of distribution of the means of production (including land) among the already existing communities of producers. Nevertheless, Marx never directly supported this variant for socialization, closing all verbal discussions and written discourses with the assertion that the path to socialization would depend upon the concrete historical and economic circumstances in a given country.

Secondly, from Marx's perspective, capitalism is weighed down by such internal contradictions that its liquidation seemed (in his days) an obvious direction for change. At the onset, elementary accumulation of capital led to the dispossession of most small private proprietors and transformed them into wage laborers. By Marx's day, this concentration of capital (which he witnessed firsthand) involved the expropriation of the now numerous capitalists and their transformation into a smaller group of substantial, grand owners of capital. Now this small number of capitalists needed to be dispossessed, and, according to Karl Marx, this was the mission of the communist movement.

Crude accumulation and concentration of capital taken together had born fruit in the form of a socialization of the processes of labor on a national and even international scale. Labor had already been organized as a collective undertaking; hence, the socialization of property could be a simple adjustment to the dominant mode of production. Karl Marx also discerned the inevitable collapse of a system founded upon capitalist ownership in the mechanisms leading to a relative pauperization of the working class. There was a deepening polarization in society: an increasingly more numerous working class living in poverty and an increasingly less numerous class of owners of capital living in comfort and affluence.

This trend had begun to slow down in his lifetime, in the 1860s, but Marx underestimated this new phenomenon, treating it as a local tendency encompassing but a handful of factions of the working class. Regardless of whether he accurately generalized his observations or not, it is true that a thesis regarding an unavoidable pauperization can be drawn from the theory of Karl Marx just as logically as one affirming the inaccuracy of such a prediction. Marx's theory implied not only a prognosis for a deepening comparative pauperization and growing revolutionary ferment but also a different variant of social change resulting in a well-to-do and substantial middle class.

Marx did not exploit all the possibilities hidden in his theoretical model. For example, he could have made better use of the theme connected with a reshaping of the workers into a class for itself. After all, since workers are owners of a commodity essential to the functioning of capitalist relations (owners of labor power), then they could do the same as the capitalists: they could organize themselves to gain a higher price for that good which they owned. This variation of the game of capitalism was subsequently undertaken by various social movements which referred to the writings of Marx in their programs, even if Marx himself criticized them strongly.

Truth be told, Karl Marx himself provided many examples of individual or collective behavior which could provoke a change in the trend and result in a turning away from impoverishment. On the one hand, the bourgeoisie, in becoming a class for itself, resigned from some of their individual interests in favor of class interests. The primary interest of each capitalist in and of himself depended upon the maximum exploitation of workers; however, the collective interest of the capitalist class lay (among other things) in a deceleration of excessive pauperization. On the other hand, the workers were organizing within political parties and labor unions, fighting more and more effectively for improvement of their living conditions. In *Critique of the Gotha Programme*, Karl Marx sharply condemned a positive stance taken by German social democrats towards similar tendencies taking place on German lands. Ignoring the successful actions taken by the labor movement which did result in improved conditions for the working class in Germany, he continued to recommend revolution to the German social democrats.

The Marxist theory of ownership *expressis verbis* precludes – but, at the same time, incongruously implies – such a model of the capitalist society in which the two fundamental economic classes (each now organized as a political class for itself) could overcome the systemic contradictions and caring for the collective interests of their members. Both capitalists and workers can take advantage of state institutions to protect their own interests, if each of them is organized as a class for itself. In the debate presented above, Marx the ideologue obscures Marx the theorist.

Thirdly, Karl Marx assumed that only social ownership could create economic conditions which would facilitate an all-embracing development of individuals and the disappearance of human alienation. He assumed and perhaps even believed this despite copious and tugging doubts which can be found interspersed throughout his writings. He thought that this would protect humanity in the future from the reinstallation of private ownership and from re-enslavement. His closest colleague, Friedrich Engels did not have such misgivings: any and all discrepancies were adjudicated in favor of an unwavering apologetics for socialization. Yet the reservations and hesitations could be many. They, in fact, could be found in the results of the research conducted by Marx and Engels into the history of how privatization ran its course in various forms of common ownership which functioned in pre-capitalist societies.

The bulk of these forms of common ownership were accompanied by exploitation and domination. Functionaries of a community held power and controlled all chances for appropriation – something typical for extreme forms of private ownership anchored in the labor power of others. Although certain elements of a bucolic idyll appear in Marxist descriptions of these forms, he disclosed their true countenance on many an occasion. With time, each of these yielded to a transformation into private ownership which was based upon enslavement, vassalage, despotism, and/or economic coercion. Questions arise: Wherefrom stemmed Marx's determination to achieve the socialization of ownership? Wherefrom stemmed his conviction that only communal ownership provides a chance for dis-alienation since all previous historical experiences pointed to the immanence of exploitation and domination manifest in the diverse variations of this ownership?

Analysis of historical forms of ownership led Karl Marx to a few practical conclusions. One is an assumption that any and all negative phenomena accompanying common ownership can be eliminated through a transformation of collective consciousness. Marx believed – as is illustrated numerous times in his works – that revolutionary practice would shape a new, general type of personality befitting the scope of the revolutionary movement and the utopian model. Marx did, however, overestimate the readiness of the participants as well as their leaders to function in an ideological dimension of collective life as predicted by the communist vision: it could only be realized at the expense of their own economic interests which were rooted in personal appropriation.

A second conclusion is a Marxist assumption that a person could safeguard himself against undisguised or disguised privatization such as had already been experienced in earlier forms of common ownership. In the early phase of communist socialization, according to Marx, domination and exploitation really were to manifest themselves in new forms. Over the longer period, however, a true socialization would take place resulting in a rapid development of production powers would ensue. Under the circumstances of plentitude and unlimited chances to satisfy one's needs, private appropriation and the building of reserves for the future would be deprived of rational justification. Therefore, a third conclusion is that the repeating of history – a retreat from already established common ownership and restitution of private ownership – would be impossible.

The controversies pertaining to the communist utopia sketched by Karl Marx have been presented neither to identify merely the unfulfilled opportunities found within his theory nor to solely criticize the path he chose (developed in deformed fashion in the interpretations of Engels and Lenin). There is also a need to recall the uncertainties which accompanied Marx in his choices. Once having chosen a direction for the application of the theory he described together with Engels in their *Communist Manifesto*, something in the way of a cognitive dissonance comes to light in subsequent writings.

Karl Marx did consider and did investigate other possibilities. For instance, although he spoke in favor of concentrating the conditions of labor as a foundation for the socialization of property, he also wrote – in *Drafts of the Letter to Vera Zasulich* – about the prospects for another way of socialization. For instance, in Russia, a significant part of the land was divided amidst agricultural communes. In this case, socialization could emerge from an association of representatives of these communes rather than a further concentration of communal land itself. Above all, Marx continuously and clearly emphasized that it is the economic content which determines the socialization of property – crucial is the way in which people find employment, and in which they participate in the distribution of the social product. Socialization is accompanied by a lack of exploitation and a lack of material reasons for the control of one person by another based upon possession.

Still – both earlier and later – Karl Marx returned again and again to those practical developments of his theory which he had previously rejected. Could this be a cognitive experiment or a toying with old ideas? That would be unlikely: very visible is the philosopher, conscious of the complexity, and ambiguity of the social world.

That said, Marx himself attempted to break through the dilemmas and make clear his verdicts. As a younger man, he elaborated his revolutionary program with Engels; as a mature man, consequential to his analyses into class conflict and the civil war in France, his theory took a more radical form, including acceptance of the dictatorship of the proletariat. And so, the circle came to a close: the old, classic, communal authorities would return in a new, despotic form promoted by the communist movement. Here, it must be admitted that Karl Marx was the man behind the route to the socialization of ownership which is associated with Russian Marxism, with the rise and fall of Soviet communism.

But he was also one of the agents of an intellectual trend which made use of other levels of his concept of property and ownership, shaping the economic and sociological theory of contemporary industrial societies. He left his mark as well on the Western European social-democratic movements which, in the 20th century, brought to fruition the social market economy, social welfare, and the prosperous welfare state. This latter path of development drew more on Marx's theory than on his doctrine – sometimes directly and sometimes indirectly, seeking methodological or theoretical inspiration, agreeing with as well as critiquing him.

What moved me to revisit and rework a book on property and ownership, one written in Polish some thirty years ago? More to the point, what moved me to issue an English-language edition of this revisit to my scholarly past? On the one hand, a deep and thorough tracing of the line of thinking pursued by Karl Marx discloses a blind and treacherous faith in the transformative power of socialization. On the other hand, more contemporary doctrines place similar faith in the transformative power of privatization. It is my hope that, through the lessons of this exposé, the reader will learn to consider doctrines (both past and present) with care and, thus, avoid such traps.

In my home country, before and after the 1989 turning point, I witnessed first the effects of radical property nationalization and then of rapid property privatization. As a sociologist of economics, I dare to state that between socialization and privatization certain key parallels are to be found. In both cases, some will win and others will lose. In both cases, phenomena such as exploitation, domination, or inhumane living conditions are possible.

What conclusions can be derived from this in-depth investigation into the concept of ownership elaborated by Karl Marx? What conclusions can be derived from the human experiences associated with the socialization and privatization of property observed thus far? On the one hand, it is worth drawing from Marx's theory because his explanatory potential can be utilized in scrutinizing processes of financialization (local and global) in the 21st century. On the other hand, his doctrine must be handled with care and caution. The views of Karl Marx represent but a part of a ladder which human theory and experience have climbed heretofore. Some of the theses and practices are worth undertaking; others need be rejected.

Bibliography

Aron Raymond (1970), *An Essay on Freedom*. World Publishing Company. New York.

Balibar Étienne (1970 [1968]), "The Basic Concepts of Historical Materialism". In: Louis Althusser, Étienne Balibar (ed.), *Reading Capital*. New Left Books. London.

Brozi Krzysztof, Winiarski Lech (1980), "Czy 'własność ogólnospołeczna' jest 'własnością'?" *Studia Filozoficzne*, 7(176), 19–32.

Engels Friedrich [1844–1845], *Condition of the Working Class in England*, <https://www.marxists.org/archive/marx/works/download/pdf/condition-working-class-england.pdf>, accessed August 2017.

Engels Friedrich [1876–1878], *Anti-Dühring: Herr Eugen Dühring's Revolution in Science*, <https://www.marxists.org/archive/marx/works/download/pdf/anti_duhring.pdf>, accessed August 2017.

Engels Friedrich [1880], *Socialism: Utopian and Scientific*, <https://www.marxists.org/archive/marx/works/download/Engels_Socialism_Utopian_and_Scientific.pdf>, accessed August 2017.

Engels Friedrich [1884], *Origin of the Family, Private Property, and the State*, <https://www.marxists.org/archive/marx/works/download/pdf/origin_family.pdf>, accessed August 2017.

Engels Friedrich [1891], *Introduction to Karl Marx's "Wage Labour and Capital"*, <https://www.marxists.org/archive/marx/works/download/pdf/wage-labour-capital.pdf>, accessed August 2017.

Hochfeld Julian (1982), "Studia o marksowskiej teorii społeczeństwa". In: Julian Hochfeld (ed.), *Marksizm, socjologia, socjalizm: Wybór pism*. Państwowe Wydawnictwo Naukowe. Warsaw.

Kolakowski Leszek (1978), *Main Currents of Marxism*. Volumes I–III. Oxford University Press. Oxford.

Kozyr-Kowalski Stanisław (1984), "Klasy społeczeństwa a ekonomiczno-socjologiczne pojmowanie własności, Część pierwsza". *Kultura i Społeczeństwo*. Nr 1, 15–36.

Kozyr-Kowalski Stanisław (1977), "Własność jako zjawisko ekonomiczno-społeczne w świetle badań Karola Marksa i Maxa Webera". In: S. Kozyr-Kowalski (ed.), *Własność: gospodarka a prawo: Studia o marksistowskiej teorii własności*. Państwowe Wydawnictwo Naukowe. Warsaw.

Kurczewski Jacek (1977), "Stosunki własności w społeczeństwach przedpaństwowych". In: S. Kozyr-Kowalski (ed.), *Własność: gospodarka a prawo: Studia o marksistowskiej teorii własności*. Państwowe Wydawnictwo Naukowe. Warsaw.

Lenin Vladimir I. (1964 [1896–1899]), "The Development of Capitalism in Russia". In: V. I. Lenin (ed.), *Collected Works*. Volume 3. Progress Publishers. Moscow.

Lenin Vladimir I. (1964 [1902]), "Vulgar Socialism and Narodism as Resurrected by the Socialist-Revolutionaries". In: V. I. Lenin (ed.) *Collected Works*. Volume 3. Progress Publishers. Moscow.

Lenin Vladimir I. (1964 [1919]), "A Great Beginning: Heroism of the Workers in the Rear 'Communist Subbotniks'". In: V. I. Lenin (ed.) *Collected Works*. Volume 3. Progress Publishers. Moscow.

Ładosz Jarosław (1977), "Własność jako kategoria ekonomiczna a prawo własności". In: S. Kozyr-Kowalski (ed.), *Własność: gospodarka a prawo: Studia o marksistowskiej teorii własności*. Państwowe Wydawnictwo Naukowe. Warsaw.

Majka Józef (1982), *Etyka życia gospodarczego*. Wydawnictwo Wrocławskiej Księgarni Archidiecezjalnej. Wrocław.

Marx Karl [1843–1844], *A Contribution to the Critique of Hegel's Philosophy of Right*, <https://www.marxists.org/archive/marx/works/download/Marx_Critique_of_Hegels_Philosophy_of_Right.pdf>, accessed August 2017.

Marx Karl [1844], *Economic & Philosophic Manuscripts of 1844*, <https://www.marxists.org/archive/marx/works/download/pdf/Economic-Philosophic-Manuscripts-1844.pdf>, accessed August 2017.

Marx Karl [1846], *Letter to Pavel Vasilyevich Annenkov*, <http://marxists.catbull.com/archive/marx/works/1846/letters/46_12_28.htm>, accessed August 2017.

Marx Karl [1847], *The Poverty of Philosophy: Answer to the "Philosophy of Poverty" by M. Proudhon*, <https://www.marxists.org/archive/marx/works/download/pdf/Poverty-Philosophy.pdf>, accessed August 2017.

Marx Karl [1847], *Wage Labour and Capital*, <https://www.marxists.org/archive/marx/works/download/pdf/wage-labour-capital.pdf>, accessed August 2017.

Marx Karl [1850], *The Class Struggles in France, 1848–1850*, <https://www.marxists.org/archive/marx/works/download/pdf/Class_Struggles_in_France.pdf>, accessed August 2017.

Marx Karl [1851–1852], *The Eighteenth Brumaire of Louis Bonaparte*, https://www.marxists.org/archive/marx/works/download/pdf/18th-Brumaire.pdf>, accessed August 2017.

Marx Karl [1859], *A Contribution to the Critique of Political Economy*, <https://www.marxists.org/archive/marx/works/download/Marx_Contribution_to_the_Critique_of_Political_Economy.pdf>, accessed August 2017.

Marx Karl [1857–1861], *Grundrisse: Foundations of the Critique of Political Economy* (Rough Draft), <https://www.marxists.org/archive/marx/works/download/pdf/grundrisse.pdf>, accessed August 2017.

Marx Karl [1861–1863], *Theories of Surplus Value*, <https://www.marxists.org/archive/marx/works/1863/theories-surplus-value/add3.htm>, accessed August 2017.

Marx Karl [1867], *Capital: A Critique of Political Economy*. Volume I, <https://www.marxists.org/archive/marx/works/download/pdf/Capital-Volume-I.pdf>, accessed August 2017.

Marx Karl [1863–1878], *Capital: A Critique of Political Economy*. Volume II, <https://www.marxists.org/archive/marx/works/download/pdf/Capital-Volume-II.pdf>, accessed August 2017.

Marx Karl [1863–1883], *Capital: A Critique of Political Economy*. Volume III, <https://www.marxists.org/archive/marx/works/download/pdf/Capital-Volume-III.pdf>, accessed August 2017.

Marx Karl [1865], *Letter to J. B. Schweizer: "On Proudhon"*, <http://marxists.catbull.com/archive/marx/works/1865/letters/65_01_24.htm>, accessed August 2017.

Marx Karl [1865], *Value, Price and Profit*, <https://www.marxists.org/archive/marx/works/download/pdf/value-price-profit.pdf>, accessed August 2017.

Marx Karl [1869], *The Right of Inheritance: Report of the General Council*. Written by Marks on August 2–3, 1869, Endorsed by General Council of The International Workingmen's Association on August 3, 1869. <https://www.marxists.org/archive/marx/iwma/documents/1869/inheritance-report.htm>, accessed August 2017.

Marx Karl [1870–1871], *The Civil War in France*, <https://www.marxists.org/archive/marx/works/download/pdf/civil_war_france.pdf>, accessed August 2017.

Marx Karl [1875], *Critique of the Gotha Programme*, <https://www.marxists.org/archive/marx/works/download/Marx_Critque_of_the_Gotha_Programme.pdf>, accessed August 2017.

Marx Karl [1881], *Letter to Vera Zasulich: The "First" Draft*, <https://www.marxists.org/archive/marx/works/1881/zasulich/draft-1.htm>, accessed August 2017.

Marx Karl [1881], *Letter to Vera Zasulich: The "Second" Draft*, <https://www.marxists.org/archive/marx/works/1881/zasulich/draft-2.htm>, accessed August 2017.

Marx Karl [1881], *Letter to Vera Zasulich: The "Third" Draft*, <https://www.marxists.org/archive/marx/works/1881/zasulich/draft-3.htm>, accessed August 2017.

Marx Karl [1881], *Letter to Vera Zasulich: The "Fourth" Draft*, <https://www.marxists.org/archive/marx/works/1881/zasulich/draft-4.htm>, accessed August 2017.

Marx Karl [1881], *The Reply to Zasulich, 8 March 1881*, <https://www.marxists.org/archive/marx/works/1881/zasulich/reply.htm>, accessed August 2017.

Marx Karl [1880–1881], *Conspectus of Lewis Morgan's Ancient Society*, <https://www.marxists.org/archive/marx/works/1884/origin-family/marx-conspectus.htm>, accessed August 2017.

Marx Karl (1968 [1845]), "Theses on Feuerbach". In: Karl Marx, Friedrich Engels (ed.), *Selected Works*. Progress Publishers. Moscow.

Marx Karl (1976 [1846]), "Wages". In: Lawrence Goldman (ed.), *Marx and Engels, Collected Works*, Volume 6. Progress Publishers. Moscow.

Marx Karl, Engels Friedrich [1845–1846], *The German Ideology*, <https://www.marxists.org/archive/marx/works/download/Marx_The_German_Ideology.pdf>, accessed August 2017.

Marx Karl, Engels Friedrich [1847], *Manifesto of the Communist Party*, <https://www.marxists.org/archive/marx/works/download/pdf/Manifesto.pdf>, accessed August 2017.

Marx Karl, Engels Friedrich [1882], *Preface to the 1882 Russian Edition*, <https://www.marxists.org/archive/marx/works/download/pdf/Manifesto.pdf>, accessed August 2017.

Marx Karl, Engels Friedrich (1936 [1845]), *The Holy Family or Critique of Critical Critique*. Foreign Languages Publishing House. Moscow.

Marx Karl, Engels Friedrich (1976 [1846]), "Circular against Kriege". *Marx and Engels, Collected Works*, Volume 6. Progress Publishers. Moscow.

Ossowski Stanisław (1982), "Struktura klasowa w społecznej świadomości". In: Stanisław Ossowski (ed.), *O strukturze społecznej*. Państwowe Wydawnictwo Naukowe. Warsaw.

Pejovich Steve (1982), "Karl Marx, Property Rights School and the Process of Social Change". *Kyklos*, Vol. 35, 383–397.

Record of Marx's Speech on The right of inheritance. The International Workingmen's Association. From: the General Council minutes of July 20, 1869, as taken by George Eccarius [1869]. <https://www.marxists.org/archive/marx/iwma/documents/1869/inheritance-speech.htm>, accessed August 2017.

Rutkiewicz Mikhail N. (1957), *Tendencyi razwitija socyalnoj struktury socjalisticzieskogo obszczestwa*, Moscow [no publisher given].

Strzeszewski Czesław (1981), *Własność – zagadnienie społeczno-moralne*. Ośrodek Dokumentacji i Studiów Społecznych. Warszawa.

Sztompka Piotr (1977), "O marksistowskiej koncepcji rozwoju – nieco inaczej". *Studia Filozoficzne*, Nr 12(145), 81–93.

Temkin Gabriel (1965), *Marks i idea pieniądza pracy*. Książka i Wiedza. Warsaw.

Wiatr Jerzy J. (1973), *Marksistowska teoria rozwoju społecznego*. Książka i Wiedza. Warsaw.

Wieniediktow [Vieniediktov] Anatoly W. (1952), *Państwowa własność socjalistyczna*. Wydawnictwo Prawnicze. Warsaw.

Polish Contemporary Philosophy and Philosophical Humanities

Edited by Jan Hartman

Vol. 1 Roman Murawski: Logos and Máthēma. Studies in the Philosophy of Mathematics and History of Logic. 2011.

Vol. 2 Cezary Józef Olbromski: The Notion of *lebendige Gegenwart* as Compliance with the Temporality of the "Now". The Late Husserl's Phenomenology of Time. 2011.

Vol. 3 Jan Woleński: Essays on Logic and its Applications in Philosophy. 2011.

Vol. 4 Władysław Stróżewski: Existence, Sense and Values. Essays in Metaphysics and Phenomenology. Edited by Sebastian Kołodziejczyk. 2013.

Vol. 5 Jan Hartman: Knowledge, Being and the Human. Some of the Major Issues in Philosophy. Translated by Ben Koschalka. 2013.

Vol. 6 Roman Ingarden: Controversy over the Existence of the World. Volume I. Translated and annotated by Arthur Szylewicz. 2013.

Vol. 7 Jan Hartman: Philosophical Heuristics. Translated by Ben Koschalka. 2015.

Vol. 8 Roman Ingarden: Controversy over the Existence of the World. Volume II. Translated and annotated by Arthur Szylewicz. 2016.

Vol. 9 Tomasz Kubalica: Unmöglichkeit der Erkenntnistheorie. Leonard Nelsons Kritik an der Erkenntnistheorie unter besonderer Berücksichtigung des Neukantianismus. 2017.

Vol. 10 Renata Ziemińska: The History of Skepticism. In Search of Consistency. 2017.

Vol. 11 Jan Woleński: Logic and Its Philosophy. 2018.

Vol. 12 Wielslaw Gumula: On Property and Ownership Relations. 2018.

www.peterlang.com

www.ingramcontent.com/pod-product-compliance
Ingram Content Group UK Ltd.
Pitfield, Milton Keynes, MK11 3LW, UK
UKHW041828100926
8556IPUK00002B/76

9 783631 667361